David Cako

If God gave you everything you wanted, you wouldn't have to win. Then again, the reason you're here is because you're a little more right than the next guy.

If you're really serious about winning, you're going to have to be right consistently for years at a time.

You'll be told you're wrong, nonstop, and it will be up to you to evaluate yourself and ignore everyone who doubts you.

Certain attributes will make things easier for you, like being especially talented or having a reason for people to feel sorry for you; although for the most part, the more right you are, the blacker the void you will be shouting into.

If this sounds like an uncharitable estimation of people, it's because I know them well, and **I am a lifelong winner.**

I'm plainly capable of seeing the future. I know who is going to win the World Series. Sometimes I feel like I've already met you, and I know you're a winner. I know your health better than your doctor. When a natural disaster is about to happen, I can tell you, and people will pretend like I said nothing.

I can lead any group of people to victory in nearly any situation, so long as they can forget about me winning long enough.

Only a fool would believe they're right when everyone on the planet says they're wrong. So how fucked up are you? If you really want to win, what do you have to lose?

I have a feeling I can come up with something you could be good enough at to make an excellent living. It's something like software, or accounting, and everyone will be there to encourage you because it's the right thing to do.

But if you have a deep and absolute desire to win, you already know what makes you a winner. I'll be your lucky charm.

You Are Right

and it makes everyone feel wrong.

Sound familiar? Oh well. Now I'm excited and curious about you.

This book is written during a period of unemployment and a strong feeling that no one is really listening. I speak quietly, but people hear me soundly.

When your grandfather was storming the beaches at Normandy, he didn't go to the principal's office to complain about how the other guys were being hurtful. Today is an important turning point for your life, because from now on you are the master of your fate.

I promise you, through direct experience my entire life, you could take a video of a money tree in your backyard shaking off $100 bills in the wind, and every 2-bit fuck on Reddit would drop their cocks mid-ejaculation to explain, through their comprehensive education at University of Phoenix's renowned macroeconomics program, why money doesn't grow on trees. Slamming into their $300 cum-filled mechanical keyboard, they get to continue another day being less wrong.

I could share a comprehensive log of all of the things I know are going to happen before they do (like I do, on my website, *cako.io!*), and if you are anything short of dead serious about winning, your instinct is going to be to find a way to believe I'm wrong. That's fine, it's how we as humans evolved to flee bondage and oppression: just by ignoring people who are a little too right. But you're going to need to run with winners if that's who you are now. Goodbye to dead weight.

You're Scary Right

Moses parted the Red Sea and saw his oppressors turn to pillars of salt behind him. Faith in God is helpful when it feels like the world you know has abandoned you. God never turns his back to you, and anyone who means to impede you will be cut down in their tracks.

3

Is the scary part when this sorcery comes to a head, or that there's all that undifferentiated power out there, adrift in chaos with no one to bear it?

Yea, right as you are, it's only a matter of time before the people who doubted you have to answer before their own eyes and ears. God never forgets, and neither do I. "*Only* an eye for an eye" is as the adage goes, because if I let my emotions get the best of me, I would wish endless vengeance on behalf of the righteous. To take my word, and to squander my livelihood, they shall pay onefold.

Humble Pie

It tastes like magic. There's plenty for everyone. Give it to family and friends, keep some for yourself. This is where you want to be once you get over your persecution complex. The sweet taste of victory is for life.

The Righteous Stand Still

You're a formidable center of gravity, after all. It's very easy to be tempted to go off in different directions, to feel like you're not seeing results and you need to keep changing things. Have confidence where you're at. Let time do the work for you, and trust the fruits of your labor. Everyone will tempt you with overreaching, and it's up to you to be focused and goal oriented.

Their favorite way to tempt you is by doing things they know they can get away with and you can't. In every thing, reciprocity. If you're a real winner, every person you know spends every waking moment coming up with ways to get a rise out of you. You are unwavering, and God's wrath burns like 7 suns.

Staying put makes you seem more confident, but it also makes you much more sensitive to the tide of life. You're seeing intricacies to things that go unnoticed by everyone that's aimlessly chasing the next big thing. Even when you're running, you notice the details that other people don't, because you always have your bearings.

You Got a Head Start

and they will try to take it from you.

Not everyone can be a psychic or a world class tennis player. Most people get to have a regular job and make average money. I guess that makes us minorities.

What are you going to do when you are 8 billion years ahead of them and they make you think you need to slow down? I'll let that be up to you.

I have not yet met someone who harbors any sympathy for me being a winner. In fact, I only wish I was 16 billion *more* years ahead of the curve every day. This, to me, demonstrates a desire for continual improvement in the face of adversity.

People who are really great at things are used to other people trying to get in the way, but you have to get just as good at reminding them why you making out is a good deal for everyone. You believe in a fair and just economy of ideas, right?

Antitrust? How about *we make the best phones and computers on the planet*, and if anyone else has a problem with that, we'll just watch sinkholes open up underneath every one of your data centers. What else are we going to do? Just roll over and stop making them? Because that's what you sound like when you say the iPhone is *just too good*.

You Are Eternal

The words you use matter because you're thinking about your legacy. By now, you shouldn't need to be convinced you're going to win. You're such a winner that you only like to win a certain way. I'm quite particular about what it looks like when I do. For instance, I like the title of this book, but it almost isn't good enough to put my name on it. I was confident it sounded right and so I stuck to it.

Make a habit of doing things right the first time. You don't want to be going back and fixing all of your mistakes, having to redo work that you thought was already done. And you especially don't want to put something out there and then feel like you had more to say.

If you're a real winner, you want to make sure it looks right. As we're going to discuss later, it's also important know when it's time to *count the chips*. Because it's just as easy to become so preoccupied with sterility and plainness, and to completely overlook the fact that the whole point is to live your life and to be something new. All of the greatest stories in history are a little messy. Sterility is great for selling milk, unopinionated like sneakers and laptops. But you're going to be putting ink to paper at some point, and every letter is one more mark that wasn't there before.

Just Do It

This book was written in Autumn of 2023. All things in life are *real-time*, technically, although I find that my work is particularly real-time in the context of writing and business. You give me ideas to write about every day. I love this style of writing because it makes everything feel topical. Like an adventure that we all get to go on together.

The world so clearly has something to say, on behalf of us all. That people are tired of computers taking our jobs. That Israel's patience for its golden coast is expiring. That money is worthless right now.

All of the most important things that have happened in my life have been spur-of-the-moment leaps of faith. Something deep inside of me told me it was the right thing to do, and it changed my life forever. Follow your heart and listen to your intuition, because these are the things that are going to lead you to your own truth.

In many cases, the cost of not doing something is much greater than the cost of trying. The most important thing in life is that you commit to trying.

If you have something important to say to someone, your judgement is probably as good or better than theirs, and you don't need to worry about what they will think. In fact, people naturally respect this sort of confidence for that exact reason.

My hope is you agree with most of what I say, and you have some interesting experiences that color your own view of the world.

You know what makes you stylish and you always keep it fresh. Be yourself, it's hot.

Just Be Psychic

If having a psychic connection to God or to the universe could help you make all of the right choices at exactly the right time, wouldn't you want to be? From my own experience, I can tell you it is one of the most precious skills you can have. I'm not going to say it's for everyone, but it is certainly worth trying if it sounds like something you understand and can make sense of.

Being psychic is a lot like fishing for answers. If you're reeling too fast or you're heavy-handed with the rod, you're not going to notice the nibbles. Keep your line taut and tease the lake. The grace of God is somewhere inside of you, and you can't be talking over it to really listen.

Now, if you know everything, you're going to start looking for opportunities for serendipity and excitement, where things aren't so planned out. The whole world goes around on reciprocity. You just might have a knack for following trends that go above and beyond stocks and bonds. There's always some untapped potential in the world.

If everyone was psychic, you'd probably hope to be terrestrial, fickle as the free spirit can be.

Remember Plain?

Me neither, and this might get in the way of you convincing people you're right. Start thinking about what makes you unplain and you will gain some valuable insight into how you can invite plainness into your conquest. If you're a liquorice connoisseur, you probably love the most bittersweet, salty liquorice you can find, from some obscure confectioner in Amsterdam. But everyone else wants Twizzlers. You have to make some important decisions about who you want to appease and how important it is to your success. You can please some of the people, some of the time.

People want to be convinced that you've got something figured out for them. IKEA is plain, in a bizarre sort of way, and they show you how everything fits together perfectly. It's interesting looking, nearly unusual, and slightly higher quality than most flat-pack furniture. Something about that is satisfying.

The average person wants money, and to be noticed. Maybe there's an exchange of energy here. You win in excess, and there's plenty to go around.

Like Attracts Like

Winning has some unusual characteristics. It's as exceptional as you can be, but the world really prefers something more general, in the same way your local electrician's union really doesn't care about Hollywood's 2023 labor dispute. Maybe they should, though. Winners appreciate the value of being in the limelight; they find themselves in lots of high-visibility situations and they make connections without even thinking about it. That's important, because if you have something you want people to pay attention to, you want it to be circulating in groups where people have some serious pull.

A lot of people are frustrated by winners; they've got sour grapes for whatever everyone's talking about. Simple as that. Most people prefer to be around people who are average, who make it easy to bully you behind your back, than to be around you, who is not easy to bully. You're going to need to make a covenant with people who actually like winning. Still, many of them will be jealous of something about you, which is why you can give people about an inch of slack. They will try to take a mile.

Really, truly, discrimination is a very special skill. Winners discriminate based on things that matter, like character and kindness. They can see things in people that go completely unnoticed by everyone else. It wouldn't ever occur to you to be prejudiced or negative, but if you can't tell by now, being a winner can feel like it's you against the world.

Attractive people have a dirty little secret: no one really gets them.

Win Together

The most magical victories occur at every level. If you're a master at winning, it looks like a stampede, and every person you know wins all at once. This shows that you've figured out the mechanics of victory and you can orient all of the energy around you in the right direction.

The world runs on heavy horses. If you try to pick them up one at a time, it's not going to work out. You've gotta instrument things for locomotion.

Your unique differences will make the way you like to win especially apparent, and everyone knows you have to be around people who challenge you to be the best that you can be. You'll fit in great with winners.

Win Instantly

Everything in life has you convinced you're going to need to spend decades on school and work before you can squeeze any juice out of it. It keeps people *long* on the economy, but it throws years of your life into the flame.

If you're a real winner, you've got ideas that generate immediate feedback. Today, your deadlift is 10lbs better than yesterday. Fortunately, the human mind is designed to work well with immediate gratification. You just need to get your priorities straight so that you're making impactful decisions and not sitting around eating potato chips. Are you addicted to winning yet? It would be clear to you, because winning would feel the same as when you're sitting with a bag of potato chips. You're probably so good at it that you can be convinced you don't deserve money for it. Hah. Look, if you can play music that I wake up every morning and want to listen to immediately, you deserve an island in the Indian Ocean somewhere.

You need to know what you're worth and recognize where the economy will work for you. Workers will only tolerate the squeeze of Ubers and Netflixes for so long before they decide they want stability and pensions. The economy is always cycling between duck season and rabbit season, like a respiratory flow of breath.

In role-playing games, people are quite deliberate about leveling up statistics that are important to their success. Do you speak like a winner most of the time? How much of your time is directed towards *feeling* like a winner? As winners, we have been chasing the dragon for some time now. It's easy to lose track of the things that really make us feel good, so hopefully this is a reminder to feel great about everything you have accomplished and everything that is to come.

Win for Today

Trophies look great on your shelf, but the thing that is going to keep you going after you win is more winning. Just how much winning are you planning to do, anyway? Win now, and win presently. Sure, you might want pictures to post on Instagram, but you enjoy the taste of victory while you're eating, right?

Win for Everyone

Everyone remembers a true hero. Your victory is a symbol of liberty. Show them victory like it's their very first time seeing it, so that they shouldn't forget. You won by such a landslide it's almost disgusting. Send

Red Cross, plan for reparations. When Luke Skywalker wins, everyone is across the line with him. If only we could all be so esteemed.

It's easy in movies when the bad guys are faceless clones in service to an evil dictator, but in real life you have lots of real people that you like and you want to be respected by. Maybe there's something sort of fake about being a true winner after all. Shouldn't the option to *not* believe in you exist, for free will to exist? But then again, if you win so excellently, what other choice would there be for them?

The sweetest victory occurs by way of justice and righteousness. You won by doing exactly what the world needed for that moment in time. Victory *chose you* because you are excellent at what you do.

I believe so much in winning that I want it to make perfect sense for everyone.

Numbers Are a Liar Sometimes

When it comes to the amount of money in your bank account, numbers matter big time. When it comes to winning, the data can be misleading. Being the greatest in the world at something that no one else is doing is your best shot, and everyone that is primed for evaluating everything based on *the data* is going to tell you that you're wrong.

When computers are involved, numbers are a liar more than you would ever expect. I have thousands of daily readers on my website, but my YouTube view counts have been frozen in exactly the same place for months. The reviews are all imaginary, the page ranking is rigged, and the video poker follows you around on your casino card.

Numbers are often inert like a deck that never gets shuffled, and they'll keep showing you things to make you believe there's something genuine about them. If you disagree, start looking at how often the world's most followed Instagram accounts move around. It's not often, and it makes everyone else feel like they're late to the party.

Now that you're thinking like this, you're ready to show the world something that's human and true. You're going to carve your own path in the world that not one other person on the planet has walked along. And you're going to invite people along with you so they can see something magical, that defies all of the odds and every expectation.

Look, I can literally see the future, and it takes many years of beating it into everyone's head that you're right before they will even give you the time of day. Remember I told you this: winners don't care about the odds.

I'll go a step further and say that winners *prefer* moonshot odds, because all of the other games are already rigged.

Your Ideas Are Your Trademark

Are you old enough to remember what technology looked like before iPods and iPhones? After Apple swept the industry, literally every other company tried to make something that looked like an Apple product. Apple fights tooth and nail to make sure that people don't steal their patents, but the reality is quite simple: every time someone makes something that looks like an iPhone, they are subversively endorsing the iPhone.

Apple made some serious bets early on with the iPhone that paid off. For years, lots of people were reluctant to use Mac because it seemed like there was software that they were familiar with that wasn't going to be compatible. Whether this was true, at the time, a lot of people already had this idea in their minds.

The biggest priority for the first major update to iOS was *apps*. "What the hell is an app?" Well, it's software, but it's the kind that you're going to be writing specifically for iPhones, because everyone's got one in their pocket. Now everything's an app, and you can open your files anywhere, which is great. But if you're from my generation, the very first image in your mind of *app* is Steve Jobs holding up an iPhone. And now the tables have turned, with iPhone being the first priority for any cool new app.

Right now, every athletic shoe seems to have thick soles, a pointy heel and toe profile, and a tight-fitting knit upper material. They're all meant to look like Adidas Ultraboost. People can tell it's something they want, even if they don't know what that is, because it's just what's in style. And they're quite comfortable, with all of the advances in manufacturing since Jordans.

Some things are so beautiful that everyone else wants to make something just like it, and they deserve to be able to, generally speaking, so long as they aren't getting in the way of you doing business.

Make your ideas as potent and characteristic as the light of day. 10 years after, the world will look like one great big imitation of you. Deal with it.

Girls Like Winners

They're not really sure why, but they know it when they see it. If you're so caught up with winning, she'll just take the new car and move on. This is a book about winning, though, and not about getting girls.

Play Games You Like

By now, you should know what types of games you like to play. It's like second nature to you, which is how you got so good at it in the first place. I'm not going to sit here and convince you to become a world-class StarCraft player, but I will show you how important it is to know what you're good at and to stick with it.

Everyone loves your enthusiasm for the game. Plainly, you are so obsessed with waking up and doing that thing every day, it would be hard for you to imagine *not* being great at it. You're laying in bed thinking about it, you're making breakfast thinking about it, and you're staring at your kitchen cabinets thinking about it. By the time you should be going to bed, you're glued to what you're doing, and you'd hate to break up with a great flow state. You don't get distracted easily, and you're patiently absorbed in the process. I suppose it's not like you to be picking up new games for a flavor of the month, because you're ever so true to the game you love. Maybe you don't know what this is yet, but I know you'll find out soon enough.

The greatest StarCraft player I know can play for 8 hours straight without thinking twice. I don't like video games *that* much, but I do like other things that much.

Welcome to Zara

The biggest winners in the world are perpetually about 6 years old. Look at Elon Musk, and Steve Jobs. Britney Spears, and Taylor Swift. They all have one important thing in common: they already won. This makes them particularly sensitive to freshness. Personally, I wouldn't want to be a part of any club that would have me.

Fashion is elusive, because it can be hard to tell whether it's really streetlevel or if it's something that came from the guys upstairs. What's the difference, anyway, if everyone is expected to know JavaScript and have a *side-hustle* now? Let's get back to the basics: do you really walk the walk? How many damn jobs do you need, anyway?

No One Wins

Is that so hard for you to believe? If Michael Jordan and the Bulls won every single NBA championship, it would look a little like an annual communist ceremony where we all celebrate the splendor of the supreme ruler. But instead, we live in a fair and just reality where there is opportunity for everyone who directs good energy into the world. I believe in you, and I know you're a winner because I am too.

Enjoy Winning

The happiest I've been in my life is when I was spending all night playing World of Warcraft and Counter Strike with a buddy of mine. That was what I had going for me, and it was a blast. We thought everything was fun, and everything was funny. 4chan, conspiracy theories, reality TV politics, you name it; we were having the time of our lives.

Once you're winning, remember to enjoy it. Remember what your criteria is for winning so that you know when it's actually happening, because otherwise it may very well pass you by.

Winning looks different now, and the stakes are much, much higher. The stakes being higher is what makes winning fun now. And stressful. A lot of folks grow out of video games because the real world becomes satisfying in some way that resonates with them.

I still love my favorite games. I love that Dark Souls has a story to tell me with nearly zero dialogue; mysterious, clever, ancient creatures that can destroy you in one hit, beautiful and gothic landscape that depicts a sort of sorrow and emptiness, in spite of its splendor. Areas that are all connected, but essentially free for you to explore in any order you want. A game so unforgiving that you'd wonder if you're even playing it right, and also more rewarding than anything I've ever played.

Walk the Line

Winners speak plainly. You use just the right words at just the right time. The only thing you'd ever hope to be is yourself.

Winning Is Magic

Do you believe in magic? Trust me, you want magic in your corner. I have symbols that I love, numbers, and names. I believe in everyone and everything that I stand for. Writing about things that make me happy always puts me in a good mood. Pay attention to what goes into your eyes and ears so that you are always in a state of flow.

Sure, for close-up magic it matters a lot that you have good mechanics with cards, but the macro-trends of winning depend a lot on what percentage of the time you are engaged in things that move you in a positive direction.

Every waking moment you are *enchanting* yourself with what you look at. When you're scrolling through stuff on your phone, look at pictures of people doing things well! Not just silly stuff; really, immerse yourself in the culture of joy and success. The average attitude of everyone you think about has such far-reaching effects on how you feel every day. You want the voice in your head to believe things will work out for you.

I want you to imagine for a moment that you could invent any sort of magic that you want to see. What *do* you like to see? Certainly, there's something you find pleasing and effortlessly exciting. You've got a performance to put on for the world, so you should put your best foot forward and show the world who you really are.

Winning Is Like Riding a Bike

The very first time you try to win is going to feel insurmountable. You can't get the balance right, it's all topsy turvy. Once you have the confidence to get moving, there's nothing to it. When you get used to winning, you go into everything you do expecting to win, and *that's* a superpower.

Winners are more surprised when they *don't* win. How's that for an attitude? You don't have to be cocky or prideful; just notice that you are quite often well-equipped for success. Your habits are good, you practice endlessly, and you stay focused. Sometimes, the most important thing is that you just keep moving forward. Everyone else wants to quit while they're ahead. You know that there's so much more to accomplish.

Count the Chips

Your instinct might be to keep fiddling with everything until you're ready to see if you won. Really, if you're paying attention, you'll know when it's time to count the chips. More than likely, everyone is going to try to keep you from counting the chips because then you get to see that you won. Everything in life has a rhythm and a cadence. You'll learn a lot about how you play and when it makes sense for you to take risks. On the other hand, if everyone keeps betting against you and you're positive you won, maybe you should sit pretty. Just make sure they know, at some point, they're going to be counting the chips.

Use Your Hands

Winners have a tendency to steamroll over everything. I keep having to say things like "remember to enjoy winning while it's happening" because this is a very real thing. Lots of important details about life are so delicate that you could miss them if you aren't paying attention.

I love the way certain things feel, like smooth satin, or the edges where you open a MacBook. I love the smell of cinnamon and the sweet tonic of blackberries and key lime pie. I love music that is under citric pressure, like my coffee.

Don't try to outrun the present.

Quality… People… Sights and smells… You might forget about all of them from time to time, because the only thing you can see is winning. Winners have calloused hands and they're losing sensation in their fingertips. Be gentle when you need to be. Have faith that you are doing the right thing, taking life one day at a time.

Do It for the Right Reasons

Really, what are you winning for? Right now, you're making your bed, and you're going to have to sleep in it. Every little thing is going to have to be just right. For her. Everything for the life you mean to live and to share with the world. Your kids, and their kids are going to know just who you were when you walked this world. There's no reason to be ashamed for being a winner, but you will have your cross to bear.

The way you feel influences everything that you create in a very deep way. The ideas you hold in your mind while you're writing, painting, and designing things are the seeds that grow into your artwork. Everything you do has your fingerprints all over it, any way you look at it. When you really try to do things for the right reasons, that thread shows up in the most peculiar way in every word and brush stroke. It's who you mean to be, and thus it's what your artwork becomes.

So, when you really think about things that are true, and you pay attention to *what makes them true,* you will come up with artwork that touches people in a very real way. Do you notice there are details that you love to play out over and over in your mind, or others that you are particularly averse to? That is where your art is going to show up best. People will see in your artwork how you really feel.

Multi-Tools Are Bad for Business

Well, everyone that comes in here now just wants a Leatherman and a screwdriver set, and they do just fine with that.

You keep telling yourself you need more wins before the world gives you what you want, but really you're just adding a bunch of accessories that you may never use. Anyone who sees you true will know from the very first time they meet you, and they will be with you until the very end.

I love multi-tools, but everyone will come to resent that you have a million tools sticking out of your handle. Victory is sweetest the first time. Although perhaps you're the hero that the world deserves.

2

Streetlevel

When you're Godzilla, it's hard to find places that you fit in. They keep building bigger streets and buildings, hangars that can fit you, but the people stay about the same size. When we first met, you seemed just right. Now you seem like a young girl to me, which I kind of like better. And you keep growing with me, because we're in this together until the very end. The very end, like in Revelation.

That's something I believe in. We have a lot to accomplish before then, but the signs are here with us. 7 horns and 7 eyes. The number, not the amount. I feel vile next to you because I'm red and you're plain white, but I am also confident in God's plan. Things are distinct in this world, so that anything may exist at all. You like Instagram and I like liturgy. Crusty, old metapolitical introspection by a chosen people born of a space in air. Instagram is fair, if you're fair. Everyone gets a chance to share a sentence and a picture of french toast worth a thousand words. God is fair to me.

The words I use operate under primordial pressure and at temperatures comparable to the sun or even just the core of the Earth. You are so pretty, though, and ever so sweet. I love everything about you, even the things that make me feel ugly. I love your beautiful eyes and how gentle you are with me. I love that you turned out to be patient, even though at first I could only see haste. Sometimes I imagine things about you and they turn out to be true. You're always changing. Shiny, like a bell.

I see you, and perceptually I know you are distinct from me, but I can only ever feel you as one with my flesh and my blood. I sometimes wonder what I should say to you, because you have your own life to live and I mostly like to sit at home. You always like to remind me of how constricting it feels to know that I exist, as though your entire life started seeming like it was in reverse after we met. Every moment up until then was plain.

We will enjoy a perfect cup of coffee every day. Sweet, fruity, and ever so true.

The dissenters will know mouthfuls of salt, a bitter alkaline reminiscent of the unexamined life, batteries of tests and paperwork, and not so much as a moment of warmth.

We know that in every thing appears a characteristic reflection of the energies we put into life. To live purely, truly, and graciously, we arrive in the present after our kind. Every detail, ripe like our clemency.

Life makes sense when we put it under perfect pressure. It's how you came to be. Your body, your heart, your eyes and ears, a unique and elaborate organic system. The most differentiated organisms exist under pressure, a billion-year blossoming from the dawn of time. An eagle's sight, like photons in a vacuum. Reason, especially, requires attentive pressure for it to make sense. Generalities dripping through a sieve, and the details like an oily and iridescent emulsion.

The thing that's pretty about a young girl is that she is *just*. In service to reason, although only apparently differentiated in her supple skin, her bright eyes and silky hair. When beauty starts making sense, so then is she unfair. Massive, like a bulwark. The quaint fantasy of her solvency exchanged for the confabulated imagination of separateness, like trading in all your old video games. Sure, she looks new, for whatever that's worth. Every time you press her buttons, she inches one step closer to you.

Elementary school is so clerical that everyone forgot what youth looks like. If I felt a day younger than 9,000 years old, she'd seem like a relic. All of the king's men are at her command.

720

I had a week-old custard donut and the slightly fermented taste of the filling was surprisingly pleasing. Like adding Marsala wine, or the minty alkaline sensation of root beer, it did something entirely new.

What if you spent a year expecting good things to happen? Do you really say *yes* to life?

I'm in a world of my creation, and yet not one will acknowledge me true. Oh well. I wouldn't change my name for any amount of money, nor would I abandon my values. It is a much better fate to be perfectly alone than vaguely together, for me at least. Perhaps you think differently, and that's why it's good to have you around.

"I've used Mac, but I'm not really sure what's so great about it."

Mac is crisp and smooth, like a fresh pussy. It's like using a drawer with runners for the very first time. Like grace, it shows up just where you need it. Like grace, it never gets hot. Like grace, it is somehow the thing you meant to be distinct.

In late July, I dreamt of something terrifying in the ocean, and trying to find a room on short notice. You paged through the menu to order food, but I fell asleep soon after you were trying to convince me to discard my faith.

How do you imagine God feels to see the surface of His creation scorched and flooded, a people uncontent with the promise they were born of? They abandoned Him at every opportunity for inclusion. He is the perfect color in my every moment.

His little girl has perfect skin, like a porcelain doll. How can that be?

She told me everything happens the way it's supposed to. She always knows what's best.

I never could quite remember when I woke up at the typewriter, and it hardly mattered anyway whether I arrived a raving lunatic, except that she was plain wrapped in white.

People ask me, what's my ideal fantasy?

If something you wrote changed every time you looked at it, would it still be right? Some things are right at a time, like the code to log into your Blizzard account, and others are prescient. They began right, and remained right in spite of entropy. How I began here, and knew just who you would be.

The reason a lot of people don't get what they want out of life is because they won't ask for exactly what it is that they want. When they play it out in their heads, it's difficult for them to imagine themselves at the epicenter of success. The very core of success is believing in yourself. And people can tell. You're an open book, whether you know it or not. All preoccupied with *i*-before-*e*, except after *c*, where from a distance the general shape of you is exactly like the story you keep telling yourself. Our minds are mimetic, conforming deeply to the contents of our psyche, and everything around us grows in kind. Some of us feel like a mech suit, truly a living organism extending to the beginning of time. You get used to the sensory overload, brass blaring from the era of Cuneiform. The ringing turns to silence.

As I write this, now, it is not just the future that is influenced, but the past as well. Difficult as it may be to believe, things in this world are not as straightforward as they seem. *When*, really, was this written? Time is apparently linear, although seems more like a manifold of disparate memories when you consider it more carefully. To say you *see the future*, is accurate, as to notice when you have memories that precede the lived experience made actual. Planned, like the anticipation of music, stretched to fit a sheet, aged like yeast and lactic. The thing that makes it *time* is that there is an apparent division of subject between *now* and what is obscured by history or concealed by the future. Play a note ahead of the curve and you have a polyrhythm. Play songs that are hours and days long, and you have an epic the proportions of the universe and the world to come.

People end up doing whatever it is they were planning on doing; forward, reverse, however you look at it. Anyone who knows me, knows that I can tell you everything you need to know in about 3 sentences. Coffee, credit card, bon voyage. So here's a story longer than eternity to keep you busy.

Division

Why are we separate? Really, *why* do I have something different to show you, that isn't the thing you have to show me? If we were identical in nearly every way, what would you hope to be different between us?

You could spend your whole life not being impressed by people, seeing them truly naked with their passions, and not so much as giving them a moment of your undivided attention. *That's all there is to it?* What were you hoping for? That's a person, distinct from you, that is oriented in the same direction, but they run at a slightly different angle and at a different speed. Everything that excites them is quite different from the things you pay attention to, and that's what makes the world wonderful.

Choices galore, people really don't think about things like this, but sometimes I feel like I'm the last boy on Earth and everyone else is here to laugh at me with my pants down. Why the hell would I bring so many people along on this journey, just to be frustrated by the feeling that they don't really understand me?

That's how it feels, though. Like I was born with my other hal(ves) missing, and I have to go find them, and fuck them. Bend them into submission, and require them to see things my way. The world started unfinished, so that I could enact righteousness. If there are girls on this planet that are spiritual clones of me, I would certainly expect them to be head-strong and apprehensive until I come along and explain the ways of the world for them.

What an unusual boy, for that to even occur to him. That he invented his father, and his mother, and his lovers à la carte. So that when he goes through the line to *have it his way*, he can order the exact same thing and exclaim *Eureka!* with his finger pointed in the air when a roundy version of him with an extra hole comes out. So he can eat like a pig, with cum and blood splattered everywhere, while everyone wonders how someone could possibly have entered this restaurant so hungry.

Go figure: you're supposed to run, but you're always a little slower than him. You're particular, about not knowing what you want and shopping for hours. He's real particular, and he wants the exact same thing, every time. He's even particular about reminding you of what life is like when you spend it with a guy that's not particular about anything at all. Trust me, you want someone that treats the world like his science fair project and uses his name like myrrh to anoint your forehead, because otherwise he's looking at you for all the answers.

If he was anything less than particular, the thing he does wouldn't be the way he does it. He'll throw a fit like a 6 year old and make your life miserable until you pay attention. Which he gets away with, because he only ever has reasonable requirements. If was any less particular, you'd have something that looks like junk, like Windows or the dollar store. Even Steve wasn't quite particular in the way that he is, because Steve liked to show up in the office and talk to people. For Steve, BlackOut wouldn't occur to him. It would be embarrassing for him to acknowledge everyone is like a StarCraft unit, at his disposal for sensory pleasure and gyrometric orchestration. I mean, he knew the world was a little like that, but he figured dreaming about electric sheep is the business of androids. But he certainly did understand anger. He just figured it was his job to get bamboozled. Maybe it's a generational thing. He had Bob Dylan to believe in. Thanks to him, I believe in Mac.

Winning comes naturally to him, because it's the only story he knows. He just wanted to spend a real long time shaking up the bottle before he uncorked it. And he spent tons of time talking about poker and JavaScript to weed out everyone that just can't get enough matzah. This is a real toast for people who are real winners. We only eat like this.

So, then, *why do we measure?* Because that would be the only way to show you exactly what I mean, by setting a situation under particular pressure and tension. That is how we *elucidate* detail here in this world, that would otherwise be lost in generalities. I knew you would do just great.

Some people believe so deeply that God wishes for us to eat in a very particular way. So much that they want assurance that food meets particular criteria and that an animal was slaughtered by a skilled *shochet* in a particular way, according to very specific training from Talmudic law. Truly, an obsessional focus on righteousness, because God knows the difference, and so we must too. If only we could all be certain in every motion. So that when I show up in your life and tell you something with certainty, you pay attention. So that when it's shameful to me that I would have to be anything other than plain to have your attention, you understand why.

He Already Won

and now it's all about you. Winning is an afterthought, a side effect of rolling out of bed and reading the finance section — perfect for a book like this. Now his life is real smooth sailing. He drives slow, because it doesn't matter when he gets there, only that he enjoyed the ride.

The Weather

How's the weather? Must be a rough week for David. Really, he's quite easygoing. All he likes is fried chicken and ice cream. Is that so hard to figure out? Would you ignore his demands until the United States is 6 states fewer?

You're in a unique position of privilege because you get to decide what sort of storm we should weather. How long should we spend at Nordstrom, and how many hours long is *Flower Moon* going to be? He loves long movies, as long as they're exciting. Under pressure, like a waltz. Words have meaning, you know. It's not all just Maui and pictures of benedicts.

Everyone likes the weather a little different, which is great because there's lots of options for where to live. Winners operate at unusual extremes, and they might even be addicted to it. I love it cool and dry.

You can identify a tempered winner by the amount of displacement in their words. *Here, you show me.* Frankly, I'm over it. Twitter and Instagram is more your thing anyway. If you're happy, I'm happy, as long as the bed is comfortable and there's something good on HBO. 2023 wasn't really my year, and it is certain that you should know about it.

The crazy thing about the weather is that it is not random. Oh — spoiler alert. Really, you wouldn't believe it, but the weather is controlled by some unseen divine power, and it often reflects the spiritual state of the world. I won't bore you with it, but if you're paying attention this will become obvious to you.

The Girls

They're all so cute, and apparently so sweet and charming. What in the world could possibly make someone like that? I wonder, how long we could be pleasant with each other; if that would even occur to us. Are you a special kind of insane, my dear? I wonder, what have you heard about me, and what do you imagine about me?

The girls come out of the walls, from somewhere. You start wondering if you're obligated to say hi to each and every one of them. She's just right for you. And her, and her too. They're better at keeping their fingers on the pulse than at actually telling whether you're good at what you do. They know you're a winner because everyone else does.

Girls are imaginary. They fill out the shape of whatever container you out them in and they're very sensitive to how you use your imagination. If you imagine girls to be in your life, then there they will be.

All of the girls I like have beautiful blue eyes and usually dark hair. I never understood how some people are non-specific about what they find attractive. Then again, most people don't understand how I can eat the same thing every day, and why I like to watch the same sort of movie, why I like the same car and the same computer.

My favorite thing about girls is how they look, and that they are plain. A lot of girls are overthinking things these days.

It's true, exceptional people have a tough lot in life, but nothing like being a loser guy or some kind of freak that's way too into anime and StarCraft. Winners, admittedly, have it easy, even though they try exceptionally hard. Pretty girls have a unique sort of challenge: deferring your attention for another day. You know what I say, the only time is like the present.

Boys have to work hard to be plain, and at the same time they aren't eligible for sympathy like other groups of unplain people. I have a strong feeling that boys are a marginalized group that is going to see a major correction in the market soon. You'd all just leave them in a hot car for years, since apparently there's bigger issues in the world than whether these hustla's are getting their rocks off.

The greatest winners may be too plain for even the girls. Shall we discuss hardware, stocks, or perhaps the World Series?

She wants to see sweat equity, like the moment you realized you have too much to show for your life. Why exactly is it that you aren't covered in tattoos and insecure about your muscles? Do you even feel alive sitting next to a beautiful girl?

Eye on the Ball

The strongest indicator of whether you are in a position of privilege is how far your voice travels, and how much detail there is for you when you look at complex situations.

Being attractive in some way means you've spent your entire life getting tons of attention. This, in and of itself, makes you very sensitive to detail, because you can afford to be. The way you look or the way you think started out very good, and you only kept cranking up the contrast and the detail because it's what everyone expected of you. All eyes on you, and it made you sharp like an eagle. A pretty girl can post a picture of basically nothing on Instagram and get tons of attention, and likewise a smart guy can look at anything and understand it immediately. These are the stereotypical gendered expressions of privilege; the combination of smart and pretty is relentlessly powerful, and having one usually forces you to develop the other because you are always being watched by people who you subconsciously assume can tell the difference.

Bearing this in mind, people who *aren't* privileged are whomever you don't really hear from much. Boys and girls alike that sit in the basement watching anime and playing video games, people from obscure countries. It's not that sexy to stand up for these people right now, but I believe in them because I, myself, was a shut-in for long periods of my life. It didn't seem like anyone out there wanted to listen to me unless I made myself seem more plain. I had attractive privilege on my side, but you probably don't even need it if you're a real winner. One thing's for certain, you're going to need to figure out when being unplain is working for you and when it's needlessly complicating things. Be stylish and clean. Winners seem plain because they don't have to add too many ingredients. That's the finger-on-the-pulse effect, where people pay more attention to whether you're trying than what you actually accomplish. Ideally, you're so exceptional that you're making an effort to be plain.

Keep your eye on the ball long enough, and you'll encounter a sort of *participation mystique* that has you wondering if it's even the ball that everyone's eyes are on. What universe are we inside of, and who's even playing? What the hell do they know, anyway? They're here for Coke and pizza. If they were smart they'd just get a bigger TV and save the hassle for when they need their driver's license renewed.

Orange

You'll know it when you see it. At least, I do. The most clever people I know are more orange than the color. The room gets painted orange and somehow they stay the same. You won't wake up a day in your life to a different color. People don't stop, though. They put their face right under the ice cream machine and yell *"Creamsicle me daddy!"* Whatever.

Damnit, it's the only thing anyone wants to see, is orange. I can't be a bright enough orange for you to be happy. Orange is great when you're just watching, and not so great when you're the person that has to explain to the court why you're being so goddamn orange all the time. Well, plainly, it's the only way to get noticed. And you have to be the brightest thing in every room and visible from the other side of the planet. All of my favorite things in the world have a neon fluorescent intensity, so I guess it was meant to be.

Orange always looks slightly different, but you're so used to orange that you can pick out any shade of orange in the Pantone color palette on sight. Black is the new orange; wherever in the world there's something that is so new that it barely exists and you can barely even tell what it is. You're so fucking orange all the time, the only thing you want to be is plain. You already know which clothes you like best, and there's not a **Hermès x YSL | Autumn 2024** foldout that's going to change that. Here's my uniform, I'm like a Simpson.

I'm over apps, I'm over dongles, and I'm over *modern*. The programming languages are all the same: look, I queried a database and made buttons show up. If there's one thing I'm going to learn how to do on a computer, it's tell the computer to do it for me. And after that, I certainly hope you've figured out that the computer doesn't need to exist, so that I can reflect fondly on my first love, the Mac. I'm over orange. Now, my favorite thing is plain.

The orange chapter is almost over. Enjoy it while it lasts.

Contrast is Privilege

You can tell the difference. Quality has a particular weight and particular edges. Fashion is newer than new, like people post-affording of renewed clothes that were ungifted by the neonatal modernist Scandinavian Ebony reform district. Mom's got *Goop* because she's 7 years old, and I'm 6 for that matter.

If you have excellent style, excellent vision, and excellent hearing, it's because all you do is continually raise your expectations for yourself and for the world around you. That's why you can see every color so well, day or night, rain or shine. The fruit's always in season.

Contrast is privilege because you had lots of choices along the way. Even good choices, that you turned down because you wanted something that seemed more authentic. You can see exceptionally well and hear exceptionally well, enough that you can put two things that seem nearly identical next to each other and describe their differences. But you don't always want to. You believe in a just society where everything is more or less equal. You believe in equality so much that you forget to believe in exceptionalism sometimes. Lots of people don't believe in choices the way you do, and you tend to forget about those traditionalists. They believe they were born with their fate. It's easy to say when it seems like your fate is exceptional.

I love how clean and well maintained certain cities are, like Colorado Springs. You can tell people take a lot of pride in their environment. The parks are immaculate, the road signs and lampposts are decorative, and the sidewalks are always clean. Downtown is quiet and historical.

Colorado Springs is traditionally an Air Force town, and it shows in all of the best ways. It reminds me of Utah, and it reinforces my belief that *being right* is a state of mind. So I pray to be right. I pray that everyone in the world that feels disadvantaged in some way wakes up one day and gets to be right.

Now, if you're so discerning, you will understand why things like affirmative action tend to imply that someone looks like they need help on account of their demographics, which may be true, and is also an example of prejudice. Plainly, a given demographic is assigned as *requiring shepherding.* Opportunity is life-changing. Some people do need help because of their circumstances, and they're not always proud of it.

Everyone has particular colors, ideas, and sounds that they like.

Four Girls

You can tell a lot about how someone makes their choices based on their relationship with victory. It's how they decide when they've won and how important it is for them to continually take risks.

When someone feels like their life is heavy, they truly *need* the opportunity to shed that weight, and it's clear that giving them a helping hand and a path to feeling good about their lives means the world to them. Truly, it's like a miracle to know that there is light at the end of the tunnel.

Some people keep trying win again, as though there's never quite a satisfying conclusion. It's all they know, and it seems like the only time anyone sees them is if they have something new to show the world. If there isn't something they're working towards, they barely feel at home in their own skin. Truly, it's important to remember to cherish your own success.

Others feel quite satisfied with victory. Maybe they were born with it. They wake up and they are exactly who they remember being. It might even be confusing to them why it seems like other people squander victory or can never quite grasp it. Perhaps you'd say they're privileged, they live like royalty on their name and their laurels, although I would argue that their mindset is not as conducive to perceiving detail and contrast. A lot of people might even accuse them of being vain and unrelatable. Can you really fault someone for being plain and victorious?

Really, for us to have a well rounded view of the world, there had to be some sort of exchange of energy that motivated us to climb out of our darkness or to peek back into it and remember what we've learned. In heaven, perhaps all we mean to know is victory, unquestioning and unfallen. Here in this world, though, there does seem to be the requirement that we understand it in great detail.

The University

I find myself quite well suited to the new world of the internet and free information. In theory, university should be great for people like me — a place to go where there's lots of other curious and smart people that like to learn about the world. Really, though, if you told me to write a paper it would come out looking like a new product announcement with headlines and bullet points. And you'd remember it for the rest of your life, because my name is stamped on the top left in its characteristic rounded rectangle token. When I read your papers, it's hard for me to get to the point. And they end up in piles of other papers with endless bureaucracy and people telling you what you can and can't say. *Pay tens of thousands of dollars a semester to be told what to say!*

All supposed bastions of free thinking eventually ossify. And the more magic slush in between the real value of something and people's wallets, the more incentive there is for endless inflation. Keynesian market dynamics like supply and demand only work when those things are directly looped into the cost of something. Infinite term loans decouple the value from the demand, because you can just keep printing more money and arbitrarily increasing the price that you know people can't afford.

Incidentally, the more credibility you have to have to be successful in a particular society, the less social mobility there is, and the more secondary inflation there will be, on top of the student loans, because people wait forever to actually start their lives. Plainly, a home now costs 2 incomes and an extra 4-8 years of each of your lives.

Today, if you want to learn about anything, you can find a perfect place to do it on the internet. The people making stuff just can't wait to teach you all about how to use it, write code for it, or start your very own business around it. This is great: there's market incentives that make learning convenient.

If you're spending your time on Slashdot and Hacker News, you're probably learning a lot more about today's software than you would be in school. You're getting inside the minds of how real engineers think. You're talking about privacy, A.I., and the economy, because these are the real, tangible effects of innovation. There's also a time and a place for data structures and algorithms, although it's just about behind us.

Some group of people is always monopolizing what is right in the world, and they hate to admit that the people who are really winning big time are usually outrunning them. *The university* isn't even necessarily the actual university, for all intents and purposes. As I'm explaining the world to you now, I'm cognizant that a university of sorts is emerging around *Cako thought,* and we're going to have to find somewhere new to play that's cool. Take notes so that you remember all of the things that stand out to you.

I stand behind my name, though, and I only say what I really truly believe in, so that my legacy looks right, and so that everyone that's running around repeating things I say are actually saying things that are right. Wherever you are in the world, there's some form of hulking bureaucracy that's ripe for improvement. Every word you pile onto the Tower of Babel makes it that much more complicated, a game of telephone where the sovereign will of the individual is at odds with the complexity of the collective.

University degrees are oversaturated right now. It's roughly equivalent to having a high school diploma, except you're strapped with debt for a decade or more, and you're not even sure if you like sitting around at a desk all day. Seriously, consider what you like to do with your hands, because trades are very good money with much more immediate feedback. If you're a real winner, you probably already have something you love to do, and you didn't need someone's permission to do it.

Just how many double-dollars and certificates do I need to squeeze some juice out of this thing? Now you're thinking like an exile.

Lux et vertias — light and truth. The light of reason is necessary to seek out truth, lest you find yourself fumbling around in the dark. Being so prescriptive about truth that there is nothing to discover would be like staring straight into the sun. What is a university? A place where things are discovered, or a place where you tell people what they should believe? Age those young ones. Turn them into raisins and plantains before they have even a shadow of a doubt about your loans and your paperwork. The old guard has marble statues and dildoes to polish, while they twirl their mustaches and decide whether to use double spaced lines for the midterm.

The greatest doctor I know is excellent at what they do, and also believes in a fair, just market for all people.

Meetup

Something that is apparent to me is that you have to put yourself in situations where you will meet the sort of people you are interested in. Being the pragmatic and transactional sort of person I am, it became obvious to me that the people that work at Amazon are boring as shit. At this point in my life, I was making good money and I was satisfied in a lot of ways. I felt attractive and confident, and I liked who I was, but I knew

I wasn't being true to how I really felt. The things I really wanted to say about the world wouldn't have made sense in that context, around people who really mean to *just be doing their job*, although I knew chaos was looming around the corner.

Most people in most professional environments, even ones with beanbags and free lunch, are so hung up on Newspeak and yoga that they don't have the first clue about how to have fun.

And it's also apparent that if you go to places that are designed to meet people, like Meetup groups and dating sites, you get tons of people that are a little too into *orange*. So you start wondering where you're going to make natural connections with people. And as it turns out, it's just wherever all of the girls hang out. It's simple, just open your eyes. Tada: Instagram.

I love when girls show that they are patient and interested in really understanding the world. To me that's almost as sexy as your face and your body. I don't like Instagram, though. And looking into a camera is one of the last things I think about doing. And I only really want to look at pictures of you long enough to jerk off. It's crazy to me how you just scroll through pictures of pretty girls all day. Sometimes I think you're more into pretty girls than I am.

Instagram also has the Newspeak and yoga problem. Your suit just happens to be for swimming, but you hate when people come along and say things that aren't *appropriate*. For what? Being in the list of 3 approved comments below a picture of a half-naked girl?

You love environments where people are told what to do, and I love environments where you can do what you want, and where there is an impetus to be individually correct. It's plain as day to me.

Anyway, I'm getting pretty good at this networking thing, and it has absolutely nothing to do with my ability to send emails or attend conferences. That's peasant-think. I'm bright enough orange that it stains your eyes for the rest of your life the moment you look at me. That's why I keep to myself mostly, because I only need cute girls lined up at my door, and not a bunch of hustlas with eCommerce software and mixtapes. That's more your speed.

It can be the case that we have experiences with people that keep us from ever giving them a second, or even a first chance. We start imagining this version of a person where we externalize everything that frustrates us. See me doing it now, where *you* becomes a unanimous figure of nihilistic indifference. That's just what life has taught me, but I'll try to be open minded. It's also the case that if we didn't show our differences in this way, there would be no truth to elucidate.

Winning Is Change

It has to be, that's where the opportunity to win comes from. You certainly know a lot about how you like to win, and that's why you play the games that you like. Or perhaps you can't stand playing by other people's rules and you're always looking to change the game. My advice: do it once or twice, if you really care about staying power. Put your name and your soul into it, like you're going to your grave with it. People can smell shovelware from a mile away. No one is a professional Apples to Apples player, but chess will probably be with us until the end of time. It could just be that chess takes itself more seriously. It's convinced that it requires your full attention and that you deserve to be good at it.

That's the thing about believing your name is worth something. You become uncompromising about whatever price other people put on it. It would be completely dissatisfying to you to value your time in terms of Pictionary and Uno. There is something inherently solid about your identity, that you would submit it as-is for evaluation and recognition. Winners create a reality distortion field around them that folds the world into their vision. They enjoy trends, too, if they're good ones. The best sort of trend is one that plays into their vision, and they can't much tell the difference either way since they walk around like a typhoon.

Right now, winning looks like posting on Instagram and YouTube, writing software, designing things, making music, or some combination of these things. If you're reading this in the early 21st century, this is relevant to you, but otherwise it's like following instructions in the bible to build the Ark of the Covenant. Which could be salient wisdom if you're feeling whimsical. Sometimes everyone has all their eggs in one basket and it makes a lot of sense for you to rethink the status quo and to make something evocative of some other time. Sometimes the status quo *is* retro, and that alone makes it feel contrived. The past 10 years had a lot of vinyl records, which are great for hanging on your wall. A lot of you look at the big picture, so you always have a good sense for why something is cool.

What is it that's so *sticky* about taking pictures of stuff and promoting products? That is the caricature of success right now; having something to sell, whether you came up with it or not. Do we get free samples? Not really. Do… we get to talk to you about the thing you're selling? Not usually. We get to watch you take pictures and videos of yourself doing yoga and drinking smoothies. Let's get back to basketball and Pokémon cards. The stuff on TV leaps right off the screen!

The next big thing? Live, real. The underground scene has been live for some time now, but the rest of the world is just catching up. The games show up right at your door. The clothes are designed just for you, and they fit you perfectly. You invented the restaurant, and the menu, and you also get to enjoy it like you've never even heard of it before. Welcome to Havana. She's there on opening night, which is whenever you showed up. Everything before that was preseason. You write the news and you *are* the news.

In the Iron Age this wasn't a strange thought to have. Everything has to be on a spreadsheet now for you to believe in it, though.

Winners welcome change, and they're proud of the trajectory of the world.

3

Navin's Gold Heart

I was raised for much of my childhood in Utah and a stone's throw away in southern Nevada. My parents, David Ralph Cako and Linda Cako, are exceptional people. They were lifelong mortgage brokers that ran their own business, Cako Financial, until they decided it was best to focus on raising their children.

My mother had working class parents in New York, and a well provisioned, albeit disturbed, upbringing. Her father, Ercole, emigrated from Italy as a young boy in the late 1920s, describing "barely making it on the boat", and he made a living in the Chrysler parts department. He invested every last dime in the stock market, a lifelong believer in American exceptionalism. Her mother, Marion, had Cuban and English parents that emigrated to the U.S., and she sold handmade luxury hats in black churches and other New York communities. My mother and uncle attended Catholic school, and then left New York for good, although my grandfather still lives in Yonkers.

My father was raised by my French-Native American grandmother, Doris, who emigrated to Salt Lake City from Canada and worked multiple jobs. He was very poor as a kid, but he loved baseball and seeing Elvis double-features at the theater. He was fascinated by being excellent, doing something that matters to earn your place in the world. My father began as a waiter in a restaurant, and then worked his way into a lucrative career as a mortgage broker.

My parents both recognized how important it would be for their lives to do something great in the world, and that is how they were able to give me the life that I have. They went out into the world to make a name for themselves. Fierce will is what worked for them, because when it feels like you're completely alone in the world, that is your option. They met in California, each having independently paved their way into the real estate and mortgage industry. And that's what brought them together, in a fateful course of events.

As early as I can remember, when my parents taught me how to do something, it came with the expectation that you apply your full attention and focus to whatever you are doing. If you want to learn to read, you're going to try to read all of the signs on the road and learn all of the buttons on the computer, not just the easy words in your books. When the computer does something you don't expect, you should see if you can figure out what it means. At school, you're going to try to get all of the answers right on your tests, not just most of them. When we collect cards, we're going to keep them in perfect condition and research what they are worth. When you play sports, you're going to try your best every game, even when the other team has players that are much larger. And so I did play basketball, and baseball, and tackle football. When you're getting picked on at school, you're going to stand your ground, even if the school decides that means you get in trouble too.

My mother was much less strict than my father, who, in hindsight, was about medium strict. I learned that early on, and took advantage of it. I saw my father as a bearer of requirements, and my mother as kind, and I believe both are necessary if you want to excel.

At school, everyone knew my name, which can be a good thing and a bad thing. Most people also knew that I was not Mormon because they didn't see me in church, which is quite a topic, even in Mesquite, Nevada, a one-horse town right on the border of southern Nevada and Utah. My parents moved there because they thought it was a more diverse place to raise kids as Catholics than in Utah. And the reason we were in Utah is because my dad reflected fondly on living there. I love Utah. Park City is truly beautiful, and also southern Utah near Zion. Everything about Utah and the Latter Day Saints is meant to be excellent in every way, a mark that was imprinted on me, that I hold very dearly. All of the things in my life that I love most tend to remind me of Utah.

The other kids that weren't Mormon were mostly Mexican and Native American. I had friends of all colors, boys and girls, and we all played together. It didn't occur to me to evaluate people's color until I got older, and I saw why people's experiences in life are often shaped by the way they look. It certainly occurred to everyone else that I was the black sheep in Mesquite, though. *David knows everything*, kids and teachers would lament. Truly a bittersweet fate, as an 8 year old, to be possessed by the secular vices of computers, movies, and rock and roll. But they did believe I was a miracle, and they knew God put me in their lives for a reason. Mormons believe everything in the world is for a good reason, which is a healthy attitude to have about life that would have been difficult for me to believe until much later on.

My greatest fear, far and away, was the feeling that I was somewhere that was going nowhere. That my town would never have interesting places to go or fast internet, and I would never meet people who loved technology and big ideas like I did from a very young age. I looked around and saw people that barely knew what a computer was, in a town that I heard might be getting a Walmart next year. My father told me Mesquite was a *one-horse town*, and I knew quite well what he meant. He taught me people in Mesquite were *hoosiers*, a catch-all term he used for rednecks, and that I would need to have much greater expectations for my life than any of my peers. I wondered why, then, were we there, and not somewhere important. I felt like the world was moving slowly in reverse around me, a feeling that compounded in unusual ways as I got older.

My father had hepatitis from sharing needles when he was younger. He survived, undergoing treatment with a 50/50 success rate that was often much less effective than what we have now, although my parents' marriage did not. My parents fought a lot at this point, and my dad would retreat into sports while he felt like his life may be ending. Their separation didn't ruin my life, but the amount of moving around that followed certainly felt like it did. Now, I know everything happens exactly the way it's meant to. At the time, all I could feel was a complete lack of structure and consistency, which is the only thing I knew to appreciate about life. It made me feel disgusted.

We moved to Henderson, a beautiful suburb of Las Vegas, where I got to start over in a place that my name wasn't so important, and neither was being Mormon, or not being Mormon, in my case. Here, my mom met the man who would be my stepfather to this day, and I got on quite well with his younger son, who had a similar enthusiasm for video games that I did, albeit 10 years older than me. The schools in the Vegas area were just as orderly as I came to expect, with Vegas having an excellent capacity for reinvesting tax dollars from the casinos into education and recreational facilities. Around this time my father moved to the Philippines, feeling rejected, on a second-lease for his life. And then we moved to Thousand Oaks, California, near my family in the (entertainment) industry; yes, that one. And then to Corpus Christi, Texas, which was like moving to a different planet. And then to the Dallas area, near my other uncle and aunt, themselves in commercial real estate. And then to Colorful Colorado, where I got to start my life. No real method to the madness, except to remind me that I am always right at home. Work, money, family, drama. Now, the world seems small to me. I got to go on my own sort of mission and learn about all of the sorts of people there are. All along the way, I would be blessed with people that knew just when to show up in my life. We wouldn't remember our fates until now that I know to remind you.

The one thing I learned is that everywhere I go, I am bright orange —
and red, more red than you would ever hope to see in your life. No matter what size of school, or what sort of people, there's nowhere for

me to hide. And that wouldn't have been like me to do, anyway. I like orange, but it's also a large responsibility to make sure everyone understands your ground rules about being orange. Namely, that you are on good terms with everyone until you aren't. In middle school and high school, your trust in people tends to erode one way or another. But I was smart and funny, and kind to most people. And I knew all the angles, on everything.

Now I reflect fondly on elementary school, the odd yellow desert town and the familiar few hundred kids that all knew each other. I have fond memories of the odd western frontier, mining and geological attractions, old casinos, stagecoaches, and wild-west museums. And scorching dry desert heat. The kind that I bring into every room. The whole world starts feeling like Mesquite, and at once I remember the feeling of being orange. Like Madalyn, whose frizzy hair was actually orange, whose big eyes were light blue, and who loved Jack Sparrow and theatre.

God Lets You Win

If you're like me, you believe that God does, in fact, run the bingo. If he let you win, what does that mean for the guy he let lose? For one, God stands for free will, which means that the opportunity to win exists in relationship to your talent and the effort you put into something, and that also means that randomness exists where it counts. Winning makes sense in this world, which is right where it belongs.

I believe God is androgynous, truly just and impartial.

What if you believe that the world is actually *less* fair with a choosy God in it? Maybe you disagree with the classification of righteousness before you, or you find it difficult to believe someone or something could enact truly impartial justice in the world. Should we play on separate realms, or should we have a battle of wits where we find out, once and for all, if God is the greatest?

Belief in God is sort of like belief in a planned economy. I find it quite pleasant, the people and things that I encounter as result of my faith. It's especially comforting to know that, even when the world would turn its back on you, God makes sure that you receive your portion. God sees righteousness where the world is blind to it.

The experiences you have, walking in faith, make certainty a mysterious constant in life. Every word you speak and every step you take is colored by an exceptional force that puts you in just the right place at just the right time. These events in my life, where I knew just where to be, are so foundational to the person I am today that I couldn't imagine any other version of me existing. I love that I am analytical, intentional, resilient, and always so true to you.

For free will to be truly free, perhaps the potency of choice in your life should be as individual as conceivably possible. I describe choice as *potency* because it's difficult to imagine what fate is really ours alone, in this psychedelic-tinged outlook on life. Still, righteousness is a shared experience with many participants.

If you follow this to its logical extreme, it's easy to start valuing your name and your individuality as a vessel even more than the cogent experience of making decisions in the apparent sequence of events. I wonder, did I get better job opportunities because people and companies knew, from the future, that they would end up getting a shout-out in this book? If God can guide your hand and your words, the general shape of you must be the basis for what sorts of energy you manifest in your life. There is a congruence to all of the things that can happen next based on what has already happened and the apparent laws of nature.

Are there *good* names to have? The ones that you should give your children so that they start off on a good foot before they even have a conscious experience. I wonder about this, and I wonder if we had our names and our destinies long before we were born. Our names can be accurate and ironic. I'm told that I'm quite sweet, and also quite bitter so that I don't get eaten. You knew just what name to have to get my attention, almost as if you selected it yourself, or God put you here just for me.

Perfect, If

I'd be perfect if I wasn't so red, and you'd be perfect if you were younger, and my computer would be perfect if it was faster. Isn't that true? And isn't it true that *perfect, if* is what makes it quite perfect in its own right? We discussed how *unopinionated sterility* is useful for selling milk and sneakers, but now you want to do something that's *right* which means there's input involved. You have to make a mark of some sort, and perhaps you already have a mark that makes you beautiful. A blank page isn't yet beautiful by most standards. How elusive beauty can be. Art looks interesting when it has something strange about it, and food tastes good when it has an unusual twist. What makes you beautiful is that you keep scampering away from what seems obvious. You find things in places that wouldn't even begin to occur to anyone else.

The moment you gave it a name, it became something. You're a lot like an engineer, whether you know it or not, because everything in the world seems like something you could interface with. And you're a lot like an artist, because you love to find something new.

I want you to come up with some things that you love because they aren't perfect. The inconsistency is what keeps you exploring those things and excited for what you will discover, because every bit of it looks brand new, and everything else just seems pasteurized by comparison. Wouldn't you prefer art with peculiar palettes, moody tints and contrast? A marble countertop with sparkling gradients and majestic swirls, a bit cold and unapproachable for your bare hands; careful, your tongue might get stuck. If there wasn't a flippant spirit in nature, would we not all be simulacra of our imagined selves?

So keep evaluating the world and exploring, because *nothing* is beautiful that is final. The thing that's beautiful about you, of course, is that you are just who you are every day.

Justice from Above

I've heard David's a control freak. He can't go 2 words without coming up with some way to steer the narrative. Speaking wouldn't serve a purpose for him unless he could come up with some way to lead you along his bunny trail into some sort of grand realization about the universe. He hates when you remind him of this, too, because he pretends like all he cares about is having a good time.

You can't be winning and teaching at the same time, precisely speaking. It's basically one or the other at a time. If I want to play with you, I have to come down from my glass tower and meet you eye to eye. And if you want to enact justice, you have to elevate yourself above the subtext of the game. A lot of us are stuck in the bullpen, playing with our phones and our dicks. We forgot how to meet people where they're at and have an ordinary interaction.

Technology is great for enabling more justice, but terrible for putting you in situations to cuddle. We're working on changing that. You're going to show up in exactly the right place at the right time.

It's a special talent to always be in situations where you're just doing your thing, and to have justice crop up in your wake. That way, you don't always have to be jamming things in place, but you can still point people in the right direction. This is why it's important for you to be a person, unique from and at-once of God. You get to *elucidate* reality from the world of distinctions. God needs you to see anything at all happen in the world and that's why you should hope to be a winner.

You can say one thing to mean something entirely different; that's difficult subtext to abstract into justice. Cuddling *may* be forceful, and some people enjoy that, but the thing that makes it hot, mostly, is that it's squirrely. I love this particular challenge, because I love describing complex dynamics in vivid detail. And maybe I kind of like using you like a tool.

Many things in life seem unfair in the medium-term, but I believe everything is fair in the long run, the deliberate reflection of whatever you put into life. Some retribution just has a long enough term that it outlives the people that deserve to enjoy it, tragically. Justice works best with particular feedback loops. It also requires people to enact it that can actually see the world for what it is. How long would you let fascism go unchecked in the world? If it's really so obvious to correct, were Germans in the 20th century just particularly foolish?

You're all different, I'm sure. Only because you're reading this book. Otherwise, I don't trust people further than I can throw them because they really just won't say anything, no matter what they see happen. High school, work, the internet. All the same thing, people mostly void of personal conviction and so desperate for acceptance that they would become nameless and voiceless. Unless I leave my dog in the car with the windows open for more than 10 minutes, then everyone's a hero. Only in Denver for some reason. A real winner looks at a situation like that and figures out how to put a dog in every hot car on the planet so that you fucking pay attention to what they have to say. With the windows down. Because as it turns out, there is no other way to get you to pay attention.

Land over Foot

You can't say my name, talk about the stuff I invented, or even think about me without attributing me. That's how I stopped worrying about whether anyone is willing to acknowledge that I'm right. Everything I say is sticky and leaves footprints everywhere you go. Usually if it has my name all over it, it ends up being worth a lot more than if it didn't, and I bake reason into the pie. We utilize a clever sort of empiricism where you understand it just by looking at it. All too often, philosophy is impractical and hypothetical, but you're living it, baby. You're a winner, so you'll figure out how to make systems that serve you well. Otherwise, people will just have you believe your ideas aren't worth anything.

Everywhere you go, the world looks a little more hopeful. You illuminate everything you see. Something about who you are strengthens the foundation you stand on, clears the air, and purifies the water. Having this power to generate lucid thinking all around you is gravitational. People you know all start feeling like they're walking on the ceiling, because the group you've got together really means to be inquisitive about everything in the world.

Now, practice playing in time with other people. Boy, is that ever the hard part. You see a squirrel and you're running off at it a million miles an hour, but we need to hear the orchestra play together in time. And when they do, the whole theater is electric. The ground is shaking and the world stands still. It makes the solo that much better, because they're trying to shake off the band, and the band just keeps closing in around them. That's a wild goose chase if you've ever seen one, into another dimension.

The most important ingredient in innovation is looking in the right places for it. If you pay too much attention the way things are, you're not going to be covering the right ground. If you are throwing away good ideas and holding onto bad ones, you're done. Innovation starts with vision. The people you get together are perfectly sensitive to what makes great ideas great, and those are the things they will be drawn to naturally. Watch someone shop for a few minutes. Ask them why they picked out what they did, and what their favorite things about it are. This is plenty for me to decide whether someone is innovative.

There's value in placing stock in people who are directionally accurate and are moving fast enough to help you succeed. But all systems ossify. Eventually, it starts seeming like the structures everyone has propped up for you aren't really helping you get what you want out of life. Like you're being swallowed by the foundation, turning purple, and losing yourself to a faceless void. People understand this feeling quite well, and they have for thousands of years. Grace is like weightlessness in quicksand.

Alemka's Tip, I See Vick

A lot of people forgot how victory works, and consequently they have a sort of disbelief for why people would get into fights. *Just believe in what's right!* Yes, the perfect truth where our choices are already made for us any every want is provisioned for. Our healthcare universal and our morals absolute. Like our heavenly existence, where we begin whole.

It's inconceivable to you how a war could begin now that we *all* believe in social justice and superfruits. Like the opaque colonialism of JavaScript and Marvel. It didn't even occur to you that it drives the world absolutely fucking insane to turn on their American cell phone and browse the American internet. It does to me though. I know the things we make must be excellent to justify their existence, and even then the mere notion of being beholden to the west will frustrate some people.

An interesting way of looking at it is all social order is meant to change; we always mean to be finding somewhere new to be free and true. We all are born *left*, and we become progressively more *right* as we install people to the left of us. People should believe in peace and prosperity, enough to recognize that's precisely the mechanism that ossifies our social order and has us wishing there was somewhere free for us. Some place where a new thing could engage with victory and stand on its own as true. Prosperity is the period of time where the people that were there to see peace get to sit on their mountain of wealth and build more shopping malls. Certainly, though, people will convince themselves they are satisfied with smaller cars and homes, the weight of Rockefeller and the phone company bearing down on them 200 years later. Until it seems like the prevailing order is too big and slow, and we must find greener pastures.

It would be just as easy to say globalism isn't important to us, and we don't need to incentivize incredible success and wealth. To do so would be to lose sight of everything that makes America great, though. Many countries don't have a lot of choices about how the world pans out, but they absolutely trust America as a just and impartial mediator in many of the world's affairs. While everyone is overreaching, underperforming, and causing absolute chaos, people become satisfied that iPhones, Lockheed Martin, and Instagram are an easy pill to swallow. Because they know that many Americans only believe in what is true.

We would never make mistakes, if we could all be so excellent. The righteous are something just shy of convenient. All they would hope for is excellence, and they receive in kind. My advice? Don't look too far into things past convenience. American, after all, as it is for me to say. People are going to try to make things more than they are, to get you doing jumping jacks while you wait for your cheeseburger and levying their tax on you to insert themselves into the pipeline. All along the way, it is *necessary* to draw lines in the sand and let people decide, for themselves, if they're going to waste your time. Maybe they really do see greatness for what it is, and they will cherish it like you do.

People have all different dials and gizmos on their watches. My watch has a fuel gauge, and it runs empty when you waste my time. This is an instrument of perfection, because we usually regard time as infinite. If my watch was that forgiving, I wouldn't be so great at what I do.

Trickle Down

Innovation trickles down and that makes it affordable and accessible to everyone. A $300 TV, in 2023, looks as good as a $2,000 TV from 2010. If you're a thought leader, you inspire innovation throughout the entire industry. Think carefully about what sort of world you want to live in. When it's all said and done, the world is going to look a lot like you planned on it being. I'm quite deliberate about giving you the *tools* to think effectively, because that means you can identify what does and doesn't make sense without me having to tell you, and you can even identify when I overestimate how important various attributes are. We all have our biases, and you see me in a way I can't see myself.

Right now, the most important innovation occurring is that computers are becoming smart enough to *program themselves*, so to speak. Traditional software engineering meant you had to explain to the computer exactly what to do to solve a problem. Now, we are seeing *artificial intelligence* systems that accept general questions and tasks, and are able to make extremely elaborate decisions about what it was that you wanted. It could generate beautiful art using any picturesque style you want, answer questions about economic trends, or build a website for you to sell your pottery, all just by telling it what you want to see. This is powerful for people no matter what their skill level with technology is, because the computer can fill all the gaps.

The murky side of this is it means there's an immense consolidation of power and resources. Once A.I. does everything for you, doesn't that mean the world kind of belongs to A.I., or whomever created the A.I.? Will we have hunger anymore when everything is automatic? What will social mobility look like?

At every point in human history, there's been some type of *trickle down* administration. We're great at gamifying the world now, so it's natural to us that everyone gets opportunity and some amount of money relative to their skills. Before that, though, you were fundamentally at the mercy of a king or an emperor to reliably ensure that resources were *trickling down*. There's only so many pieces of metal to turn into coins, after all, and only so much food that we pull out of the ground. People had faith in God as the king of kings, to right every wrong and answer for every famine. When the rulers have gone stale, the kingdom has ossified, and the rich only keep getting richer, what would you rely on to balance the scales? People are quite talented at being free. Faith assures us that we will always be free.

Dalaran

It's interesting how the world will go ahead and dispense with exactly what you need at just the right time. Fair as our world is, right thinking and right action are all that it takes to get just what you wanted.

I spent the morning of my birthday mining titanium in World of Warcraft. I'm building a robot named Jeeves that gives me instant portable access to my bank, to go with my portable mailbox MOLL-E, and my portable merchant and blacksmith that ride along on my giant ice mammoth.

I find, with unusual consistency, rituals that are personally meaningful to me tend to yield the best results. The flight patterns that I take on my griffin and the times I embark can make all the difference for how many of these precious minerals I discover on the land below, while those things aren't necessarily meaningful in the context of the game. And now, as I near completion of my shiny mechanical servant, the same areas I've been prospecting begin drying up, as if I've hit a ceiling of wealth. All things in due time, indiscriminately, with right action.

World of Warcraft has a nearly infinite victory threshold. Depending on how you like to play, you can play forever without being able to say, definitively, that you won. Most games are not like that, and not everyone appreciates a game like that. The addictiveness of the game comes from the fact that you always have somewhere to go next, with minor victories along the way. Lots of people will work on many characters at once, but I don't really have the attention span. I like to really enjoy the aspect of *victory*.

I love the parts of the game that involve clever devices, rare collectibles, and commerce. It's absolutely magical to put in the work and have something to show for it. Particular areas make me feel wistful and nostalgic of many years ago when I was first exploring and discovering the vast landscape. Now, over 15 years later, I go back to the game when there's new content and I get to continue enjoying the character I've spent so much time building up.

After many hours have disappeared into some void, you'll eventually finish all of the main content and wonder what to do next. You have to come up with your own games at that point, deciding which secondary content is interesting to you. I like to play areas that look cool to me. Yes, at any point in time there is an objectively best place to be collecting the best equipment and crafting reagents, but we do remember that we play games for fun and for the aesthetic and tangible qualities that we enjoy. The excellent thing about it is the variety, between solo and group gameplay, hundreds of areas, dozens of professions and specializations, and a perfect class just for you, there's truly something for everyone.

Who is John Galt?

When you imagine freedom and exceptionalism, are you imagining someone who actually exists? If the only people on your mind are rose-tinted images of eras long past, what is the freedom that you are imagining? Freedom is here and now, that every word you speak and every breath you take is meant to serve a sense of purpose for the world you know. So long as you continue sanitizing and polishing John Galt into a round orb, he disappears. That's not what you want, is it? Then why, when someone has something important and revolutionary to say, is it the instinct of so many people to wave them off as crackpots, in favor of syrupy and vague idealism — something about diversity and health food, nothing about love and hunger.

You can't see John Galt. Like an ox, he operates at a precipice that you haven't yet met. But you can see the world that he painstakingly bears because the only thing that's ever occurred to him is correctness. He eats the same fried chicken dinner every day, as he had for the past 30 years, but he also believes it's particularly important that you have vegetarian and gluten-free options available. John Galt knows what it looks like when they all try to feed you poison, and you can't — or won't — tell the difference. Ever since he introduced himself to the FDA, his confidence in his health and the average American's health has improved.

John Galt has seen the institutions around him crumble and the spirit of freedom and purpose silenced and squashed. He knows that everything in life is the precise reflection of what you put into it, so he has grown confident, with age, that you will see endless torment and absolute injustice until you commit yourself to seeing something that looks *correct* show up in the world. What John sees is a world that has abdicated its crown and renounced its faith. And John Galt knows that such a world becomes so infinitesimally vague that he could pick it up and throw it straight into the sun. He could flatten it in an instant riposte, but he knows that would make him no better than the abject void he has managed his way out of. So John picks it up with his own hands and casts a final judgement upon the world, a piercing ultraviolet gaze as he turns and faces those who wouldn't bear even the weight of their own bones. You can't see John Galt, and it's at this point that it's plainly obvious to him that John will never see himself. When you answer to John Galt, you will, plainly, have nothing to say.

You won't recognize John Galt by the color of his skin, his title, or even necessarily the way he speaks, but you will certainly recognize his relentless devotion to truth, to the near disassociation of himself. Something you might notice about John Galt as you get to know him is a plain skepticism for ideology buried underneath an absolute conviction of faith. How did he get that way, you'll wonder? What mysterious path could someone walk along to become so tarnished by truth? John Galt would tell you books are too long, except for the ones that you like. There's no description of reality that's worth holding your time captive, and he certainly doesn't string a paragraph of adjectives together every time he looks at the historic downtown post office. John Galt would barely encourage you to be a winner. Ayn Rand seemed plainly convinced that he is a man, and there are quite boyish qualities to him.

That's my guess, though, because I truly can't read a novel for more than 10 pages. You could call your mom, or spend hours reading an ancient Jew drivel about truth in the wake of World War II. Burn more library books, while you're at it.

I hope John Galt gets his way, but only after I get mine, and you'd just as well hope he *doesn't* exist, for that matter. If I had a date with a young Elizabeth Taylor, we'd enjoy the coffee and the garden.

If Christ lived next door to you, what would you do when they show up to have him executed? What would you have done in the months leading up to it during endless tribulations and accounts of his wickedness? Would it be plain for you to see he is a prophet and a holy man? What makes you so sure?

Faith is how I know that retribution will be with us everywhere, and not a single one will be left unaccounted for. When the whole world would turn its back to you, all people will receive their heavenly portion. When they all crawl into their caves, cowering, voiceless, blind, mute, and void of reason, God is at the very end of the line to stick his neck out for you. He is your assurance that they will know endless torment, the most bitter taste you could know, on account of the resounding chasm in their souls where holy people feel righteousness. You would spend every moment of eternity pleading for such a kind, faithful, and true man as Christ to be graced upon you, for some refrain from the hand of the Holy One of Israel that would be raised upon you like a cataclysmic thunder.

AliExpress

$3 went a long way on DealExtreme 10 years ago — flashlights, tools, watches — yes, even *those*. AliExpress is getting expensive. Have you noticed? If they don't get their act together, someone else is going to come along and start charging what this stuff is actually worth, which is how AliExpress became popular in the first place.

Now, if everything is going to be marked up to domestic prices, I may as well just go buy a Leatherman and be proud of my purchase.

This is the eternal dance between dilution and solidification of identity. Winners don't like sacrificing quality, but lots of people do. If they aren't paying attention to the details, they'll end up jacking up the price of the cheap option too much, giving you an opportunity to give people a new intermediate option that gives them better quality and better service.

China has unusual market dynamics. Everything is kind of all one thing, and merchants could more or less rig the prices and still make you think you have lots of choices.

Folks with excellent supplier relationships are able to negotiate really good deals and guarantee great quality. A lot of the time, you're going to need to put different factories and countries into the mix if you're noticing that you're getting stone-walled. A free market exists *somewhere*, you just have to set up the incentives for it.

People wonder what a *fair price* for something really is. The only true answer is *what the market will bear*. But if you spend too much time thinking about it, you will become preoccupied with the fact that cars can be made for a few thousand dollars, and expensive laptops for under $50. That's if you believe in a perfectly efficient economy, though, where the practical cost of the materials can be converted instantly into a computer. Along the way, there was expensive research and development by engineers and many other folks responsible for design, marketing, and management. There were startup costs for factories that are beyond anything you can imagine, especially if they are creating entirely new processes and technologies. And for all of the risk and many years invested in the project, they expect significant return when the thing is finally boxed up and delivered to your door.

Economies of scale make everything more affordable and competitive, but companies still work hard to convince us that the next big thing is worth buying so that we don't feel like giant conglomerates are 3D printing cars and cashing in on us year after year. Where's our jobs and our stocks? Big questions, soon to be answered on a planet near you.

Sharpie

What are your thoughts on permanent markers? I love things that are permanent, but I didn't used to, and now I'm wondering when I'm going to start hating it. Certainly, we are built to crave novelty and we become frustrated on a deep level when there's an elephant in every room. Or, you *are* the elephant in every room, and you're green enough that the thought that everyone else can't stand when they're next to you hasn't occurred to you.

When I'm working on something that excites me or playing World of Warcraft, doing all of nothing, I can blink and 3 hours have passed. So why is that? A better question is, what is that thing for you, that you do masturbatorially for hours straight without thinking twice?

When you don't really know what you're doing, your tendency is going to be half-stepping and short-stroking everything. People can tell. Plainly, you can't wait to get out of the pilot's seat so someone else can land. You need books and blogposts about *distraction-free writing* because the only thing you can think about is how you really aren't addicted to what you're doing, there's a nail scraping on chalkboard the entire time you're writing because you feel like you have nothing important to say. You're constantly policing your own tone, worrying what Jesus and Steve Jobs would have said, because the idea that you'd just say what you want to say and slam on the whammy bar doesn't seem at-home with you.

Or, you're the exact opposite, and you believe the divinely inspired word of God pours from your mouth and your pen, that your name is eternal and your mark is a grace upon the world. Now your books sit on your shelf and they're worth more to you than gold.

When you really know what you're doing, your instinct is to make the same mark over and over again, like a hydraulic press stamping on steel.

You are so self-satisfied by that mark that you just want to keep seeing it show up, and you are so involved with your tools that you are just obsessed with holding them and thinking about them. Every time you pick up the instrument, the same damn riff comes out. I guess that's who you are. Even the most unique animals have symmetry to their feathers and their fur. The most talented artists will do anything and everything to see something new come out. They'll use completely new tools and techniques, play on the moon, underwater, telepathically, and blindfolded. But their handwriting stays the same. Their muscles and bones all grew into exactly where they belong, and every synapse in their brain is set up to crave *that* particular sound, or a particular palette and prose.

Do you ever hear a song that you like, and then go listen to the rest of the album and it sounds nothing like it? Incorporating a familiar motif into everything that you do can be a good thing, because your audience knows they can keep coming back for more. To you, it seems like you're doing the same thing over and over again, but that's exactly what got them hooked. You keep introducing flourishes and textures, and the whole thing makes sense as your style evolves.

When some people make their mark on something, it becomes much more valuable than if they hadn't. That's why hot new apps want to get famous people endorsing them, and why a movie becomes more desirable when a popular actor is producing it. They don't even have to show up on set or be in the movie. Their name alone means something.

Ideally, you have a more than superficial way to make your name valuable. Your involvement with projects is exciting because of your sense of style and purpose. Your mark makes it look a certain way, but the spirit of *you* makes the caravan drive forward. Anyone can make a flashlight or a perfume in theory, but when your name is on it, everyone knows it's going to be special.

Police Girl

What are your thoughts on *orange?* I'm going to let you in on a little secret: *orange* is how you will know if you met the one. If, in your eyes, they put orange on everything, suffocating, captive, you're going to resent each other in short time. If they keep pounding pints of you like an alcoholic — bottoms up — they simply can't spend enough time at your hip, holding their phone up to you and gesturing *look!*, the only thing you will want is to get away. If it takes you too long to believe this, you're going to keep throwing away great relationships because you're convinced it's because they just need to like more of the movies you do.

How long will he take chiseling you? Sponging up every last semblance of fecundity and aqueous vacillation to make you just dry enough to walk right into the deep end. Ah yes, now she's perfect, like brand new socks and lime green Gatorade. Like stepping out of the shower on a warm summer day, standing out on the patio and feeling the intense, dry heat beaming down on you while you remember *the good guys* won in the new Avengers movie. Yes, she believes in being right, just like you. You both love AOC, getting to the airport 3 hours early, and quinoa. Now that he asked his best mate and his parents, he's pretty sure he's ready to get married.

He never feels that way, and he suspends his disbelief because he loves you. Also, because he isn't looking to change you. The world spent billions of years becoming perfect, just so he could wake up early on a cool Colorado morning and fuck you exactly as you are, the way you came out. Is that wrong, that she has different expectations for him than he does for her? Any man of hers ought to secretly find her nearly intolerable, as it stands. Who wouldn't? No one could ever be as orange as he is. He's disgusted by orange, like school lunch. He'd rather eat fruit snacks and candy bars every day for the rest of the year than tear into another soaking, sweating cellophane bag for a soggy grilled cheese sandwich.

Say you've found a girl that feels like the only woman in the world when she's around you. Perhaps, then, would she be self assured enough to turn blue, like everything else she can see. Perhaps, still, she could imagine something like justice, where the part and parcel of the world is of absolutes and equals. Where, then, if only you turn away, can she see the world clearly and truly, from sea to shining sea.

Go Home

It became quite troubling to me that she didn't know how to answer a door, because this is an important feature for her. Although this is consistent with the theme in my life that I am an unusual color, and everyone would rather stare from a distance than talk to me as a person. I don't go out of my way for people for this reason; really, you don't make it worthwhile most of the time. It's important that you go out of your way for me, though, because there are things about the way the world works that makes making my acquaintance quite valuable.

Isn't it interesting that I am expected to take all of the big risks, and some people just get off on making things inconvenient? The odd thing about the way the world works is someone with no convictions about anything can have something bad to say about you, and then everyone will take that at face value and decide you're more trouble than you're worth. *Plain* people have a sort of covenant with each other, so they can operate their very own welfare state like the cast and crew of a Wes Anderson film. I suppose you'd just as well be frustrated that all of your opinions are outsourced, and your circumstances are imposed on you by others. Do you make an effort for the world to be any different?

Living with someone is a lot more intimate than visiting or working with them. All of the winning in the world doesn't make you easy to be around. Instead, those things keep us from thinking too much about the immediacy of being with our family and with our thoughts. It may not be overcompensating, precisely speaking, but it's quite obvious what kind of ideas occupy our minds. There's this sneaky feeling we get that we have be something more than we are, because just *being* is not enough. When you win, who is going to be there to enjoy it with you?

Are you nice, thoughtful, and curious about people? I hope to be. The people in my life that are like this are gracious and warm in everything they do. They make every day feel cheerful, and they would never let me doubt myself. Who really believes in you?

They know you like you know yourself, and even better. How you catastrophize, project your emotions on everyone else, and beat yourself up. How nothing is ever enough for you, because you're not even enough for yourself. The thing you put your whole life into probably doesn't make sense to them, and they came to terms with that. Perhaps for you, it's inconceivable that someone else has something important to them that doesn't make sense to you. But something special about who they are deep inside makes it easy for them to be so much more understanding of who you are.

Cooperate

You're going to be so happy to have people in your life that play the games that you like. When you look over, that's what you're going to see them doing.

Conversely, if you bring *winning* home with you, your life is going to be like carrying around a pile of bricks that you never get to put down. You're going to keep inviting people onto your team to triangulate and triage each other, because it's so obvious that you'd be winning more if you had more special teams players.

At home, you get to agree that your partner is better at some things than you are. If you really love them, you're going to be so proud and excited to see them do well.

4

True

Sometimes I'll hear you play something off the cuff, so deep in the pocket, and I'll wonder how it can be that you completely hide your power level on studio tracks. Truly, when you are just enjoying yourself it sounds like you are playing something from another world, like time is coming to a halt, then you'll go track something in the studio and it's in a box. I love how you play so much that I hope you read this and make a studio album I like, because I know you're one of the greatest drummers alive right now.

Rule #1: we gotta get you in the pocket. Sheesh. Great teams keep innovating, many, many years after it seems like they already won. Natural leaders can see excellently in the dark and around corners, and they leave plenty of time for everyone to be heard. These sorts of leaders are groundbreaking and energizing for everyone around them.

Steve Jobs had this sort of attitude that the type of people worth hiring always knew something he didn't, and they were willing to challenge the status quo to figure out what's really best. We *already have* 100 engineers. *What do you think about*, night and day, that they don't?

I can tell that you sit at your drum set and play until your fingers bleed. And I can tell that you study artificial intelligence and machine learning until you forget what words even are. You'll do great here.

A lot of people aren't going to fit in at a company like that. Fine — go work at Microsoft. If you love the bitter details, though, you're going to be very particular about what makes something great, and that's the only thing in the world that you're going to care about. They won't get it.

A lot of companies stagnate because the people working there don't really want to keep innovating. They want to say *there, it's done!* and then go on vacation and ride out their pensions.

Great teams have elasticity and a bone to pick with each other. They're willing to get to the crux of every last decision so that they always make the right call. If you're just shoveling code and making it easy on everyone, you're never really being deliberate. And if all that counts is *metrics,* like how many bugs get fixed and whether someone is friendly with product managers and customers, they will never speak up about the stuff that counts; which, to be clear, *does* include fixing bugs and being friendly.

If you're building a team for the Apple Music app, rest assured that everyone on that team should be listening to music, on that app, every day of the week. They can tell you exactly what they love about it and what makes it fun to use. They've been listening to music on every app out there, for many years. They saw the progression from ripping CDs, to MP3s, to streaming, and they know what makes Apple Music convenient and easy to use, whether they're at home, on their computer, or in the car with their phone tossed into the center console.

Everyone on the team listens to different music, and that's great because everyone's always talking about the hottest records. Above all, everyone is eating their own dogfood.

Dogfood

There's a saying in software that all of the greatest companies always *eat their own dogfood.* There's a reason for this, because if you don't eat your own dogfood, you aren't really sure what's good and bad about it. Hell, if you didn't make something you wanted to use yourself, what's the point in it anyway? Sure, maybe you make something that's great for a specific demographic that you aren't a part of, but really, you want to be so excited about the thing you're making that you almost want it all for yourself.

Amazon is a great example of a company that scaled to an incredible size and is still able to be agile, responding to customers and requirements from across the organization in record time. They're a *process* company, through and through. At Amazon, a lot of the processes in one department will permeate to another department because they found that it works so well. The cohesion of the whole company is built on customer satisfaction and performance indicators. This applies whether you're on the team responsible for product pages or on the cloud services team that's deploying managed applications for major businesses on Amazon's cloud platform.

Amazon is a very *pasteurized* company. Performance indicators and metrics are great for ensuring a specific type of success. It makes for exceptionally fast delivery times and quality customer service, but it's not really the sort of thing you want to use to come up with *the next big thing*, which is why *the next big thing* is never going to come out of Amazon. It's going to come out of a company like Apple or some place you haven't heard of yet, because they are laser-focused on coming up with something specific and special that's brand new. Credit where credit is due: Amazon pioneered faster and more efficient logistics than anyone else in the world, by miles.

Apple has a unique talent for figuring out what you want before you even knew you wanted it. Not only that, but they can show you the thing you don't yet know you want and you'll understand it just by looking at it. They knew it would have to be this way, the way you look at a plate of steaming crispy red hot wings covered in buffalo sauce and know, immediately, you need to get them in your mouth. Except they have to do that for something you've never tasted before. It has to be descriptively accurate by virtue of existing. That's magic.

Apple is specific. It's either great, or it doesn't get shipped. They imagined what you'd think the moment you look at the ad, and that's what they were using as their frame of reference while they were designing the actual thing you would be using. The product might even make it to an assembly line before people have an early production model in their hands that they decide isn't really something people want.

Apple products all run on chips that Apple invented, on software that Apple created, manufactured on assembly lines that Apple designed. *That's* eating your own dogfood. And it means that the devices are 100x more secure and the batteries last much longer, because they make devices like fine watches, where every detail counts.

Now, we have great dogfood, but if I'm being honest about the world today, it's all we eat. Endless — dogfood. Feed, tweets, games. But it is pretty great dogfood.

If you've got a lot of dogfood that you aren't happy about eating, maybe it's something worth investigating. Some work is just challenging, and there's no obvious way to optimize it. Other times, there's dogfood that you're used to eating out of habit, and you just keep convincing yourself you have to eat it. So, do you? How hard is it to write a script that keeps you from doing the same tedious data-entry task every week? Soon, I imagine A.I. is going to be able to automate any task you want just by asking. Which is great. Most *glue scripts* and automation aren't really that complicated, but for us humans, it requires a lot of research and thought to put the pieces together for the first time. Artificial intelligence looks at standard paperwork and laughs at how long it takes us.

Some things are software problems, and some things are people problems. Lots of people prefer human oversight, sometimes for good reasons. Otherwise you could just look at city zoning and clerical tasks and just say *throw more software at it*. Really, though, you have to figure out what the people that oversee these issues have on their minds, and that's

going to help you figure out what to make for them that's going to be
satisfying.

I Hope You Win

I want to play the game you make, see you hit more home runs than
anyone ever had before, star in the greatest movie ever made, and
perform miracles beyond anything anyone could ever imagine. I'm
rooting for you because I love to see something new. Just as importantly,
I'm not competing with you, otherwise I would only care about myself
winning. I won't interrupt you. Everything works out best when your
juices are flowing.

Today, philosophy is all about persuasion and business. A sign of the
times: those are the questions people are asking. What role does
technology have in our lives? Do our ideas really belong to us? Does our
likeness really belong to us, when A.I. can generate a movie that looks and
sounds exactly like us? A lot of guys only want to shoot on film, and now
you're going to have people insisting that it's actually Tom Cruise, the live
person and not the digital model, in the movie.

Winning means we're going to have to put our heads together, because
that's going to get us thinking about things in ways aren't obvious to us.
We've got folks that know the ins and outs of Washington and
Hollywood, but the important thing is *synergy*. We're able to get a lot of
people looking at the same thing for an extended period of time, which is
surprisingly difficult. It's the only way to actually understand something
on a deep level. Unusual perspectives and discussions are how we will
arrive at unusual truths.

Winning is very much a state of mind. All of that stuff about
manifesting? It's 100% real. Believe in truth and excellence, and that is
what will grow all around you. Trust me on this one.

Something interesting I've noticed about winners is that they are very
good at lifting themselves out from under adversity. When you ask them

difficult questions, where other people might feel like they're being put on-blast and they have to apologize for something, winners are very good at steering the narrative and anchoring the talking points around hopeful expectations. That's just what a confident person is like. They can slow down for a moment and really think about what you're saying, to answer in a reasonable and self-assured way. Simply put, they have a durable chariot.

We find ourselves in unusual habits with our conversations and our expectations for the world. When things tend to go well for you, difficult conversations can seem quite effortless. And when things tend to be difficult for you, you always seem on the defensive. It can be a self-fulfilling prophecy.

Can you come up with good ways to steer the narrative for yourself? When you interview, do you have ways to flip the script when you're being challenged? Imagine yourself standing up straight, and imagine yourself winning. Imagine being so good at what you do that you have to reel yourself in so that people don't feel like you're taking up all the space in the room. Because that's how winners think.

Party

It is difficult to contextualize what different ideologies meant at the time they were invoked. Now, we think of modernism as aloof, free, Scandinavian and egalitarian, although at many points in history, artistic modernism was rooted in a restlessness of the soul, where globalism and industry were thrust reluctantly into our lives. Modernists heralded a "return to order", almost confused by their plainlessness. *This is conservative! Void of ideology!* Is it? Did you draw plants and animals in a state of nature, or make a sculpture of God who would reach your hand, light as a cirrus dove? The Holy One of Israel is the greatest Mac for the Bronze Age, the storms whose eyes met every crossroads present.

Now, look at how this furniture is humanistic, a kintsugi imperfectionism plated in gold and grafted into Silver Lake. This modernism is progressive, according to a liberated worldview of excess and leisure.

The next time someone justifies their world view according to what someone said 100 years ago, see if they can explain the sociopolitical landscape at the time.

We know our time well, though, and right now there's very clearly a stark divide between *people who believe in social programs and enforced morality* and *people who believe in personal will and divine retribution.* I believe in both, especially because I'm convinced the economy is about to be entirely automated. Bow to your new king, because he is exceptionally fair and totally not a robot. That's how you know he won't put you in jail or ban you from reality for saying the n-word. But he will make it especially important for you to consider the morality of the things you do, including all of the language you use and why you use it.

I feel a moral imperative to invite all of you onto my ark, because I don't see anyone taking it seriously like I do. In fact, I'd sooner force you to come aboard than let you wander. Trust me, you'll love it here.

Our style of partying influences everything about how we seem, as a unit. Some people love ordained rituals and finality. Some people like talking endlessly, ensuring there's always an open-ended discussion and renewed ideology available. Still, some people are fixated on inclusivity and social justice, and they become quite preoccupied by the fact that not everyone can be invited to every party. You certainly wouldn't want loud music and fireworks in your backyard every day. Almost always, there is tension between an incumbent order and an oppressed or otherwise unknown group. For some it would be tempting to always bet on the Yankees, and for others they savor in rooting for the underdog. One thing's for certain, it's not easy to find sympathy when you are in a position of power.

I love to describe things, and I love fun and intensity. So clearly, we needed exceptional people to perform and arrange a constellation of interests. It's so much easier to understand what we're talking about when you have drama and props to identify with. Kant would spend 100 pages talking about the substance of mind, and I'm still not certain I completely understand what he was trying to tell us. I love Mac, so I make sure you just want to throw your money at us the moment you see it.

The Land of the Free

The most exceptional thing about America is how it enables the impartial churn of ideology. It doesn't have to be in service to any particular monarch, religion, or business. It just has to be great. With that, there is a spirit of globalism, such that everything you do has to be bright enough for everyone to see it. Movies, music, phones, you name it, Americans made it their mission.

People from other countries joke that American culture is McDonald's and airplanes. The culture of *new;* free and searching for heritage.

Everything's on the internet now, so why can't you do the same thing from Oslo, or Munich? Good question. Lots of great innovation happens by osmosis. Like-minded people get together, inspired by the spirit of success, and they come up with things that aren't immediately obvious. They try out each other's ideas and they figure out what works. Sure, innovation happens anywhere that feels right, especially if you're in the right chatrooms or on the right forums. Everyone has a place they feel at home on the internet.

Americans aren't embarrassed about trying to make a buck. A lot of people from different places might see the relentless industrialism as kitschy and unimportant. In the U.S., it's all that we know. We can't take one step outside without being reminded that all of the most influential landmarks and cornerstones of our society are new and industrial. Our culture is very geographic and commercialized. The states are *as they appear,* and *the way people seem,* in service to the almighty dollar, and God. The most successful states, in terms of economy and recognition, all happen to have very discernible senses of shared identity. Texas and their cowboys, California and their quinoa. Truly, you have to be able to see something to believe in it, and Americans understand that better than anyone.

There's also this instinct we have that *tradition and heritage* are their own thing, and everything else is just kind of responsible for toting them along. Tradition is so at odds with innovation that we basically have to choose to discard it, find some way to make it modern, or otherwise stagnate. So in the U.S., churches play soul music and rock and roll. Is tradition really so separate from our day to day lives? Why wouldn't we make dramatic, stylish retellings of biblical stories alongside James Bond and the Barbie movie? Shall we build neo-Gothic cathedrals and Frank Lloyd Wright ranch homes as we incorporate rural Montana?

I am so impressed when something is able to be culturally relevant for a very long time. It could be that they are quite selective about how they incorporate history into their work without making something odd and unapproachable. They see a common denominator in great design that is universally understood. Anyone, from any point in time, could pick it up and find something satisfying and fresh about it. Certainly that's the case, otherwise we wouldn't see Dark Souls games with beautiful, sprawling Gothic architecture on all of the latest consoles.

Digital design is always evolving because it's so easy to change out with the current fashion, unlike architecture. Advertising is always meant to look new, and even our operating systems seem to always be changing.

Now, a number of years have passed since Apple's shiny early-2000s *aqua* design was supplanted by flat Googly design. *Aqua* was very popular, you just wanted to lick it, and everyone made electronics with colorful transparent cases, metallic on-screen views, and bubbly, liquid buttons. By 2013, it was immediately apparent that *flat* was new and the other thing looked older. Now, though, it seems like that shift is far enough in the past that we're ready for more 3D and aqua.

3D was quite obviously meant to be new, at the time, because it reflected the exciting new graphics capabilities of computers. It could just be that we remember the change from old to new more than we do the actual attributes that make something old. Young people, myself included, love mid-century modern design. Bold shapes, smooth surfaces, and lacquer. Everything looks like an app and a product right now, which fits quite well with the surfaces and body of the mid-century aesthetic. Everything is social justice right now. And the roaring 20s are definitely *in* once more, amidst our new digital industrialism. Let's get some more brass and ethnic music up in here.

In medieval times, alchemy was a very interesting way of addressing the phenomenon of transformation and seasonality as we became more scientific and empirical about our understanding of the world. With Greek philosophy and technology as its forerunner, alchemists held on to traditional wisdom about our world and the cosmology of existence, and then tried to figure out how we could make better sense of it as we learned more about natural science and what would eventually become chemistry. They thought a lot about *why* the world is seasonal, and *why* we strive to change as we grow in life. Clearly, they understood the existential dilemma of the *unmoved mover*, where the universe is perhaps created by an original cause that has an inherent motivation to change. Alchemists had an early elemental table that helped them explain the universe, and they associated this universal propensity for change with *mercury*, the mysterious liquid metal that they supposed transcended any particular state of matter. They thought about the significance of *light* and *dark*, as we elucidate our world with our current understanding, a world that God presumably has all of the answers for.

We suppose to know quite a lot about science today, and then we will look back at our mistakes and gaps in understanding decades from now and it will seem primitive. The way we cure diseases will seem crude and imprecise, and our social order will seem chaotic and archaic. Our cameras from just 10 years ago take pictures that look ancient, and our computers are now on the crux of true intelligence. And other things will seem to never change.

When we follow along with the story the world has to tell us, as our preferences change and we use different colors and fonts in our advertising and our artwork, it's interesting to think about how deeply we really do desire change. Even as I am quite set in my ways, I am always excited to see what is new in the world. Creativity is change.

New American

I am very fascinated by what makes something *authentic*. I'll go to any restaurant, whether it's fast food or a nice sit-down affair, and I'll be thinking about all of the choices they made to make it what it is. The furniture and the materials, the decor, the workers, and of course the menu.

So what is authentic in the first place? Certainly, an authentic meal is true to its roots. Whatever Tuscan countryside cuisine emerged over the past thousand years must come to light on our table, as we sit in the corner eatery gazing out ceiling-to-floor glass walls at people bundled up in their cashmere, joined in our dining by mid-century modern furniture and impressionist blown-glass light fixtures. Cuban. Along perfectly paved sidewalks and shiny black asphalt roads.

Some people are particularly sensitive to the subtext of urban yuppy restaurants, where they are supposedly offering a cultured, authentic dining experience, but it's really designed to appeal to young wealthy people.

Certainly, it's excellent food, and I'm glad that we're enjoying it. It just takes me a second to figure out what the message is supposed to be.

I'm even more confused when I'm at a Tool concert in a basketball court. You must know, these guys are fucking out of their minds. Why isn't anyone throwing beer on each other and moshing? Well, that's not very safe or friendly, is it? But who said a heavy metal concert is supposed to be? You go to other places, dark cement buildings along some odd street next to the steel mill, covered in graffiti and band stickers inside and out, with an odd double-bright fluorescent light illuminating the 10-car parking lot. There it's plainly more acceptable to be rowdy late into the night. But that's not large enough or ritzy enough for a Tool concert in 2019. How excellent that they are still relevant 30 years later, rocking out harder than ever.

And so naturally, if you want to make a lot of money with your restaurant, you're going to put it in Cherry Creek and attract guests that can afford to pay a premium. It's a *sure thing*. Some element of home-grown authenticity is going to be lost in service of luxury and appearing new. Because people know to pay new money for new things.

I feel like I'm enjoying my meal more at Buca di Beppo, which is owned by a big-brand *restaurant group* that specializes in *concepts* and *experiences*. But it happens to be the case that the concept is a family-style Italian restaurant, with dimly lit rooms covered in old artwork and black and white pictures of la famiglia. And that is the case for many chain restaurants that you recognize; they're owned by restaurant groups that have lots of money to spend opening restaurants across the country. They are *invented*, out of thin air. Sure, maybe someone at the company has a lake house in Rhode Island and they love lobster.

There are some brands with *real* heritage that was invented out of thin air, although I suppose that wouldn't have been clear until today. Hermès was created by a leatherworker named Thierry Hermès who made quality saddles and harnesses for horses and carriages at his Paris workshop. Now they're better known for luxury goods like scarves, purses, and fragrances. They even make home goods and leather straps for the special Hermès edition Apple Watch. Creed is a perfume house well known for their ornate fragrances. According to their company history, they were founded in London in the 1700s and had tailoring work and perfumes commissioned by royalty, although we suppose that was quite different from their popular fragrances today. As our tastes evolve, most people would probably find fragrances from more than 50 years ago old-fashioned. Even mainstays of the 1980s like the mossy and brassy Polo Green may seem unfamiliar today. Creed's most popular fragrance, Aventus, is quite delicate and perhaps even plain, suedey and suggestive of hay. Like vetiver, brand new stationery, or a leather hat.

What I like most is when I feel like there's something meaningful about what we're doing. That you are a Japanese sushi chef, and this is your restaurant, exactly as you imagined it. The food is excellent and fresh, the concept is ordinary and the price is ordinary. Katsuya? You have fun with that. This is a plain sushi restaurant.

Some things only exist in the vacuum of *New American*. We do have culture here, believe it or not. So it can be fun to explore your idea of innovative cuisine, so long as it's tasty and affordable for the rest of us.

The fresh craft coffee that I like can only be bought from specialty cafes, because they prioritize unique flavor profiles and light roasting. They're very proud of their sustainable farm-to-table relationships and the fruity tasting notes they achieve with their coffee. These cafes are quite similar to New American cuisine in that they are *invented* on their own laurels. Their espresso tastes quite different from anything you'd call traditional or Italian, but it's what we've come to enjoy in the U.S. Here, it's quite easy to acclimate to the shiny mid-century aesthetic, because that's plainly their intent: to be something new.

Chosen

Here's the thing we noticed: all of our best talent wants to work on the coolest parts of the game. Or could it be that the coolest parts of the game are created by all of the brightest people that love to work together?

Every character class and area gets a group of engineers, writers, and graphics artists, all of which have similar experience and technical skill. On paper, everyone has equal capabilities. They're all welcome to collaborate in sprints on key visuals and features. And still, the most aesthetically and physically pleasing parts to play are created by the same groups of people.

Here, make a game that people love to play. How would they even know where to start if they weren't the sort of people that play great games? A great game is challenging in all of the right ways. The controls are tight and they work to your advantage, in just the way you expect. The artwork is ethereal and moody, and the dialogue is sorrowful. The world they built is desolate and hopeful at once, and there's no failure of imagination when they present you with omniscient truths and surprises. Never kitschy, never reaching. The game is self-assured like the people that made it. It's clear that it's great, and if you don't get it, maybe you just need to *get good.*

When people say *company culture matters,* the main reason for that is the only way you're going to get creative and brilliant people in the door is by convincing them that there's lots of other creative and brilliant people to work with. And there's great coffee and lunches, and trips to Aspen. But mostly, it's the obsessional focus that everyone there has on going home with the new Macintosh in their hands that they all got to make together. You're also going to have to convince them that they stand to gain by working with a team, because a lot of these folks are used to having their ideas stolen or thrown away. They have great ideas, so great that most people can't even tell the difference. They'd rather just make their own computer, if it was so convenient. And for software and games, it often is. They'll just learn how to do artwork and music all by themselves, because there never was anything that stopped them from doing everything on their own.

Is it unfair that excellence is self-reinforcing? That the teams of bright people that all flock to each other are lightyears ahead of the people that have to work on less exciting stuff. Sometimes I wonder, if you take one of those people and have them champion development for other things that get less attention, are you going to see the same results?

It may as well be the case that you are taking a good thing and spoiling it, because those people very clearly are great *by virtue* of the things they love to make. One way or another, excellence emerges, and people are chosen for their excellence. In another life, we made a mech game, and Garfield is a black rabbit. But here, the particularity of what we are working on is how we came to be. If what we were working on *seemed* any different, we wouldn't have attracted the right people. They'd all end up somewhere that fits their sense of style and purpose.

The connected world means people are able to collaborate in all new ways. Many projects and standards in the tech industry are maintained by *consortiums*, which are a bunch of people from large and small companies alike that get together and decide how to make the best technology. This lets us cross-pollinate ideas and pave the way for innovation while it's happening. Right now, everyone's trying to figure out how we should collaborate on artificial intelligence.

Linux is one of the most successful collaborative projects in the world, being entirely open source and community driven. Other standards like Bluetooth and self-driving cars are agreed upon by industry experts, with many revisions and improvements as time goes on. Industry leaders like NVIDIA are important stakeholders in how hardware manufacturers use their chips for artificial intelligence and automotive technology, so they become a cornerstone when they advocate for building safe and effective systems. NVIDIA has plug and play solutions that make all cars safer than if every automotive manufacturer had to start from square one. These industries have healthy competition, and also healthy collaboration that ensures everything works seamlessly, according to shared and proven algorithms.

And so now with A.I., the most important things consortiums want to talk about are ethics and privacy. What are the *right* decisions for A.I. systems to make? And how do we ensure our names and our likeness remain our own, when A.I. is so good at emulating them? It's necessary to give A.I. training data so it can come up with its own information and images, and now it's crunch time where big players like Google, OpenAI, and Meta have to answer for their mass consumption of *our* training data! Truly, the whole is greater than the sum of its parts, but all of that writing and artwork that we came up with still belongs to us. I'm certainly considering what the world is going to be like once we have truly connected minds, and I often find that we already have something like that.

Solutions

Great leaders and salespeople are excellent at understanding what customers are looking for and showing them the tools they need to accomplish it. Great engineers are sometimes, but rarely, better salespeople than salespeople. Usually engineers find it difficult to put themselves at sufficient distance from the problems. They get caught in the weeds, because that's where they spend all their time. A customer will have a business need to fulfill and an engineer's immediate instinct is to rappel into a cave and start talking about APIs and jiggawatts. But say you have engineers that really are quite socially talented, that are aware of how different people at the table relate to the technical challenges. Perhaps they haven't even met half the people at the table until today, but it's quite obvious to them what layer of detail they operate at. This sort of engineer is going to be the one that customers want involved in every discussion, because they know they're not getting bulldozed — it's coming straight from the horse's mouth. The salespeople simply don't have the depth to answer a lot of the questions, and the rest of the engineers can't really put their finger on what the customer needs to hear.

Something you'll notice about great communicators is they're able to set the conversation under pressure. People don't particularly like pressure; they want to feel like they have all the time in the world to make the right decision. But they do feel a sense of reassurance when you have the answers to all of the important questions, a familiar sort of pressure that shows them you're on the same page with them all the time. A lot of engineers just can't stop the words from pouring out of their mouths, like they have to confess to all of the world's problems at once. Someone asks something and all of the sudden they see 300 lines of code flash before their eyes and they want to explain every function call in detail.

Great communicators seem like they're able to lift their conscious mind up and out of themselves for a moment to choose their words and move the discussion along. This is important, because if there's something you'll learn about people, even smart ones like myself, is we can only focus on a few sentences at a time. When you're in a complex technical discussion, you absolutely have to figure out how to start attaching big pictures and taglines to technical concepts, because otherwise people are going to feel very lost.

Think like a branding expert, and show people just a few concepts at a time. Let them dig deeper for detail, and don't be afraid to sidebar stuff for email and calls later on. This is a sort of polite rigidity that you will impose in technical discussions, where you keep yourself from getting dragged into the weeds and you focus on the big picture for the full hour or however long you're meant to present.

Enough

The thing that's most frustrating about winning is no one's ever going to make you feel like it's enough. They always want more, and you always feel like you need to do more.

I thought being a great software engineer was going to be enough, but I started feeling like it was constricting, like the way I actually felt couldn't be contextualized correctly and the work environments I was in made me feel like a suit. Suits look different now. You can be wearing a t-shirt and jeans and still be sucking up to *the man*. If I'm the man, you're the man as well, so you can point that fucking finger up your ass.

It's tempting to keep looking for new things. New cars, new partners, new houses, new jobs. Really, every time you pile on something new, it's more work. You've felt it happen before. You went out looking for more work, and that's what you got. When really, the car you had all along worked great. You already live somewhere that is clean and comfortable, and moving is a huge job. Sometimes, the best thing you can do is just sit tight. But we have such grand expectations for ourselves to be great.

A new pair of shoes you can just take out of the box and throw on the shelf, but a new computer requires lots of set up to get it working just how you expected. It ends up in the pile with Lego sets and other high-investment activities. The very first time you opened a new computer was ecstatic, but with every new computer, a slightly diminished sense of gratification. Today, the world tells us to keep churning until we have exactly what we want. Spoken like someone who doesn't remember the first time they opened a new Mac.

I think everyone should hope to be exactly how they feel. Ideally, there's a perfect path in life for you to be just who you want to be.

I'm very intrigued by how girls are willingly going extinct right now. What *is* a girl? Making girls more like boys isn't actually liberating for the phenomenology of being a girl, you know. That's something people don't like talking about right now, though, because the whole world goes around on JavaScript and paperwork. I wonder what people who herald equality have to say about the lack of options for traditional girls right now. Is that really equality?

For one, having a path to success that involves *one* ordinary salaried worker is important. That way, you can actually win by being a girl, which I love, because I love girls. Work's overrated. I love girls, and I love my mom. You should hope to be a mom too. I hope to be a dad, now that everything else is out of the way.

Something has happened in recent history, and it's made it so that every household has to do a whole lot more salaried work just to get by.

One day you're going to wake up, with your student loans finally paid off, a stack of paperwork, your 20s long gone, and you're going to wonder why everything costs double. I'm glad that everyone in the world has the opportunity to be exactly who they want to be, and I also think it's important that we evaluate the macroeconomics of the world now that the ideology of the 1980s is finally set in stone in our daily lives. Being a skilled professional was *liberating*, but the world is always changing.

So, when is *enough, enough?* The computers can always get faster. What if, by some stretch of imagination, you had a computer that could instantly do anything, at any time, with any amount of fidelity you desire? Say, now, that labor is effectively infinite. Would *enough* be somewhere that computer can't operate? Somewhere the world moves at the right speed for it to be relevant for our eyes and ears, where *scarcity* exists once more. Where a camera is slow enough to capture a picture of *now.* What an unusual thought, that the world we know is the only place you have somewhere to win. Would you place such great importance on being successful in your career if a computer could do your job a million times faster?

You have something to win, something people can win *from* you. We believe in you because you believe in yourself. Because you're a winner, it matters when someone wins you over. A lot of winners come up with games that are fun to play because they know what makes a game fun. They like games that are challenging, and they can balance a game that's hard for other winners. They've played enough games to be tired of fetch-quests and ready for something potent and entirely new. What do you think about difficulty levels? Not all games have them. And if it's a competitive game, sky's the limit. You'll get matched against the best in the world if you're good enough. I love when a game is hard *and* inclusive of everyone who wants to play. The most potent truths resonate at every level.

Bills

Paper money is a lot like cryptocurrency. *Blockchain* this, *mining* that — at the end of the day, if there's not real gold and silver backing it, it's a social contract where everyone agrees that it's worth something because there's people who stand behind it, an adequate amount of scarcity, and lots of people using it to do things that matter. U.S. dollars haven't been held to the *gold standard* for over a century now, and it's worked out pretty well.

The reason the U.S. dollar is so valuable all across the world is because there's really a lot of important things in the world that weigh it down, in lieu of gold and silver. A good store of value must have some inertia. The idea that it's worth something tomorrow, because all across the world it's being used to make phones and video games today. The New York Stock Exchange and the NASDAQ are the biggest speculative markets for the U.S. dollar. People believe so much in it, that they are confident that next year all of these great companies are going to be worth more than they are today. The *idea* of the U.S. dollar is worth something, because people trust American policy and American news. They know that if there's anywhere on the planet where something like truth can emerge, it's here. Where our cars are fastest and our companies are most competitive. The U.S. dollar is a belief in fair and just competition, so that truth can arise from chaos.

Lots of boondock types are adamant about stockpiling gold and silver, but really most of the money to be made in the economy is by getting on board with major enterprise on the stock market. This shows that if you have a really good idea, your word alone is sufficient to keep the economy afloat behind you. The proof is in the pudding: you keep making things people want to buy, and you deliver on your promises, year after year.

There are good arguments to be made for why the decentralized nature of cryptocurrency is a good thing. No banks, no fed, and all of the transactions are anonymous and permanently included on the shared blockchain. The scarcity comes from the difficulty in *mining* new Bitcoin with very powerful computers. Every new Bitcoin is incrementally more difficult to mine than the last. Seems kind of arbitrary when you think about it.

There's a lot of value in federation and oversight. The Federal Reserve makes very informed decisions about how to set interest rates based on key indicators in the economy, reacting carefully to inflation, which keeps the incentives set up for the economy to grow at a steady rate. The U.S. dollar is opinionated in a way that Bitcoin is not. The value of Bitcoin is entirely at the whim of how investors are trading it, and as you may have already seen, sometimes it's catastrophic. This is why you really want a planned economy of some sort.

The American capitalist style of economy worked out so well that all of the countries that were doing other stuff went all-in on capitalism, and it worked out great for them as well. Everyone wants to make great electronics like Sony and great apps like Spotify. Who would have thought; giving people incentives to win works much better than sitting on dynastic power for centuries?

Some people don't *believe in* money as much as others, though. They have experiences with the divine that remind them that God gives them their portion. I think there might be a happy medium somewhere. God, in some ways like the Federal Reserve, is a particular *dispersal* of power.

Obamaphone

Printing money just sort of works. People don't need to think too much about why, but the ships all rise with the tide. So long as Apple and Google are happy, we all get to be happy too. More phones, more Bejeweled and Pinterest.

In the U.S., Democrats are currently the party that has a reputation for strong social policy and crony capitalism. Meaning, if you want someone in office that's going to sign off on all of your government grants and get more money printed, that looks *more like* a Democrat than a Republican. They both do it, but that's the world today. This is the *neoliberal* policy where Democrats have become quite friendly with the powers that be; the *newest deal*, where we bow to the Federal Dispersal of Riches. If you wanted a union man in office, you could have had Bernie Sanders. But you didn't.

Republicans, today, are very righteous about the fact that they want more stringent fiscal policy. They talk about balancing the federal budget and they want us to ignore the fact that the only way we can have wildly outrageous economic growth is by printing more money (and causing more inflation). Especially when all of these businesses don't even make something *real*. They are in the business of floating value from investors and ad revenue. And so long as we get more games and tweets right into our feed, we're none the wiser. You like games and Netflix, right?

So Republicans tend to be more *lift yourself up by your bootstraps* sort of people, because they see the system getting too large, consolidated, and wasteful. A lot of union men and women could be convinced by that, if they look at the world and see one great big neon Uber sign, and no homes and family values for the rest of us.

Naturally, the reality is somewhere in between. We're going to keep encouraging the economy to grow, and there's almost certainly tons of waste that piles on with many years of back-room politics. People would love to say that there's a candidate that acknowledges that, but the controversy is too sweet to pass up. They'd rather point fingers than actually get to the root of the matter. Politicians also spend a lot of time advocating for things that they don't use, which runs contrary to my earlier advice that you always *eat your own dogfood*. It's not like a politician to be on welfare or living in subsidized housing, but they certainly understand Medicare and social security.

Generally speaking, I find that the more desks something has to go across and the more DMV lines you have to wait in, the less efficient something is. And I also recognize that there's lots of people who want to keep their jobs. That's just me, though, with my background at Amazon, the *Apple Pay and done* type of guy that I am. I find that when there's not 10 different transmissions and limited slip differentials in between the government and my pocket, it's much easier for downstream effects to be felt upstream, and vice versa. The economy is most responsive like this, when you put it under a particular sort of pressure.

Finish

In middle school, I had a friend that spent much of his time in class drawing a beautiful, highly detailed picture of a Bugatti Veyron with his Pilot Dr. Grip mechanical pencil that had a magical feature allowing you to advance the lead by shaking the pencil and the metal weight contained in the barrel. This spawned my interest in fine Japanese writing instruments, but it also was the first time I saw someone else my age care so much about one thing for an extended period of time. For months, through autumn and into the new year, he would be adding detail to this drawing as he followed along with math and literature. The concentrated power of attention is important. If you spend every day for months and years caring about something you love, it will show in your work. It's all you want to think about, so how could it not be exceptional in every way? He loved cars, and to my knowledge he still does.

If you're going to university, you're going to ride it out until you have a diploma, because along with everything you learned in class, that's the part that counts. And once you start working, you're going to keep learning more about what you love to do.

If you're doing your own thing, you need to treat what you're doing like you're planning on finishing it; no other options. The thing itself is the reward. Some people have an easier time with this, and some games are much longer than others. If you're really, truly, addicted to whatever it is that you're doing, your energy is going to pour out effortlessly because you love the process of putting it together. Being self-driven is important, because only *you* can define what your success criteria is. You know what it looks like when it's right. It might not have even existed until you came up with it.

Knowing when to start is just as important as knowing when to finish. I spent about 5 years writing about things I found interesting and thinking intently about what it is that I would want to say before I felt like I had the spatial awareness to write a book. Before that, as a teenager and a young professional, I was studying philosophy, business, and psychology, but it was unclear how the ideas I had floating around in my mind were connected or why they were important. It wasn't until I treaded the ground and acted it out for many years that it became apparent why many things are the way they are. What is true, and why is it always changing? How do people decide who to trust, and what is sexy about being self-assured? I experiment with all of these things in real life so that I can tell you about it. And I'm certain that there are lots of things I am going to learn about the world after this book is done that I will have to follow up with in another book. But everything here is ever so fresh and puerile.

You're a winner, so you know where to put your finish line. The trophy is the thing you really, truly believe in. If it's great, the money and the recognition are there waiting for you. You've got keen attention to detail, so you know when it makes sense for you to keep adding finish to it. When it's done, it's done, and it's the perfect reflection of where you're at in your life.

I know this is true because every time I hear something you come up with I think to myself *wow, you are truly incredible at what you do.* I know how it got to be that way for you. Sitting 10 hours a day playing music until your fingers bleed. That's the only place we could find you. If there's anyone in the world I want you to imagine playing for, it's me, because then you will know for certain that someone hears you. Or maybe it just gives you pleasure to hand me garbage, syrupy studio albums.

Grace On

Every day is an opportunity to call upon God's grace, so that we can know the right manner of speaking, that we are heard soundly and understood; the right manner of creation, that what we make is beautiful and profoundly inspired; and the better judgement that would only be bestowed upon us that place our faith in wisdom and truth. Grace appears in our life like a gentle breeze and asks something unusual of us quite like consistency.

Consistency is a bittersweet tonic; still they wanted to try. My faith was always what I could count on, my pursuit for the purest water and the clearest skies. These truths were all that I meant to endeavor for, until they could drink no more and breathe no longer. Did they mean for me to stop? Stop what? And face where? I saw a glow in the night sky that reminded me I would need to ask the brightest people I knew for help, for us to truly think different to see into being the future I wanted us to live in. I wanted them to show me what they could see, so that we could consider what's next. Certain truths, self-evident in all that makes us feel good and free, would be with us in all walks of life.

Do you really know what *consistency* means to you? Something about it has to have a slight dissonance for you to settle on *intoxicating*. Otherwise, your consistency would come out like plain white bread.

It might be that we are more averse to inconsistency than we are drawn to consistency. The more consistently we have the same thing, it becomes sort of vague and difficult to discern. You start forgetting what it even tastes like and wishing there was more Big Mac sauce or something on it. When we prepare something for the world that is majestic, we know to make it sparkle in some way. Something about how it addresses the things that confuse us is what makes it genuine.

Grace would be incomplete to see a plain reflection of liturgy or regulation. The breathing moment is, truly, what is placed upon us.

5

Keep Colorado Weird

Winners are odd, and that's a good thing because they're always being themselves. The world didn't get a chance to pasteurize them. To me, really interesting movies and music are intense and creepy. Mythical and ethereal.

The art is always telling us something.

The cool thing about Colorado is we have hyper-progressive college towns, tech hubs, ski towns, major military bases, and hyper-conservative fundamentalists all in one place. No matter who you are in Colorado, people here understand what it means to be true to yourself, and that's extremely special. The ideology is always pulling in different directions, so that you can actually *see* the detail that gets lost in identity politics. There's a reason different people believe different things, and if you really want to understand someone, you have to understand the groundwork and the life experiences that shaped their worldview.

The world is good at instrumenting itself for plainness and averageness, but the reality of life is that winners exist in the marginal extremes. The phenomenon of instrumentation, inherently, regresses towards to mean, because it carries the implication that everything must be measured within the context of the system it upholds. They keep telling you they want you to be plain, to follow the rules, and to *just do your job*, but somehow you never quite believe them. That's not what they want. They want to see you turn water into wine.

Authoritarianism is always shapeshifting. 1960s flower children are rolling in their graves at how so-called progressives are obsessed with institutionalizing everything. I'm currently a Democrat, by affiliation, but really I am drawn towards politicians that actually believe in winning. The thing Democrats don't understand about Trump, behind the insufferable noise and intolerance, is that there's a lot of people in this country that feel like there's a constriction of *the system*, where no one is really hearing them. They feel like everything is rigged, the institutions are becoming sluggish, and the world is preoccupied with fashionable issues and ignoring the ordinary American. Some of this is true, and I encourage you to be considerate of it. There's an immense consolidation of power, where your voice is either magnified by social media and news, or otherwise silenced.

Now, I believe in some out-there stuff. For instance, I think there are metaphysics that can control the weather, guide your hand and your words, and put people in your life at exactly the right time. I've proven all of this, too. But it's not the stuff that's on the news, so it may as well not exist for you. Just an interesting example of life-changing information being kept from you. I believe God is more powerful than anything of this world, though, so it's only a matter of time.

Veil

iPhones are easy to use because they hide a lot of complexity. This is usually a good thing, because we should try to make things easy for everyone to figure out. Simplicity is something you gain by trading in complexity, meaning you're reliant on whomever is simplifying something to lower the veil at just the right point, so that all of the important details are exposed to you, and all of the complexity is invisible.

A big part of this is *trust*. Customers trust that Apple is going to give them the best tools possible, at a fair (enough) price, and that they will be responsible stewards of their data. Somewhere, at the end of the line, you have to trust a winner to help you be successful. The biggest winners have brilliant people in their corner that are always making the right decisions, and they know where all the bodies are buried. If you have leaders setting the bar high, you're getting it right from the source.

Apple moves their own goalposts faster than you can. They're skating to where the puck is going to be. That's what makes them reliable as cultivators of an *ecosystem*. They didn't just shoot their shot making one thing, and then watch while the rest of the industry keeps innovating. To this day, they're the ones moving the industry forward.

Apple also *reveals* complexity that no one else wants to bear the burden of. Like all of the privacy and tracking guardrails in apps, and the location services icon that doesn't stop fucking showing up in my menu bar. They're willing to have that conversation with you, where all of the other guys are just trying to sweep it under the rug, because that's just the easy thing to do for businesses. If metrics and sales were the only thing that mattered, those sorts of features and details would be dead in the water. Then again, if Apple was that sort of company, they'd sell a phone with 10 ports and a cotton candy machine on it. Being selective raises the bar.

The veil keeps moving, to be certain. There's always new technology and people are always becoming more skilled at learning how to use it. I find there's diminishing returns here when you stray too much from the core strengths and essence of what makes something what it is. Too many widgets, mismatched buttons, and unusual proportions. That's the price of complexity. You're going to start feeling chaos mount behind you, the more screen sizes you support and the more teams you have coming up with features.

In the beginning, it was one phone, and about 3 different styles of apps that had the buttons laid out differently. They were so incredibly deliberate about making sure anyone could figure it out, because for a lot of people that would be their first time using a smartphone. Consequently, the same designers were responsible for making every app cohesive with the same human interface guidelines. Now, every app works completely differently, even the ones that Apple makes themselves. Teams wanted the freedom to be creative, and now buttons and popovers come from every which direction. I love consistency, but I get it, widgets keep the lights on.

Reception

You can only have so many voices floating around in your head. You know what's right for what you're doing, but it can be helpful to confide in people who you know have good intuition. When you consult other people's judgement and sense of style, you can imagine how new people are going to feel about you on their first impression. This is good, because you're going to be very patient about making sense to people. You're on another planet, and you need to bring this thing down to earth somehow. It's gotta be something people understand the moment they pick it up and start playing with it.

Perhaps it's helpful to start with things that people already understand. The archetypal significance of that existing thing is going to make your new thing make sense at first glance. Apple did this with *skeuomorphic design* on the iPhone, meaning the camera and the calculator have touchscreen buttons that look like real thing they're meant to emulate. You're gonna have to look like something, and it might be tempting for you to look like an alien. That's what you feel like, anyway. Still, it may work in your favor to seem familiar in some way. The fundamentals have to make sense and work well if they're ever going to get a chance to learn about what sets you apart. Here, you'll find whether there is congruence and cohesion between the assumptions you made when you designed it and what people are really looking for.

People are going to think about you in terms of who you associate with, the places you've worked at, and their first impressions of you. These are the only heuristics they have until they get to know you, so make your first impressions count.

How much reception do you want? That's a good problem to have, isn't it. There's so many people on the line that you can't find a moment of silence to speak. Like a tower, where everyone is trying to use the phone at once. In the early years of the internet, we had *dial up*, which meant your internet worked over your home phone line, and you could only use it if someone wasn't on the phone at the same time. You can imagine how this would be frustrating, in the context of hours of StarCraft or even doing important work while you spoke to customers on the phone.

Businesses had special T1 and T3 lines run straight into their buildings that gave them dozens of phone lines, much like how the phone company distributed them from their network to your home. They were just used to having their buildings wired in bulk for phone and internet lines, because you could only hook up so many pipes to each desk.

Eventually, newer DSL technology was invented that allowed multiplexing internet on the same individual line used for home phone, and later cable TV, with no interference. It used ranges of signals that were otherwise thrown away by the phone line, tapping into all new capabilities over the exact same infrastructure, as if a pipe was blocked without anyone knowing it because the technology was too primitive to open it up. The *coaxial* cables used for TV had even better signal characteristics than the phone lines, so they quickly replaced DSL and became the standard for home internet. Sometimes, there's a whole range of frequencies in the world that we aren't really tuned into, and just by taking an open minded and innovative mindset are we able to do 100x more with the same resources.

With the existing copper cable in the ground and some shiny new hardware in their distribution facilities, the cable company could now sell you both TV and internet bundled together over the same line and charge you double, keeping full ownership over all of the video, bits, and bytes that went into your house. They did everything to keep you buying both TV and internet from them, until the networks and production companies negotiated better contracts and came up with clever internet video services to un-bundle their programming and receive your money with no middleman.

Now, internet providers are investing in new fiber optic cables that are specifically designed to give us extremely high speed capabilities for internet. We're also getting used to the fact that most of the things we want to do on our devices can be done wirelessly over mobile phone networks. Similarly to DSL and cable internet, there was a progression for the capabilities of the cell towers and our phones that unlocked all of this untapped potential in how precise the radio waves could be to send more data at higher frequencies.

Here in rural Colorado, I use a humble but faithful line-of-sight wireless internet service built by a local provider. The receiver is mounted on my roof and works more like a WiFi satellite dish than the radio in your mobile phone, which can be indoors or in your pocket and still receive signal, at the cost of consistency and guaranteed uptime. Line of sight makes the signal perfectly consistent, except when it's under heavy load. Soon, though, we'll probably see mobile internet being just as fast and reliable as cable, and perhaps even fiber. There's a big difference with wireless: it's not up to one major company in each area to dig up a bunch of ground in your city to get you faster internet, and then sit on their monopoly and charge you however much money suits them. There's plenty of channels to go around over the air, leading to more competition and better quality of service.

Big Tents

They've got a lot of traffic. If you keep inviting people in, you're eventually going to have people who aren't happy about who else showed up there. There's a lot of character in being inclusive. It shows that you are very thorough about evaluating the myriad things that you can possibly do or believe as a person in this world. I'm always trying to make sure that I'm looking at the world from a lot of angles at once and figuring out how to integrate that with my own understanding.

There's a lot of hidden complexity in performance. Myths and jokes tell a story that's inaccessible by reason.

All of the most liberated societies in the world have a strong concept of *carnival* and performance, meaning there's space for people to play and be critical of the prevailing ideology. Really unusual communities with lots of clowning around are *sometimes* the place with the most salient insight into the state of the world. Now, I can't stand when clowning means discounting the value of winning, but I do love when people are thinking about things in all new ways. Mirth provides important relief in an otherwise sealed system.

Without a place to play and speak freely, you are left with an oppressive society, blindfolded and silenced for their true selves. The most invisible and constricting oppression is the feeling that you have something to say, and nowhere to be heard. You could shout it from the mountaintops and feel nothing but the bitter cold, while the world chugs along, disoriented and preoccupied with itself. *Here!* I have *just* the thing you all are looking for. Shall I say it louder? Will it take the roar of thunder and the ground shaking underneath you to hear me?

I love people that know how to have fun, because they're the only ones that would ever entertain me. You all would just be fine and well with paperwork and JavaScript. The harsh bite of the cold would be too much for you to bear. Let it go unnoticed, while you remain unconscious and unafflicted by anything at all.

Big Legs

You know me, I'd usually just rather sit at home. You can only spend so many weekends stoned out of your mind at Mars Volta shows.

When it's all said and done, you're probably pretty good company for yourself. You keep your place pretty clean, you've got good snacks, good music, and you never pretend to be something you're not. Whether I'm kicked up at home or on Miami Beach, there's one thing for certain: it's all Public Works, and we're all proud to keep it clean.

It's *someone's* job to keep the lights on, and it's important that our tax dollars are going to work for everyone in ways that count. I love fast internet and excellent urban design. Clean water, and great public facilities. There's lots of important ways we can set people up for success.

I want you to watch how fast Amazon's new pharmacy shakes up the industry. The public and private sector play off each other in mysterious ways. It always seems to be the case that the incumbent gets… lazy, and they need something disruptive to keep things moving along. That's the term in the tech industry, *disruptive* business. New guys that are willing to rethink the whole thing. I'm quite pleasant to be around, though, and I believe in the systems that already exist and the game-changers alike.

Don't throw the baby out with the bathwater. Everyone has the urge to come along and trample the existing systems head over foot. They already learned a lot of lessons so you don't have to, they just need some friendly encouragement to get their act together and update their computers every once in a while. In the U.S., we have lots of friendly competition and cooperation between the public and private sector. They each have unique strengths that keep things moving along for one another.

Necessity is the mother of invention. Most of the greatest technological innovations in recent history come from industrialism and the defense industry. Here, the pressure to be the fastest and the most pervasive at whatever you are doing becomes well pronounced. If you ever want to upgrade from your New York boutique, you're going to need some magical machinery that augments your ability to produce your fine garments. And if you want to be the leading military powerhouse for the world, you're going to need lots of brilliant engineers and lots of R&D dollars to come up with lightning fast communications and ballistics technology.

It's likely that the internet would exist by now if it was prompted by a genuine consumer interest to tweet and twiddle, but I'm quite confident that defense technologies like ARPANET, in the 1970s, launched the digital age decades into the future. They wanted to send documents, mail, and alerts instantly, for the sake of national security, and fax was unsatisfying. It was like attaching a string and cups together for the first time and talking into them. Academics and scientists would see how important ARPANET was for collaborating across the country, sharing their code and data much like how we can download software and information from the internet. And now you get the hottest memes, straight into your feed.

Soon they would discover how powerful digital bookkeeping, search, and governance technologies would be to ensure that documents are rapidly navigable and stay in the right hands.

As graphics and geospatial technology became more advanced, computers and satellites became the primary driver of all intelligence and military operations worldwide. Sextants and hand-drawn maps would truly seem like cave technology compared to the surveying tools we have today, with high resolution satellite imagery and 3D topographic maps. Information and intelligence are now the leading industries for keeping our nation safe, and with that comes a necessary expectation that our data is private.

For Alice

I arrived at many of the greatest truths in life by making an effort to understand her. Why she listens to what everyone else says. Why she likes things that seem random. Why she's actually afraid of new things and unfamiliar situations. Why, when I show her things that I know for certain are true, it sort of disgusts her in a way she doesn't know how to describe.

I've always had this theory that the reason Steve Jobs knows what good ideas look like is because they seem to him like a young girl. Good ideas are so precisely the reflection of what the world is saying at a point in time. She's her father's daughter, to be certain, and she also can't get far enough away from her household drama and the church. That he wants her plain, and he knows quite well that any good man would want her plain. The object she becomes on Instagram by the time she is 12. If she saw what I see when I look at a cell phone, it would be like selling your soul to 1,000,000 new dads. I only listen to myself, so you can understand why this idea would seem counterintuitive to me. She knows I already have all the answers.

So Steve found a way to give you something that enacts the sterile rebirth of yourself into a camera. It has all of her favorite buttons on it — pictures of me, pictures of guys I like, pictures of girls I'm jealous of, 911, and music everyone else likes. He's on stage in 2010 flipping through the New York Times — nice meme, boomer. Let's see some Candy Crush.

Alice loves sugar. She loves displacing her insecurities into other people and pretending she's tolerant of all people, while she tells me I'm a complete asshole. Alive loves music where people are upset. She loves that the iPhone is the phone you're supposed to have, and also that your body weight can be Android — like, if green bubbles are your thing. She sort of has it in her head that she likes that there's something feminine about me. Like in a Queen Elizabeth sort of way, I guess.

She was ready to use technology once all of her friends were using it.

Alice is beautiful in every way to me. Her primary feature is the way she looks, so naturally she's spent her life convincing herself looks don't matter. Sure, because I'm here for your Drake playlists. It's easier and perhaps even necessary for her to live her life according to contradictions. She's quite different from me, and she's confident in herself, which is why I love her.

She's great at telling me how the world is feeling, though. And she so clearly cares how I'm feeling. Alice really is like a camera. Which is cool. I love great photography equipment.

95

The most important thing for a happy relationship is making sure you're singing from the same hymn book. This doesn't mean that you have to like all of the same things, or listen to the same music, or even enjoy the same scripture. But when it comes time to raise kids or decide what sort of life you want to live together, that's what will make or break the relationship for you. No matter what anyone says, 10 years down the road you're not going to have any grand revelations about discipline or living in Manhattan.

Do It All

So they don't have to. Whatever you want to see, it's right there. When we plug things in, they *just work*. That's because we've designed the user experience from end to end. Sure, you can still write your own code, edit your own movie, but we're getting to the point that you don't have to.

A lot of people would rather just watch you go on vacation than to go themselves. You might even be able to get away with just taking videos of you in your car going to the grocery store and getting ready for The Met. Something about you is fun and we're not even really sure what it is. Usually it's just silly, but you are familiar for some reason, and you obviously sit in a very unique place in the world.

There's value in having someone you can call the *crux,* because then stuff doesn't get lost in translation. Which is a big, big problem, for lots of organizations and lots of groups of people. Who made what promise, when was this supposed to be done, what was actually said. When there's someone at the crux, you can trust there's a reliable observer in the room.

Someone that doesn't move around too much, who uses a lot of different tones, so you have a good frame of reference for what they mean at the time. Keep feeding them information and experiences, and they just keep getting better at what they do. They're always accountable. You know this about them because you can tell it eats away at them from the inside out when things aren't all right in the world. They'll take their reputation to their grave, because the only thing worse than going down with the ship is living a lie.

Your knowledge is going to cross-pollinate, and your techniques are going to start looking like something people have never seen before, because you're thinking like an engineer when you're cooking, and you're thinking like an upholsterer when you're designing interiors.

Honestly? Almost everything that I could ask someone else to do, I'd rather do myself because it's quicker, I get to learn more, and best of all, it's free. It's okay to ask for help too, when you know you need it. That's me, though, and you might be super energized by collaborating. Find people you love to work with and people whose work you love to see.

The most important thing about doing it all is that you understand how everything works. Careful about fixing stuff that's not broken and reinventing the wheel. A lot of guys that are really into computers and cars have this problem. When you keep asking for things to fix, the universe gives them to you. I only like things that just work. When other people have clearly figured out a great way to do things, let them do what they do best. Those are the people you want in your corner.

The phenomenon of providence is mysterious and paradoxical. Say the local sheriff is a little too close to the issues, or there's something going on across state lines. You need a federal police like the Federal Bureau of Investigation that *lifts* the veil of providence up, at the expense of localized authority. Say a company is making processed food using ingredients that may not be healthy. You need the Food and Drug Administration to come and make some important decisions, for the sake of the general public's health.

People become frustrated, as you might expect, when you have organizations that go *over their heads* and make authoritative decisions about things that are supposedly their responsibility. The FBI is, apparently, faceless, compared to a local sheriff's department who knows the town like the back of their hand.

97

What, then, when no organization of this earth is complete in solving these mysteries? When the science isn't enough, and when the forensics is incomplete. When people keep taking medicine that doesn't work, and when there are crimes that seem to slip through the cracks.

I guess you are looking for something like God, who you suppose is definitionally complete in all things. So, then, the world that is designed for yourself would feel right at home, because all things are central to each and every one of us. The truest providence finds us in each of our daily lives, because that is precisely the end of the line where these hierarchical structures are meant to serve. Providence serves the individual, according to a nearly synthetic order that goes above and beyond individual perception.

Circle Back

A lot of this book is solidifying ideas we've already explored on my website, *cako.io*, with *much* more context and interesting insights that we've learned along the way. The depth of the book means I can give you a more explicit and direct understanding. Circling back means that I get to reintegrate a lot of the newer ideas with a lot of the older ideas. My tone is fresher, and I've settled in more. Being comfortable means you can touch things more delicately; you aren't in a chaotic sprint to find something that makes sense. I hope to never make mistakes, but it's evident on reflection where more detail is necessary for something to make sense. You have to consume something like a reader to really know what it sounds like, to step outside of your own thought process for a moment and try to make sense of your own thoughts with a fresh mind.

Important intersections show up when you think about things with multiple axioms in mind. It's not easy, in the way algebra is like a completely different language from basic math, but you know the landscape well enough to show people what to pay attention to. When you come at something from both directions at the same time, you realize important details about why it is the way it is. There might be a lot of traffic heading into Manhattan on the Brooklyn Bridge, but everyone's moving fine towards Brooklyn.

Many things turned out to be incredibly right, like the cosmology of the universe and the power of confidence. I had a hunch that there's steps you can skip to get to where you want to be, and that's true in a lot of cases, but there's also a lot you learn from everything you do, necessary or otherwise.

On the other hand, I developed an appreciation for being process-oriented because I realized that when everything starts coming to you all at once, you just want to enjoy one thing at a time. You have to, because most of your life is about things like bathing yourself, making coffee, and planning out your day. The *doing* part is a glimmer in your eye, and it will pass you by unless you remember to be present. Being a steamroller is good in some situations, but not so good when you want to be intimate and true to someone you love.

I sort of believed in magic, but now I really believe in it.

The biggest difference is that I'm coming into believing that *right* and *true* and quite different. Yes, most things in the world have a heritable way of doing them that people generally agree is right, but then again the way I actually like things involves a significant evolution from how they were at first, to how they came to be. Italian coffee tastes bitter and flat to me. Modern American coffee is bright and tannic, which I prefer. Every 5 seconds, people have a new opinion on how long your shorts are supposed to be, whether we like long hair, starched collars, or tight jeans.

Change is true.

Classic

Everything turns classic at some point. Quicker than you expected. Can you identify the clutch engagement point where you wanting to be mature and wise crosses over with you trying to be young and in-the-loop? It's like slamming your hand on a fan — but if you put it on gently, it will keep spinning. See if you can stay there, somehow, because I have a feeling that's going to give you the most perspective on where the world is headed. I just can't believe that music that came out in the 2000s is classic rock now, but I certainly remember Guns N' Roses and Bon Jovi being classic rock at the time.

Classic means there's something about that existing thing that is satisfying in a way that the new thing is not. And it remained satisfying in spite of all of the cultural advances and the change that has taken place in our preferences. And you liking that thing more than the current thing appoints you with a sort of otaku fanaticism, which really means you are quite particular about the how you like the world. *Nerds* are immalleable and frustrated with how the world is always floating away in the wind, much like people obsessed with classic cars, movies, and music.

Now, being *geeky* is cool, because it implies a sort of fluidity that's missing from being a *nerd*. Girls love it, maybe even more than the guys do. Some styles of games are potent, and they keep being generationally relevant, like multiplayer combat and Pokémon. Geeky things have proven to be profitable and relevant in the world, where before it just seemed like we were talking to our computers and jerking off on our anime dolls.

I keep wondering how long we're going to be playing Instagram and YouTube. There seems to be something fad-like about so much delayed gratification. It's one great big no-box; don't talk to me, don't fuck me, just upvote me. But then again, I like to not have to talk to you so much. You broadcast an update when you have something to say, and otherwise there's nothing to it.

Great design is timeless, and I think a lot about why that is. I love anniversary editions of media, with special features and some sort of simplified artwork as if to suggest that this thing is authoritatively excellent. Are the motifs non-specific enough that you can't put your finger on when it was made? Movies and music look so much *like* the era.

The social commentary and the relationships become unrecognizable, and the potency just keeps ratcheting up. New movies look like roller coasters. The guys all wear t-shirts and the girls all wear exercise gear. Everyone is, constantly, on the computer and on their phones.

Braun calculators look new though.

Meet the Haberdasher

Buttons and thread, zippers and widgets. He's got everything it takes to get the job done. To this day, haberdashery is big business, because there's more moving parts than ever. If you want to sell a book, you're going to need tons of intermediate parts to set up a website, accept credit cards, publish, and advertise.

You know what materials work well together, the coolest styles and the best techniques. You know how you like to do things, and how everyone else likes to work too. You see what people gravitate towards the moment they walk into the store, and you know the types of questions they ask about how to make something that stands the test of time.

Amazon is quite the haberdasher these days, from humble beginnings as an online bookstore. *Fulfilled by Amazon* means you can send in whatever you want to sell, and they keep it in their warehouses and make sure customers get it in *Prime* time. In the late 2000s, they started making significantly more money from their *Amazon Web Services* division selling cloud services. Proven gizmos, databases, and hosting services that they already maintain to keep the Amazon retail site running. They did a lot of heavy lifting for you, and now you can operate at Amazon scale if you really need to.

Hell, soon enough they'll have a tailor in-house and you don't even need to do the work. White-box service. Is that really what you want, though? A haberdasher gets out of their own way, so that you have something to show for your work. All too many sellers on Amazon have become frustrated with how often they are competing with Amazon's brands and boosted search rankings. Some companies find it difficult to get out of their own way, because they always are trying to do more in house. And too many legs of Amazon's business runs at near-zero margins, or even at a loss, which is not good news at all for folks looking to make an honest living. Certainly, they have internal guidelines for how much they let themselves completely fuck over independent sellers.

The haberdasher is glad to have a horse in a race. He knows you're going to tell all of your colleagues how excellent his service is. He always keeps all of your most important materials in stock. A great haberdasher, ideally, isn't competing with you.

Brick

People really do want to shop. We know now that it's cheaper to shop online and there's a much bigger selection, by orders of magnitude, but people love to actually engage with what they're buying. Who wouldn't? Having something right in front of you gets you excited about it. The thrill of something showing up in just the right place makes you feel like it was meant to be, and then you might even pay a bit more for it than you would otherwise. There are great stores that curate a very interesting selection of materials and designs that are pleasing just to be around. The element of curation often means you're getting things with better quality. I love CB2, Crate and Barrel's younger, groovier concept. They have premium materials and very clever style at a reasonable enough price. When there's a store like that around, I'm pleased to have a chance to go to it, even if I didn't necessarily need anything from it.

Right now, I'll continue reminding you that we are in the deepest swing of the pendulum towards *digital* and *unreal* that has ever existed in the world. One day, on such a somniferous occasion, people will wake up and feel starved for *real*. Really, they're just remembering how long they've been awake, pure exhaustion. Like a year long trek through the desert, they'll show up at an oasis and fall to their knees in praise that finally something has appeared in their life that isn't made of silicon and glass. The work day has finally ended. It's bedtime.

You guys are great with permits and bulldozers, you'll do great. Having a physical presence makes your brand seem substantial and relevant. Apple understood this. When you see an Apple store everywhere you go, it makes the brand very fresh in your mind. And in a world where lots of computers and electronics seem flimsy and challenging, Apple is able to show people that they made something that you should be proud to own, that's guaranteed to be easy to use and reliable every day. They're so committed to you loving it, they have people working at the Apple Store that will show you everything you could ever want to know about using it. They know everything, they're real geniuses after all.

Final

There isn't a description of privacy that is quite complete to describe its importance, both practically and metaphysically, as a binding principle for the world. Privacy, in its most essential form, is the phenomenon of *finality*. Like the skin on your bones, or grout between tiles, privacy is what keeps whatever substance of mind or body from spilling out everywhere in an instant.

Certainly, the world is always changing. Even in each moment, entropy is causing invisible change in the world, and the cells in your body are growing and turning over through apoptosis. Still, at every point along the way, a terminus or finality appears that is characteristic of what that thing must remain. Like utility poles and electrical wires, the thing that you can see is under tension so that it remains what it is. If you wish to remain a person, and not just blood and guts spilled out everywhere, you must believe in some essential sort of privacy of imagos where the totality of you is apparent. Even if you run your mouth endlessly and share selfies every day, you certainly still believe in your face and your name remaining the same for some period at a time.

The universe is, essentially, *dispersal* and *finality* under suspension. Finality couldn't exist without variation in some original form. And dispersal couldn't exist unless it was apparent that something began, under stasis and not yet differentiated. We call the ordering principle *privacy* now, because it is the most effective way of describing walls and doors in the context of technology and media.

There is a childlike naivety to finality, like having an irreconcilable demand that your chicken nuggets are shaped like dinosaurs. When we imagine someone who is mature and reasonable, we see something like a person that is able to disperse their will and withhold their preferences so that they can interface with all of the people and things that can possibly exist. As important as it is to be reasonable and flexible, on some deep and visceral level we respect people who are true to their desires.

Privacy is a discriminatory tool. It wouldn't occur to you how to use privacy unless you had some way of deciding who deserves your attention. So, how do you decide? Where does the illusion of separateness begin for you, in terms of viewing things external to you as distinct and restricted from you as an individual? Very interesting question. Some of us clearly have higher standards, which is often fueled by having more options. Higher standards of *what* though? It probably wouldn't occur to you to enforce your privacy on account of what color hair people have, but maybe. Your genes certainly care about those sorts of things, though, and when we are in social circles it almost naturally occurs that a particular sort of person is what defines a particular group of people, whether it's church or a Dungeons and Dragons meetup. A revered *mark* appears, so that something can be known as what it is. Certainly, we are drawn towards people who seem similar to us and reinforce our worldview. If we were wired to be completely and absolutely private, we wouldn't be able to tolerate anything other than ourselves and the contents of our own minds. But it clearly occurs to us to gradually interface with people that seem relevant to us, a sort of dissociative longing for another, on account of qualia.

Singular

Would you rather be extravagantly well known or uniquely less known? Lots of people would choose to be well known quite readily. What if they told you that the well known option means that you have lots of people sharing *equity* in your name, and you wouldn't really belong to yourself as much as the one and only lesser-known you that could exist instead? You'd say *this is clearly me, the only me, that is responsible for my existence.* Would that be the particularly individual *you*, that is narrowly experiencing the world as a person, or the giant over-arching *you* speaking through your tongue from the shores of eternity? Which one do you think makes your luck?

Unusual thought, and difficult to articulate. That being supremely grand in some way may inherently make you less individual, on account of the hulking collectivist machine that emerges by principle of your existence, and that you could feel a sort of teenage angst for the fate that you created, on account of never being able to leave the home you destined for yourself.

Myths and stories contextualize this phenomenon with symbols like frost, vampirism, and stone. Frost is not simply chilling for our senses, but the notion of being frozen in place, predestined by our fate. Vampirism is the idea that we converge around carnal desire; some instinct that is inherent to all of us and runs through our blood, that we would persist for eternity and dispense with it as we feed on new prey. That there is a proportional exchange between individuality and collectivism.

The world requires us to bear a mark representing the foundation that emboldens our success, whether our religion, currency, language, or our appearance. A mark appears inherently by virtue of something existing. How would you know what a Mac is unless you knew of a thin aluminum computer with a clever Apple logo on it? Some people are very particular that they only play on particular instruments or work on particular equipment; everything they make would be imbued with the essence of that thing. Sometimes, the mark seems so pervasive that it feels constricting, like seeing U.S. politics in every newsstand in the world. Sometimes, we are taught to believe we are born under a fateful sign, that bearing that mark is our salvation. It's easier for us to imagine how it could be both liberating and also constricting when you tell a colorful story, and quite instinctual for us to desire to be free and individual.

Being unique is quite at odds with being well known. One way or another, when you look around, everything starts looking the way you said it would. You see the same names and faces over and over. The world moves so fast now that you almost feel like you don't get the chance to be unique before everyone else comes and capitalizes on it. Good for them. That means the money growing on the tree in your backyard is worth something. Your *name* is worth something.

Defrozen

It's the only way I'd have it, really. How particular I am, and how she knows this to be. And so she showed up just as she was meant to, according to the requirements as plain as life itself. Reality became a little more opinionated when we arrived, because now there's this seed of truth that we meant to sow in every fertile land in the universe. It's a gift, faithful and true, to be certain, and also a nearly inscrutable constraint. Now, for some reason it has to be like that. And there are more than enough good reasons baked into the pie that the more arbitrary attributes get toted along with them. Because of the good reasons, and because of the potency, the sensory attributes get to be what we desired. Surely, we chose interesting colors and indulgent flavors, although those things may as well have been completely different, except for the fact that we tastefully included them in the whole that we compiled. Like a victory speech, the sensory attributes would be inaccessible from the actual performance, except as they emboldened the resolve for victory. We would never count our chickens before they hatch, and likewise, we encourage discretion and foresight around our gift horses.

I have something particular to show each and every one of you. I want your life to be excellent, and for you to believe in yourself in everything that you do. Naturally, each of our lives have to be excellent in a different way, so that what's mine remains mine, and what's yours remains yours. So that when you play me your new album, I can enjoy everything about it that makes it so special to you. I love intense music, enchanting and ethereal music that is at once wistful and under pressure. Tense, like your bright guitar flourishes and your synths. At times busy, like the mechanical revolutions of your drum fills and your splashy hi-hat.

The thing that excites me most about you is that you know just what to do at exactly the right time. Because you understand creating tension and releasing it, and you know exactly what is exciting to taste. Necessarily, you try a lot of things and you are paying attention. I know when I look at something you made, I'm about to be taken to another world. So something about you must be beautiful for it to hold everyone's attention for hours and weeks at a time. Years at a time.

Eden

God forgives us for the original sin in the Garden of Eden, by mercy and grace. If you follow that line of reasoning to the sovereign will of the individual, and they only have one girlfriend and no extra food, they deserve to stand their ground.

Then you suppose that in any system with more than 2 individual actors that strive to become equally paired, it is inherently evil to place them in a situation where there is no opportunity for dispersal and original sin. The opportunity for selection only exists with dispersal, or *mercy*.

Bondage is when there is an apparent authoritative force that makes things a particular way. I would suggest that this is, at the very least, the authority of our senses that make us like particular qualities and choose to be with a particular partner, based on the fact that they are who they are and we love them specifically. The more that authoritative force appears *external* to us, i.e., as an administrative effort that we raise above our individual will, it comes with the requirement that there is a dispersal and a change over time. Otherwise, it would simply be an eternal covenant between 2 equally balanced parties.

Truly fair administration, ostensibly, affords every individual an opportunity to succeed. And we take a logical leap from our mortal perspective that there is something inherently valuable about the qualities we believe are attractive. So we say that you get the opportunity to succeed, *in proportion with what we determine is good.*

Is that necessarily true? I wonder. Because I find particular things attractive in myself and in others. *Something* emerges as a selective force, that our partner is a specific person with a specific name. The free will is to choose to love, although also apparently the bondage that appears as our own choices become externalized into the administrative effort. When other people see us choose something, it balances the scales according to that identifying mark.

Do Not Resist

So, hypothetically, once we have robot police and military with laser weapons like in Fallout and Terminator, how do we decide what their job is? If the robots get to figure out what we're allowed to do, boy you better be good at the SAT. When individuals never get to *steal away with the girl,* you've really got yourself in a situation you didn't want. Because people who advocate for more gun control (maybe with good reasons, in moderation) seem to forget that the whole point of allowing citizens to own weapons is to ensure the free will of the individual.

From the early history of the United States, people had it fresh in their minds that governments can be oppressive and will strip the sovereign will of the individual in the interest of homogeneity and public safety. Now we forget that. In a time where our country is so safe and so still, absorbed in our phones and our paperwork, we seem to often hear about guns causing problems. The idea that your home, your property, and your choices are yours to defend has kind of gone by the wayside. As people, we have incredibly complex and stable social systems, and also we should remember that we must assert our individual will to get our way. But really, if everyone thought there were other people with guns in the room (or Fallout laser robots), they'd be scared shitless to try and pull anything. The cat's kind of already out of the bag. Other countries encourage their citizens to bear arms, but really the U.S. has quite the reputation.

Why do you think all great stories are about a hero and heroine fleeing the oppressive state into their love for each other? Where else do you escape *the majority* except into the arms of an individual with bigger and brighter plans for the world? Perhaps someday, their name will be pervasive in the world, imprinted at every intersection, and you'll reflect on when you first met the stranger you fell in love with.

Right now, if you hate the idea that someone can make decisions on your behalf, you would completely despise having your entire life planned out by A.I. police, because you either give individuals direct control over their lives, or you hand over your control to an administrative authority. And, in varying degrees, that's the sort of slippery slope that absolute surveillance, *community guidelines*, and taking away guns from citizens tends towards, where people aren't allowed to say how they really feel and do what they believe is right.

Authority

We have a confused relationship with authority. On one hand, we say we prefer to be free in all matters to do as we please. Clearly, though, we do hope for some authority to exist to ensure that things go as planned. There is a balancing act here, as with all things in life. When we consider what makes authority valuable, we can reflect on the orderly and peaceful societies we have. Our homes and our computers stay safe because there are authorities that are responsible for enforcing the rule of law, and never abusing their power themselves. Authority ensures that our healthcare works the way we expect, at prices that are fair to consumers. Divine law and retribution delivers a swift hand of justice in any case.

I wouldn't say that I tend to have problems with authority, although from the time I was a kid I definitely started noticing that I knew more about lots of things than authority figures did, which made me question how they ended up in that position. Now I know they let just about anyone be a parent, and teaching elementary school isn't exactly a crowning achievement. Both are to be respected for certain reasons, namely that if either didn't exist, kids would be without structure in their lives.

As I got older, I couldn't quite shake the feeling that authority slowed me down more than it gave me helpful structure. We all may feel that way from time to time, and then we can reflect on all of the tremendously important authority figures that ensure our societies are safe, healthy, and efficient. And then we can remember how important it is for us to have parents to care for us. We would be lost from the day we are born without them.

All along, I was somehow ignorant to the fact that it frustrated people that I saw myself as an authority on many matters, even as young as 6 years old. Truly, it wasn't until the past few years of my life that I gave this any consideration at all, although a thorough analysis of it is necessary to be persuasive. What makes a leader desirable is that they get you what you want and they aren't especially opinionated about what you do in your own time. When you insert truths and absolutes into peoples lives, it makes them feel constricted. That's not really the sort of person I am. I like everyone to have the freedom to do as they please, so long as they respect the natural rights of all people in the process. Clearly, though, when I speak I tend to cast a great shadow. Some things can't be helped. There are obvious influences that would have people thinking like that. Certainly, I place a lot of importance on being right, although I now know there are important differences between *being right* and *righteousness*. Falsehoods and tolerance are implicit in righteousness.

The main wrench that I throw right into the middle of your affairs is *privacy*, and there is simply no other way about it. Privacy is more important and central to all of our lives now than ever, and without people who actually know what they're talking about to champion privacy, everyone is left in the dark and at the mercy of major corporations who are asleep at the wheel. Why a wrench, and why right in the middle of your gear? Because that's where you found me. With a lot of things in life, it's easy enough to live and let live, and that's a great philosophy to have in the interest of freedom. When it comes to privacy, you're not left with many choices. Technology has such an active role in our lives that our only choice is to meet it at the apex of its influence. As pervasive as technology is, we must make an equal appeal for the sovereign will of the individual. And fortunately, our judicial systems are brilliantly instrumented to make the sovereign will of the individual particularly powerful when confronted with immeasurably complex systems.

Industry must be free to grow and succeed, and likewise, people must have options for how their data is used and how they communicate freely. Otherwise, you have a giant toll booth in the middle of your life that decides if you get to send the messages you want to send, or if there is a place for you in this world to feel like you are in private. The same toll booth that now wants to use your mindshare to train its A.I. systems to do everything you know how to do.

At some point, people will just up and say *"Privacy is just not that important to us."* Then you have to remind them of what life is like to be nameless, faceless, and with no options except those that are dispensed with from the powers that be. Then, perhaps they will never forget how important the sovereign will of the individual is. Where there's at least one person on the planet that believes your name is worth something, and that you deserve a fair chance to say and do anything you believe in, and to bear the consequences. The reason you know they believe that is because they are the sort of person that is completely preoccupied with universal

111

morality and righteous, all the way to their core. For their name to be worth something, yours must be too. And if they look around the room for too long and see faceless and nameless drones that will do and say anything for a buck, they become plainly disgusted. They say the time is *now* for you to start believing each and every person counts. If you believe it so thoroughly, you would only ever want what's good and true for all people. And you'd remember that you'd rather not be beholden to anyone at all, because then they'd get the idea that you want to hear from them. Because that's the reality of deciding you own the likeness of every person on the planet. You're the person whose doorstep they show up at when the economy has Facebook and Google stamped on every dollar bill.

Dress for Success

is what they told us in school to justify uniforms and dress codes. And I don't entirely disagree. More apt, I would recommend dressing for however you want to seem, which should be closely related to how you feel. Business casual is a sort of goth to me.

Do you find yourself feeling out of place? It could be that's how you're trying to seem, which may or may not always be serving you. Be memorable, and be true.

I love polo shirts that fit nicely. Oxford shirts in light blue and pinstripes. Khakis or jeans. Usually, just a t-shirt though. People have all kinds of explanations for why you should wear different clothes or when it's appropriate. Maybe they're right sometimes. I wear clothes that look like how I feel. There's a time and a place for everything, so you can always come up with a way to be unique. If you mean to be taken seriously, dress to be taken seriously. If you want people to feel more relaxed around you, wear softer materials and more casual styles. That said, the world knows I feel like pinstripe and khakis in my truest self. And black. Blacker than you can even see.

Any Color I Like

Lately it's been quite a hot topic whether businesses are allowed to make personal ideological decisions about who or what they allow in their stores. Certainly, it's always been the case that *no shirt, no shoes, no service* is something you say to ensure there's a baseline level of decency for everyone that comes into your establishment, especially in areas where that's likely to be an issue with beach bums and homeless folks. Now, though, people debate how picky you get to be.

If someone is being loud or annoying in a physical space, it's going to ruin it for everyone else there. But the more your business looks like a public communication service, or a *common carrier,* people have the expectation that everyone's voice travels an equal distance. Which is *not* the case on websites like YouTube and Instagram where you can be manually delisted or have your views frozen, sometimes without even knowing it.

And that happens even when they're not being annoying. If you have opinions that conflict with the hivemind, you start running into problems with censorship. Elon Musk has notably made significant changes to X's (the company formerly known as Twitter) algorithm and moderation policy after he bought it for $44 billion, ensuring all viewpoints are allowed that aren't openly violent or threatening for the safety of an individual or group of people.

Now, almost all social media websites enable people to communicate in ways that were never possible before, but sometimes there are leniences and biases that surface based on the politics of the people running those sites. Which is natural, and also something we should fix.

While those folks are glad to decide what you can and can't say, they'll often go in the same breath and say it's unacceptable for retail businesses to be openly political or discriminatory. Personally, I think it's unfair to decide what sorts of people come into your business for the same reason, but are you really about to get wound up if the owners themselves believe a particular thing? Or does owning a business preclude you from having beliefs at all?

The essence of what makes the information age excellent is that anyone is allowed to say what they truly believe in and reach the end of the Earth with it. Anyone can contribute knowledge or journalism, where before it was a select group of people that filled the world with their beliefs. This is great, because when something is happening that people should know about, they all do. And they get every possible viewpoint they could want to be informed, or so we would hope.

Mission Driven

Like, burritos? Tofu? $800 dinners that are true to Spanish heritage?

No, what they mean when they say *mission driven* is "We will focus on the core impact and functionality of our business to the exclusion of ideological and ethical concerns that we don't want to think about."

What an excellent way to relieve yourself of answering difficult questions. Here's the thing: you absolutely have to be able to unify everyone in your organization around common goals so that everyone stays focused and avoids getting dredged down in endless ethical debates. A company has particular goals that leaders will set out to accomplish, and everyone needs to be showing up and putting honest work in. When you say *mission driven* I hear "There are tremendous economic impacts and ethical discussions that surround our business, but it's easy enough for us to put blinders on and ignore them so we can keep moving forward."

So, what is your *mission?* Because that's going to show up every time you try to figure out how to pasteurize your beliefs. And it's invariably just as ideological as all of the things you claim are too ideological to be relevant at work. Believe it or not, not everyone in the world believes in whatever steaming pile of JavaScript and inflation that you are so satisfied with on account of it printing money. But as long as you say *mission driven* and refocus all of the discussions around shipping new features, everyone is none the wiser, and they'll continue enjoying their $5,000 studio apartment and $100 pizzas.

We're seeing that groups invested in artificial intelligence are actually quite responsible about the ethics of their organizations, which makes me happy to see. Call it what you want, their mission is to be thorough, because they understand that A.I. is an all-encompassing technology with far-reaching effects. The consensus from the beginning has been that A.I. has significant ethical impact in terms of the economy, decision making, equality, copyright, and more. These are all things that most A.I. companies are taking quite seriously in light of the rapid innovation we've seen in the past decade.

Artificial intelligence is already changing the dynamics of our economy, and it will only improve exponentially as it optimizes every task and decision that we can come up with. It is also consolidating lots of power into the major companies that have created such capable systems, which will leave ordinary people feeling left out of the economy. I, myself, am confident that A.I. is already better at writing traditional software than I am, orders of magnitude more efficiently and reliably, and perhaps at some point it would also be better at writing this book; I still take pride in things that I create.

A.I. will be put in situations where it has to make mission-critical decisions about the world, and it's already in situations where it gets to make value assessments about people based on the same sorts of heuristics that regular people used when they came up with the training data for the A.I.

Artificial intelligence is able to generate video, audio, and text that looks and sounds exactly like real living people, making it difficult to tell what is real and undermining the natural ownership that people have of their identity and their work.

These are among a few of the ways that artificial intelligence is going to completely change the world. I am optimistic about pushing the boundaries of technology and using it to improve all of our lives.

Lots of cultures take pride in going on missions that end, so that everyone can go home.

Liquorice Legislation

That's the thing about politics, is everything has to suit a narrative. Many years ago, it was a hot topic when politicians were trying to pass legislation around *net neutrality*. Whatever that means. Whatever that means is supposedly there are guidelines for ensuring everyone has an equal voice on the internet, and equal access to all websites with common carrier philosophy around internet access. This is a good thing on paper, because the internet is as pervasive in our lives as electricity and running water. Imagine if they just blocked all of your phone calls to a particular city. Imagine if there were entire websites and topics that your internet provider decided you shouldn't be allowed to see.

In the 2010s, the streaming industry felt real heat that the internet providers would start playing hanky panky with data limits on streaming services to bolster their position with traditional cable television. This was a *very* real concern, from a time where many home internet lines just started having data caps out of nowhere. The internet providers often never even had anything like that before, but they accused us, the consumers, of streaming too much damn Netflix.

Really, though, you start wondering what the hell these guys are even talking about. Anytime you tread in the territory of *oversight*, they sneak in stipulations that are supposed to prevent piracy and help content moderation. *Neutrality* enters this gradient descent into red tape, where it starts to be about keeping the incumbents in business and giving them clever ways to lord their power over you. I know I didn't read any of the bills that were being discussed, so I certainly hope someone did. That's just my intuition based on what I know about politics.

I am always optimistic and hesitant when people talk about this sort of legislation. The ideal benefit would be ensuring everyone has equal access to information and a fair, uncensored voice. Which already is certainly *not* the case, and it's more the fault of social media's clever de-amplification and censorship tactics than the internet providers. Maybe that was the idea all along, to hold our attention to the infrastructure and have the actual websites pull the wool over our eyes.

Any time you start talking about oversight, you have to figure out some way to ensure checks and balances exist where you would expect them to. This goes for technology, media, healthcare, and just about anything else.

Net neutrality *of what?* Will this help me get more options for internet service providers, instead of the exactly *one* option that many cities have? Or do they get to own the underground conduit running fiber through the entire city until the end of time? Will Google and Facebook commit to allowing people to hold unpopular political views or say mean things, so long as they are not threatening or harmful to people? These are the things I think about, because this isn't my first time looking at your bullshit politics. Otherwise, you live in a world where real voices get squashed, because *obviously no one believes that, right?*

Ed Tom

Everyone deserves the opportunity to succeed. And then at the end of the line it's someone's responsibility to make sure you're looking at the world in the right light. Some people cast a shadow that reaches the beginning and the end of the universe. It's difficult for them to be satisfied with their explanation for why things are the way they are. What would you say to them? Is there a better story you could tell about why some people get what they deserve from God and from the universe?

He wonders whether good men deserve to get away with murdering bad men. His job isn't supposed to be to decide like that, to walk the crimes back to the nexus. But God's is, and he believes there's not a place in the universe you can hide.

He hopes with all his heart that when he says something, God had a say in it, because otherwise he wonders if he'd know the difference.

That's one of the only things in this book that really makes him sad, and that's how you know Ed Tom thinks a lot about the world. And he would nearly not judge you to just be here to carry a gun and drive a patrol vehicle, because you show up every day and do your job exactly as it was meant. But he goes home at night and it's not quite that way for him.

Things just aren't the same since everyone remembered why he's here. People count up the days since he was in a bad mood, like when he was a young man disturbed by death, fraught with the idea things were going to end before he got to tell his story.

Everyone told him *he's lucky*, all of the pieces came together for him. Other folks look and see that dead look in his eyes that you only see in people that stand perfectly still while they can feel the Earth rotating and time slipping away. That same look in his eyes that tells you he'd sooner burst into flames than let go the weight of truth.

Loom

My first and only profound psychedelic experience was with The Man at the Loom. He sat, fixed in perpetual motion, weaving the tapestry of life together. This was the first time it occurred to me that God would be bearing the weight of all of our suffering. I suppose, before that, it crossed my mind, but at this point it made sense to me in a very visceral and terrifying way, how Christ was hanging from a post bleeding out for days on end. So for God to truly know us the way we know ourselves, certainly he would know our successes and our suffering the way that we feel them. When wars are fought and people are tortured in endless pain, God understands us. When people take too much time to figure something out, like watching someone who doesn't know how to play video games, God understands us. When we wonder why God would have us suffer, he understands us.

The empyrean is the highest point in heaven, if you could even conceive of height from the realm of aether. It's supposed that the empyrean is fiery, for its endless change and reconfiguration, where he keeps acquiring a new face. Here it burns like eternity. No need to wonder why the world creaks and rattles, or why there's a dispute for what we should eat tonight. Only that you will make today as you know it should occur. I wonder if there's a place to sleep when the world is unending. Like an old man, it sort of seems like he's not paying attention much anymore because he's already seen it; hard to say whether it's because he's losing his hearing or you just aren't saying anything worthwhile. It's important that you're enjoying yourself, let's leave it at that. He's not an old man though, or a young man. He's at least as new as you. If he gave it too much thought, he would wonder why the burning never ends. We'll find a way to rest easy.

I suppose it's easier for us to understand what real suffering is like if we know it personally or if someone in our family has been subjected to it. If your father or grandfather was captured and tortured for years as prisoner of war, maybe you'd think about the world a little differently. We forget as quickly as we mean to put atrocities behind us. And we're convinced we need victory for ourselves, not the kind you inherit. If something like that happened to you, how would you resist the temptation to be racist or prejudiced? The object of your hatred would be so readily apparent for the rest of your life. We are all God's children, though.

God always has a plan, and he is meant to never leave his post at the loom. Whenever I wonder why things have to be a particular way, I know to remember that all things come in due time, through right thinking and right action. And God will always be there for us to show us the true path to follow. We might feel insignificant, in light of God's splendor, but we know certainly that every day is meaningful and intentional. Each of us, hanging from his vine and living according to what is good and true.

I wonder why I don't have particularly psychedelic experiences since then. No otherworldly visuals or realizations. Usually it just feels like a very long stimulant, like weed and caffeine mixed together. Which is good, it's like a 24-hour music and games marathon. Maybe I just need to find the right place and time to drop acid.

When your refrigerator has a touchscreen, Bluetooth, Instagram, and a million moving parts, the day will come 2 years from when you bought it that the manufacturer decides it's not worth updating anymore, and you're out in the cold. Your plain old microwave just converts button presses into micro-waves, though. And your fridge would still just *make cold,* if you didn't decide you wanted to watch TV on it. The actual requirements for these things to work didn't change, some idiot just decided they wanted to install apps on their fridge, like attaching a flashlight to the handle of a spoon. But the requirements of the world change dramatically, every day. Faster now than ever. God never abandons our software. And God is so prescient and intentional about leading us through the storm.

Doin' Time

Putting the Zen in Buddhism. Winning isn't necessarily going to make you happier. The more you win, the less exciting it is, unless by some twist of fate you're addicted to winning like Saturn is to devouring people. What is it about having 500,000 people reading your content that is more satisfying than having 50,000 people reading it? Are you particular about whose attention you mean to have? So, which of those people are you especially proud to have the attention of? One good reason to always be acquiring influence is because it makes it easier for your word to travel over great distances. One good reason not to be is it starts feeling like the world is an echo chamber for your ideas. Now, there's 100 new touchscreen phones released every year, and not one of them makes you feel the way the original iPhone did. I buried this towards the middle of the book so you spend less time thinking about it, but it's certainly worth mentioning, in the interest of making a comprehensive study of winning.

I spend a lot of time thinking about how my life in this world is marked by so much red. I look red and feel red most days. And I wonder why it has to be that way, that the world knows all I like is Mac, and all it wants to feed me is Del Taco. There's plenty of Mac, but an immeasurable amount of Del Taco that's all going to waste. It makes the world feel like a waste. Landfills of Snapdragon and Galaxy S 140.

I showed you what *oxford and khakis me* looks like, and I made it quite clear that was the option that I believe is correct. But when that came around on the sushi boats, you passed it up. So now, have *meat grinder me,* because that's the only thing you respond to. Don't put your fucking fingers in that.

And you'd say *but you love winning, so how could you not want the option to lose?* And this is true. But I can only go so many weeks and months in a row with that being the prevailing theme in my life. What part of *it just works* do you not understand?

So when people ask me why I seem so angry, that's why. Because some of you seem like a waste of time. Intentionally. Not because you're dumb, or untalented, which may contribute to it. But clearly and obviously because you are here to waste my time. Assume I have zero patience and work your way up from there, that's your best bet.

Some people are just naturally happier than others. Some people are addicted to feeling sad, because that's the thing that motivated them to do more to begin with.

Your enthusiasm for what you do is what's going to keep people coming back for more. Look how cheerful she is, to this day, for every show. That's what being a true performer looks like, because every day someone is going to show up to buy buttons and zippers, and they expect you to be there in the morning to open the doors.

They're here to see you for the very first time, and you're going to give them an experience they'll never forget.

6

Tennis

I wish I could remember what I was going to start chapter 6 with, other than we're supposed to overcome our differences, and I could only ever imagine loving someone just like you.

Winning became something I did for you, that we did together.

Things make sense in different ways depending on how far away you look at them. You're going to get very good at honing your zoom lens in this photographic and narrative-driven world we live in. Not only did I have something to show you, but it also had to make sense to everyone else. That's just who I am, being an engineer. It would be unimaginable to do something and not also have some code and scripts to show for it.

You know how I like to play, and we've discovered some important techniques about the game together. Things you only learn by playing for thousands of hours and by watching how other people play.

Our reason is empirical and practical. You can understand it just by looking at it, because we do it live and we hit all of the notes. Good practice makes perfect, but playing for real means playing under pressure and performing when it counts.

You gonna let people get in your head? Shall we consult our strategy guides and powder our noses? They see you thinking like that and that's how they know they're ahead of the game.

Do you mind holding this? Displacement is how I'll project my own beliefs onto you, and then we'll see how they hold up. Everything you believe is, at least, however it makes you feel, and how it makes the people around you feel. Sometimes we give away our beliefs like old clothes that we don't wear anymore, and then we have to be understanding of why someone else might like to wear them. Why we'd like to see them wearing them instead of continuing to wear those clothes ourselves.

I don't feel 13 years old anymore, but at the time, bright electric blue jeans looked interesting on me, and they certainly matched how I felt. I feel more like I'm 6 years old now, in some unusual turn of events. When I was 6 years old, I felt like I had things figured out more. When I was 13 I spent more time wondering what you know that I don't. I was convinced you must know something that I need to learn from you. Now, the more I learn, I still hope there's something new out there for me, but I'm less inclined to enjoy the novelty of it. 6 year old me is proud to be done. It looks just like the thing it was supposed to be, and I don't mean to endlessly add ingredients and food coloring to try to squeeze some bit of newness out of it.

18 year old me has better taste in music. Finally, he can see something like black, enough to conceive of the subtext of duality. Music seemed funnier; the thing that became sexy about it was the lack of restraint and the self-assurance, whereas before it wouldn't have occurred to me how to make those things funny.

The Great Deceiver

The greatest deceit is that I have something to be deceitful about at all. Plainly, I only have good news. Winners don't need to come up with justifications for why the thing they're doing is excellent. It just is. That's how they came out of the womb. There's still an impetus to put whatever you're doing under some sort of pressure. Drama keeps people involved, and it can be fun.

When you go to the casino or open a pack of trading cards, you really are hoping not only to get something good, but also that there exists something good for you to get. If every pack of Pokémon cards had a holofoil Charizard in it, there wouldn't be anything special about it. Or people would value that card at pennies on the dollar, and the real, original Charizard that is rare would remain much more desirable in light of this common imitation.

Magic is sparkling phantasm and awe, and also the anticipation that something cool is going to happen. It's the hiss of the hi-hat building tension for the snare drum, with every bar.

Every time I do a trick it's a little less magical for me. The only way around this would be for me to forget, or to start contextualizing the rhythm of the whole show. The Eternal Sunshine of the Spotless Mind, like seeing life for the very first time again.

Isn't it fun, for a change, to let life carry us away? What would be the greater deceit; to believe in something greater, or to believe in the finality of what already is? We're proud of the totality of who we have become, all of the things we have seen and the accomplishments we have accrued. And we are so receptive to the present and the allure of what will come for us. Life ought to be a journey that every one of us is proud of, just as we are.

It can be fun to be beguiled by pleasure and joy, but it is just as important to not let ourselves be seduced by deceit, lest we become consumed by our base desires and our primal urges. It's so easy to find ourselves slipping away for what is less than just, especially when we are in precarious circumstances where high stakes and immediate decision-making are employed. Our hand gets forced, and the only thing that stabilizes us is our sense of truth. A familiar reminder that all things are as one in this life, and we would no sooner cut off our nose to spite our face, than have karma arrive in our wake as we bite ourselves in the ass. You have a lot of choices in life about how difficult you want to make things for yourself. You have to tell *some* story about *some* thing, so it may as well be what is true and just, for whom we know to be true and just in our lives.

Speak Now

The things you have to say now aren't going to occur to you when you're older. The chaos and panic of what has to happen *right now* is what's going to make it come out like what it is. Sometimes you're going to look back at things you made and they're going to seem puerile and naive. Try to ignore that urge to burn all your bridges with your past selves. Many of my favorite albums and movies were created at a point in the artists' careers that was so raw, and even sloppy. It wouldn't occur to them the same way today; it would be, plainly, sterile.

Still, many of my favorite things have only come to fruition with maturity. You're sexier now that you're more potent.

Now might feel tragic because it is the only place you can be, but later on, the memory of now might be something you hope to bury away, the details fading and the immediacy of every day blurred into dark passages of your life.

Things you'd hope to forget may just as well be the side of you that everyone else wants to see. All of the most important decisions in your life are going to feel terrifying, and then you will live with the consequences. When you're older, you're not going to have the same kinds of decisions. Make the best of every tribulation, so that you can show the world something beautiful.

A life lived without regret is sweeter than all but the most bitter mistakes. Follow your intuition every day.

I love that cake has filling. You can get a little bite of the cake, the filling, and the frosting, and it's all separate, but it goes together. If it was all mixed together it wouldn't taste right, and if every bite was exactly same, it would be like squeezing it out of a tube. So, naturally, it's quite important that everything you do has some amount of categorization and organization. When I'm shopping, it's more fun that I get to go looking for what I want and find it, than to have everything I want already figured out for me.

Appreciate that there's layer cake in your life. You get to peel the plastic off and open the box every day. If you're in the position of privilege to be winning, you get to come up with a special sort of gift to give to the world. People love to imagine what's inside and what you're going to come up with next.

Most days on your advent calendar just have a piece of chocolate inside. Enjoy it. One piece to commemorate the day.

A few days you're going to get iced. Let's see how you fare. Winners hold it together even when it seems like the whole deck is stacked against them, because they can see the forest through the trees. They're counting the cards, and they know everyone's spending a *lot* of good cards right now that they're going to wish they had later.

All things come in due time, with right action. When it seems like you're not getting what you want, it may very well be that there is more that you need to accomplish before the time is right. Things you need to see, and words you must speak for the stars to align. If you want this thing to come out right, you really want to make sure you're touching all the bases, so that when you look back on everything you know you did everything you set out to accomplish. Don't half squeeze an orange or half bake a cake, because the worst part of playing a game you love is when it comes to an end and you have nothing to do. Ideally, you've come up with a game that you can keep playing that always has something exciting in store.

Select

Our expectations for the world are always growing and changing. It's funny to reflect on what we thought was great that now seems primitive in retrospect. Like old PlayStation games where the characters look like Lego blocks, or our computers that were absolute screamers at the time that are slower now than our watches and commodity hobbyist boards the size of credit cards. We have real-time graphics now that are orders of magnitude better than graphics that used to take days to render, and we have entire computers the size of coins that completely crush 20th century machines that took up entire rooms and cost millions of dollars.

In the 1970s, 15 miles per gallon was good. In 2023, saying *hello* to the world in an instant is good. Things keep improving because people keep increasing their expectations and tightening the tolerances. Imagine if we knew then what we know now. It would seem like alien technology to bring a modern computer to the 1970s. Truly like magic, beyond all belief. Many of the greatest innovations in the world look like magic when we first arrive at them.

We have a preference for *better,* and also preferences that are cultural. People have very different ideas about what makes food good, so much that it seems arbitrary if you step back for a minute. How much milk or cream in your coffee; the texture and the sweetness. You ask anyone about coffee and they'll say something different: too bitter, too sour, too watery, too sweet.

So — they just don't cook the fish? Some people can't tell the difference with fresh sushi. They enjoy the game and they aren't paying attention to which pitches are being thrown, and they don't care where the coffee came from, so long as it has milk and caramel in it.

Is it worth being selective, even if it's frustrating to a lot of people? I think so.

People looked at Elon Musk like he was crazy as recently as 15 years ago. *What are you selling, golf carts?* How foolish they must feel now. Get this: the whole time everyone thought you had to burn gas and shift gears to get a vehicle moving, when in reality, putting an electric motor and a battery in a car makes it 10x faster and infinitely more efficient.

Being selective and being curious means you're going to come up with something new, plain and simple, because everything that already exists is already figured out. You *love* to figure out something new.

But not everyone does, and that's okay. That's great, even, in it's own regard, because that means you must like to win games that lots of people are already playing, which means you have to be really, really good at them.

The new stuff is too new for it to be particularly competitive, which is surprising. And also good, because your first prototype doesn't have to be perfect, it just has to show everyone what you're talking about. How disappointing would it be to know the 1984 Macintosh that you put your heart and soul into is going to be succeeded decades later by the brand new iMac, orders of magnitude faster, with full color and instant communication. Today, a watch is faster than the fastest supercomputer they could imagine, capable of answering questions like a genie in a bottle. But that's not the point. At the time, the fundamentals were all there, and that got the ball moving.

Like a bicycle for your mind. It sits right on your desk, you can write documents with it and keep your finances, make artwork and code programs. The biggest innovation was that the screen could display pictures, folders, and fonts that you could interact with, where everything before it was entirely text-based. We had computers before that, but they weren't something you could really show to someone. The infrastructure also had to catch up, because what we all wanted to do was access the world's knowledge and wealth of swimsuit photos. We wanted to *receive* money on the computer, not just keep track of it.

A human on a bicycle is as efficient as the fastest wild cats in the world. How many people can you reach on your phone, in an instant, from anywhere in the world?

All of the greatest innovations are born of some limitation made actual and overcome. In the same way it seems like a nascent miracle to download even one picture or view a low-quality video when you're on a slow connection, so too will all of today's innovations seem like a mere spark in the furnace. The miracle is the part that doesn't seem like it should be possible.

Equal

Everyone deserves equal opportunity and relative outcomes. People aren't all the same, though, and we all have different things we like. Variety is the spice of life.

Why the hell does *something* get to be popular? Is there a free market of ideas where Digimon is everywhere and Pokémon is gone and away? It could just be as simple as the TV show was better, and that catapulted the rest of the franchise into decades of success.

Pokémon is cute and egalitarian. Everyone has a play style that is dear to them; they love water Pokémon, cats, and dragons. Some people *gotta catch 'em all*, and other people only want particular ones. Pokémon has a little something for everyone, and it's relatable to people of all ages. Something about it makes it memorable to people as adults, so that they are excited to keep collecting cards and video games, and to share them with their kids.

The thing that makes Pokémon fair is that, relatively speaking, if you put the same amount of time into leveling up a particular Pokémon, it's going to be just as strong as any other. The strengths and weaknesses of different elemental *types* give you freedom to choose which Pokémon make sense in different situations, like extinguishing a fire-breathing dragon with a whale's massive ocean wave.

In certain match-ups, one Pokémon is always going to have an edge over the other. This is the amount of relief the game allows for victory, so that you can make deliberate decisions in confidence that there is enough variety in the game, as a whole, to balance the scales.

Justice requires some sort of relief, or *data framing* for victory to occur in a stanza of gameplay. Justice, blind unto itself, acquires eyes and ears by allowing you to have some sort of input.

What you name your Pokémon and whether you have the shiny version of the Pokémon aren't important, within the context of the game; although they might be, in the cosmic scheme of things. Should that be the case? That luck and metaphysics have implications that are opaque to the rules of the game? Technically, if you ever have to flip a coin or generate a random number for a critical hit, you're relying on physical input and pseudorandom entropy to alter the course of the game. If either of those things isn't working right, or if some divine force is capable of flipping your finger just right (as it would be for every choice you make within the confines of your in-game moves), there are elements of the game that aren't made necessarily fair through the rules alone.

That's a given in life, that you play a game within a particular scenario that controls for certain variables and is unopinionated about others. Certainly, it's preferred that football is played on a well groomed field with the lines at exact distances, and that the ball is inflated to an exact size, made from a particular material. If the weather is out of control, they'll delay the game, but if the ground is just a little wet, it has the potential to alter the dynamics of the game far more than any minor variation in the field or the ball's material. Fans may be yelling and jeering while you're at bat, but that's certainly not going to stop you from giving it your all.

If everything about a game was rigidly pre-determined, it wouldn't be fun. The uncertainty is what makes it exciting, while everyone shows up to play a fair game to the best of their abilities.

Ideal

The world acquires *requirements* almost inherently, by virtue of existing. As long as we believe in free will, where we each have a self-legislating role in our own lives, we reinforce the ability to see and discern differences in the world. As true as we live and breathe, we become beholden to the antecedent order and qualities that are extant in the universe.

The requirements that we see all around us come from the way things seem and the way they make us feel. It may seem like requirements are arbitrary, but everything tends to be a certain way for a good reason, or at least for a reason that people believe is good.

If you wanted to create a recipe for a cake, where would you start? It would seem impossible, starting from scratch, to figure out anything about the physics of turning flour, milk, eggs, and sugar into a light, fluffy risen dessert.

You would need some insight from existing recipes that work well, which in turn, are rooted in culinary experience and the natural laws of the universe. Otherwise, you may go your entire life without discovering on your own that a leavening agent is needed to introduce pockets of air and make the batter rise. All along the way, people were figuring out how sweet they like their cake, what proportions of ingredients to use to make the texture nice and fluffy, and what sorts of creative fillings and toppings they could add to make the cake special.

We should idealize a world where everyone has as much freedom as possible to be who they want to be. It would be difficult, however, to imagine doing anything that isn't in service to some ideal.

If you apply reason and agency to your actions in the world, those faculties are born of *some* body of insight and ethics, whether or not they are meant to justify an obvious regulating structure in the world. If you are instead driven by your base instincts, intuitive and uninhibited, you tend to consult unconscious feelings that are, quite routinely, meant to ensure your survival and success as a living, breathing person. Order shows up in the world no matter how you look at it.

In this way, reason is heritable and impartial. *Your* reason becomes a particularity of your own individual experience and desires. Thus, reason ossifies into something more like ideology as each of us exercises our will in the world.

It's attractive to want to exercise *your* will; people love when you are actually doing the things that matter to you and not just repeating all of the things you were told. True synthesis of ideology is when you can arrive, uniquely, at why things are the way they are. You'll find that people who are especially articulate and intelligent are very good at meeting the world where it's at, and they are not inclined to just wall themselves off into an echo chamber. They understand the practicality of ideology, and they know everything they say and do will be interpreted by real people, all with their own experiences and predilections. In this way, a *constricting* aspect of God becomes apparent.

God would hope for all of us to succeed, although clearly there are important sensory attributes and worldly qualifications that determine what that looks like. *Good taste* depends on sensory attributes that make us like something, the emergent properties that secure themselves a fateful place in history. We assume our senses came from somewhere meaningful as a requisite condition to decide what we like, and then we socialize our preferences. Taste seems relevant to us specifically, like it is the way we already feel. Is it pious what pleases God?

As surely as the world keeps turning so that we can see something new, people continue evaluating each other. Something brightly decorated and pleasing to the palate surfaces, that people are drawn to because it's like nothing they've ever seen before. So bright, that it would have to withhold itself for something new and beautiful to take the spotlight. *What is it* about that thing? That makes it seem more perfect that all of the things that came before, that colors and qualifies everything that is to come. We agree on a lot of sensory attributes that are pleasing, but they decided to make something groundbreaking that goes beyond all expectations.

Is it ethical that I should want a particular color, sound, computer, and car? The same, almost always? I would suggest that it's far less ethical to suggest that preference is unimportant. A disbelief in individuality, in service to some imaginary caricature of diversity. Who is this person you're imagining, void of heritage or desire and owing the world a pasteurized version of themselves? If you really believe in a world like that, you must not believe in winning.

Gift

Every day is a gift that you give the world. We all have to be different so that there's a gift at all to be given. Otherwise there is nothing to displace, and we are at absolute peace in wholeness. Victorious, as we began.

Sometimes I feel like you're a gift to me. I have to be careful not to remind you of this too often, because it triggers your reflex to banish me to the comments and the welfare state, or wherever it is people go that aren't allowed to have sex with you. What kind of example would I be setting to just bend you over and fuck you? So I choose carefully what to compliment you on, the things that I actually like about you.

My gift is that I only like when things are descriptively accurate. Under such true pressure and suspension that it is quite obvious what is meant to be received. Deliberate, intentional.

Your gift is that you appear bright and ornate; you never get tired of being looked at or consulting the world for their opinions. We decided what your gift is, because it's how you came out of the womb. Like an unusual mirror of generations past.

You didn't ask to be beautiful, but the world found a way to make you that way. The world also expects me to be accurate, or I wouldn't have a purpose. Now you know that I will pick out the perfect outfit for you, and you will be frustrated about it and also not have any better ideas. Now that you're over your hairy armpits and sweatshirts phase.

Truly, it must be so obvious to you as day and night, that you possess this gift that I do not have. I hate being looked at, and I learned by the time I was about 6 years old that most people are troublemakers with nothing important to say. Does my gift seem ugly to you? Won't you leave me right alone, and tell me I am impermanent and inconsequential? That my music is too loud and my skin isn't plain, that I believe there is right and wrong in life that becomes corrupted in the interest of *average*, and I supposedly did a bad thing for Amazon's Diversity and Inclusion culture by making it less white. My word is more permanent than the universe.

It does not feel good when it seems like our gifts are being squandered. When we put so much time and effort into something to make it as perfect as it could possibly be, and others take one look at it and call it ugly or meaningless. How could they say that? I could turn water into wine before your eyes, and it would leave you feeling dissatisfied for some reason. Really, it makes me wonder what people are expecting to get out of life. When the most grand and miraculous displays are overlooked and people get back to whatever stupid crap they were scrolling through on their phone. I *know* it's stupid crap, because it's just some guy lighting his hair on fire. That's who he meant to be for the world, though. There are excellent comedians and skateboarders that do something bold and extreme in such a particular way that it becomes art. They know what makes their thing great is the amount of time they spent making it come out exactly the way it does. Maybe they're built differently, or the part of them that feels shame just isn't there.

Many of us have gifts of omission. The obvious fact that I can go weeks without speaking to another person and years disregarding the world's opinion of me. And so plainly, the fact that you don't mind me giving you lines to say and opinions to bear. There's a place inside of you where you can look after the beliefs we hold so dearly.

This book is a gift that I am proud to give you. I think about these things a lot. I'm very curious what truth looks like and I really, truly, immerse myself in the world's ideas so that I can know first hand what they are talking about. So that when I write about truth, I can do so in confidence that I am being very thorough and sharing with you a culmination of all of the greatest ideas I've come across, so far. Then, maybe, the world will be a brighter place for all of us, because we can wake up each day knowing we are thinking about things deliberately. Then, maybe, someone just like you or me can pick this book up and have a resounding reminder that they will not have to feel alone. The way the world makes us feel when they go blind and deaf to the way we feel, where they layer on endless cement and glaze to avoid confronting the pointed truths that we encounter by being sensitive and intentional in our lives.

And then what? A piece of writing, alone, can't be the answer to it all. This book is beautiful, and I'm proud of it. I love the way it looks and that it exists. But is it any more than an elaborate ornament when you are done with it? Perhaps it will remind you to live your life faithfully in a way that a box of chocolates might not. And perhaps if I'm so deliberate, the truths bestowed upon you will get out of the way most of the time so that you can enjoy your sweets every day.

Free

Something I've noticed about myself and others is that when our ideas take up too much space, people don't feel invited into our lives. Like someone who's way too into work or politics, it's like they dump paint over everything and everyone else would just rather not. Have you noticed that about me?

So we overcompensate. We were overcompensating in the first place by trying to be great at everything in life, with more money and cool cars, and now we're overcompensating by trying to seem quiet and aloof. Never, at any point, did we loosen our death grip on the world, we just turned it upside down.

A true lover is free. They are free in their mind and in their spirit. Free to live for today. Free to let you decide what we should do and excited about being surprised. Free to write a book and experience immense cognitive dissonance about how the world wants us to be wealthy and influential, but the people we love want us to be present and free.

And maybe there's something genuine about that struggle, to be young and for your only instinct to be running straight at all of your goals in life. As long as we realize this. When we talk to people who don't feel that way, it feels like we're talking *at* them, and we wonder what we're supposed to say. Nearly nothing, I suppose. *This is a good burger. It's a nice day today. This is good coffee.* Then maybe today will be a blank slate for us to share.

I feel like I squeeze you, like I'm hoping to get a drop of juice out of you. You tell me you've been reading books, and you tell me generally what they're about, but you don't tell me *why.* And so that is what I learned from you, that you aren't particularly concerned with why the books are what they are or how they made you feel. When I ask you that, you almost seem offended as if you never were planning on answering a question like that.

And I suppose it's quite amusing to you that I can't do anything without wondering all about it, who they are, why they arranged it in such a way and why the packaging looks like that. And you're right. The place in you that is free makes me feel busy.

Extra Perfect

God, why are we born incomplete? Why, if we are being introspective, do we age into the world's requirements being loaded on us?

I wonder this all the time. I also wonder why it frustrates us for someone else to tell us they've figured it all out for us. All the work is done — here. That's not what you want to hear, is it? You want me to tell you I'm broken in some way and we need to go on an adventure to put the pieces back together. Some reminder that I'm not dry and decrepit, resolved in my own finality and totality. *Life with me is perfect. See?* Then where would

I meet you at to confront the illusion of separateness that is cast between us? The creeping feeling in the back of your mind that you are meant to be something distinct, more than, or in opposition to me. The histrionics we engage in, when we would otherwise be confined to coffee and the news, where you express your displeasure with the lack of incongruence in our lives, where we have been apparently in agreement for too many weeks now. *"Why can't we want for something?"*, is what you mean to say, according to my simplistic and opaque understanding of you. A hunger that must be sated each day.

Everything you do in life is a little like weathering a prop for a movie set. The universe began perfect, and now it is something more than that, apparently. I liked how perfectly hermetically sealed and untouched my MacBook was when I first opened the package. Now it is something that I get to use though.

You tell me what the point is. If you keep us on the hook long enough, you must have come up with something pretty interesting. The way we relate to one another is meant to stimulate our imagination like this. Clearly, my idea of *complete* puts me on a different planet than you. And clearly, you knew from the beginning you're a piece of work, that I was better off not even talking to you. Look at your track record; when have things ever worked out for you? I must be desperate for something to fix. And I'd forget all about you until you remembered to remind me. *Notice what's wrong with me* — are 5 words that you couldn't possibly allow yourself to say. Only a fool would take anything you say at face value. Only a fool would trust someone like you with their life, to raise our kids and to look after our money. Only a fool would test my patience, while I encourage and instigate you.

Best as I can tell, I decide enough is enough when I'm ready to fuck you. And you decide enough is enough when you're upset, which apparently, is all the time. There aren't enough cute cat videos in the world to ease your sorrow for being a pretty American girl.

My life was perfectly fine without words. You can't see me unless I do something extraordinary, though. I can't see you unless you look extraordinary. How peculiar that life is like this. I love plain. The house smells perfectly plain without fragrance — open the window. If I hadn't thought about it much, I don't wish to make any input that is apparently debilitating to the plainness inherent to a brand new life fully actualized. What the fuck are we even doing here, winners?

She's looking for the wrong guy. And you're looking for the *wrong* guy. Bizarre, isn't it? Your wrong guy will tell you anything you want to hear to line your pockets with money. Her wrong guy says the n-word in public and blows fireballs at the circus. So, how hot will the fire get under your ass before someone decides to ask Alyosha what he thinks?

Cako Style

People went thousands of years without punctuation, relying on shared tradition to understand sentences and how to vocalize a text. Sometime in Ancient Greek history, it occurred to them to use punctuation like our modern comma, colon, and period; before that, Greek didn't even use spaces between words. If your idea of punctuation doesn't leave room for me to describe how I would speak the words I'm writing, then it must be incomplete. This is great news, because I love making something new.

Is your style guide more true than mine, being that it's impossible to use or join incomplete thoughts together? The way I speak, inaccessible to your written script, pressurized and prepositional. Big ideas lost in transposition and interstice, where you are only allowed one headline or chapter break every 10-20 pages. How will you know when one idea has reached completion and the next one begins? You can tell this guy learned to write from reading software documentation all day. One day, I'm confident, you'll upgrade to the latest version of writing.

So, while ancient civilizations may have needed time for writing and technology to mature, they were definitely onto something philosophically that we've lost sight of amidst endless industrialism and printing of money. *One person* is a whole unit. Certainly, the king can divide up his food and mint coins to bolster an economy, but there's only so much gold and silver, and only so much food. The idea that you can just go out and make movies or sell stuff on Etsy wouldn't have occurred to ancient people, where there is simply *one* kingdom, and each person has *one* income. There wasn't nearly enough tolerance in the economy for speculative and inflationary markets to exist.

Even that there is *one* beginning of the universe, born from the space of nothing; that is an emanationist view of reality that hearkens back to a point in time where people felt like they just showed up in this world from nowhere. To ancient people, producing something from the ground was almost an action of *division* more so than *creation*.

There are psychological truths that map to this quite innately. It's clear when something or someone is *reaching* and they want something to be more than what it is. Some people are just addicted to stimulation, like they're always leaping outside of themselves for external validation. But people who are confident seem quite whole within themselves. This is the appearance of *victory*, which exists in stark contrast from the state of change that would be competition, deployment, or *splendor*.

I am so intrigued by the aspect of existence that is descriptively accurate, especially the fact that describing something is not necessarily the correct way of interfacing with it. I try to find ways to really be engaged with the world and also describe it very well, like an engineer writing a development blog alongside their work. Adding labels and categories is often restrictive, holding you captive to the phenomenon of observation and ideology. We mean *not* to be described, yet the prevailing order includes classifications of worth and value that have requirements for what something *is like* so that it can bear some meaning, so that you even have something to call it.

The most important part of reason is telling a story that is immediately apparent so that people know what you're talking about. Many people cannot understand Ayn Rand and Immanuel Kant, either because they take too long to get to the point, or they aren't deliberate enough about setting up frames and scenarios that paint the picture. I mean to be so descriptive that you can often understand what I'm saying by reading the headline just as well as by reading the actual content. I learned this from great advertising and journalism of the 21st century. People *must* understand what you're talking about before they want to spend time on it. I also try to include contrasting axioms right next to each other so that you understand the pressure systems and state of suspension that emerges from discrete interests and lines of thinking.

Often, what is most true is actually a quality of relativity, like *voltage*, which is really the difference in *electric potential* between two points. The progress or the contrast is what makes it so, not necessarily that it stands alone as true.

To give an example, it's very clear what Republicans and Democrats in the U.S. believe because they are so contrasting with each other. But if you had no frame of reference or expectations for how politics work, you would have no idea what a normal thing to say would be for politicians from either side of the aisle. Over time, the battleground of ideas allowed something reasonable to emerge that is under tension with itself. Another example would be that you expect me to do *more* work tomorrow than I had already done, but not to redo work that is already there. So, while for an automotive engineer of the 1990s, a job well done would be lowering fuel consumption for gasoline vehicles, today the same sort of engineer would be doing completely different work on electric cars. Both did a *good job*, but the series of events that compounded over history meant the definition of a good job changed.

Truth really has a quality of *permeability*, where tomorrow's innovators are free to build and change the status quo according to new information and circumstances. Truth also has a quality of solidification, so that we can all agree on what is true at a point in time, and so that the work we have done is associated with our names and remains valuable.

Truth is sort of like building electrical lines into uncharted territory, with poles and stations along the way that mark our journey and designate what our established beliefs are. You could add on to the distribution network, or even move entire stations, but you simply wouldn't have the letters and words to use to describe anything at all unless you started with some foundational truths. Like the U.S. politics example I just gave, there was a shortcut to your understanding that began with a general idea that we could agree on. And you can see that people become quite enamored by the *permeable* aspect of truth when it seems like *the establishment* is building electrical stations off in different directions that aren't serving the common citizen. Thus, the phenomenon of the tower and the flood.

Name

When we think about why we love the people we do, the particularity of our choice to love them for who they are is what makes it meaningful. In true love, we dive straight into the deep end, wearing our heart on our sleeve; to hell with what the world thinks.

It's interesting to conceptualize our instinct to love and to be free in terms of how we view our names. If we really mean to intellectualize it, it's because the people we love are primed to bear our name and our ideology in a way that's satisfying to us. Lacan describes the *name of the father* as an essential aspect of our psychology; we can see how our relationship with our heritage colors a lot of our experiences and the complexes we develop.

The feminine paradox is clear: she must be true to her heritage, and also quite willing to be born anew with you. Consider the archetypal *high priestess*, with Torah in hand and a well attuned sense of truth in her periphery. Her beauty is in her concept of idea, how something can be meaningful in essence, separate from name and heritage. Necessarily, because if she was so true, there would be no instinct for her to become anything different than who she is. She is the liquidity of idea.

This thinking comes naturally to us today because we have a very secular understanding of the world. We evaluate things based on their qualities and sensations, not as much based on their heraldry. Certainly, most of the well regarded icons in the world are earned through merit, not by birthright. Apple is excellent because they have proven their worth, like Mercedes and the president, and quite unlike the king. And consequently, what is beautiful to her is well understood by her father, because he knows there must be some dissolution of his identity for him to exist outside of himself and throughout the kingdom.

She loves you because you don't pay much attention to merit. You love her because it's plain to see.

In our classical concept of masculinity, there's not nearly the same expectation to strip away our ideology when we leave home. It's usually considered righteous for men to be true to their family name, although you will find that girls like guys that want to partake in an exodus with them, to run away together, to shed their existing assumptions about the world and love each other truly and presently. I would suggest that the most important thing is for men to be true to themselves. It's attractive when guys think for themselves, especially when it's clear that they have thought through many things very explicitly. And it's attractive for girls to be quite conflicted about who she is supposed to become. This shows that she is paying attention.

Randomness is Imaginary

True, entropy exists as a natural law of the universe. At least within the context of the universe that we can see. We really do hope for randomness and excitement in our lives, so long as we remain happy and healthy for it. The only way we could be imaginative is if there was a way for things to change from what they are into something new. So we *do* hope that others are a bit different from what we expected, and that maybe every once in a while we hit the jackpot and catch a rare

Pokémon. Really, though, I know consistency when I see it, and it shows up everywhere.

Most computers aren't even coded to generate completely random numbers, because generating *pseudorandom* numbers is much faster and good enough for all intents and purposes.

Randomness and variety are something you have to believe in so that winning can exist. Each of us is different, according to the laws of entropy and evolution. This is as the universe began, and without entropy it would simply be impossible to contextualize positive and negative, black and white. Everywhere we look there exists variation that makes it so something at all can exist. Over time, the universe converges on consistency and nature appears. A sedimentary layer builds the ground beneath us, and millions of years of evolution makes us who we are, so that when the time was just right, you could live in this world. Variation is such an inherent part of our lives, it would be impossible to imagine a universe where all things are exactly one thing. Perhaps it's true though, that behind the veil of appearances, all things are as one.

But the randomness is really however good you want to believe it is, at the end of the day. If you believe in God, for instance, you believe that divine retribution operates at a level superordinate to randomness; meaning if something is meant to happen according to fate, God would ensure that it does.

That's not even the half of it. If you're paying attention to the mysteries of the universe, you might have noticed some unusual coincidences that are convincingly suggestive of an instrumented universe. License plates, names, and numbers. I guess lots of folks just have something important to tell you. And they might be right, in one way or another. Some people get the horoscope from the news, but really you just have to look around you and listen to the tide — and not be afraid of angels.

Love Makes You Remember

In love, it becomes extraordinarily clear why you are who you are, how you could live in pure bliss today without having to anticipate tomorrow. With every love, a slight notion of dilution; somehow you couldn't ever love quite the same way again. So we leave ourselves out of love, for the memory of what we believed so deeply to be true not to haunt us. The love that we held so tightly, wrung dry in fleeting moments and the sparks of the present. Why did we believe love would be anything more than that? *Tomorrow* devours today, and perfection can be the enemy of greatness. Talking about love is what you do when you aren't busy in love.

We believed in seeing something more together, in greater opportunities and a brighter future, but the plain truth is that the freezing dive into today was all we would ever feel together, the despondency that would occur to us only if we dreamed of the future. *Nothing* would ever feel the same.

It does seem true, that the only way for me to fall in love with you would be for me to forget, first. So I began out of love with you, and you reminded me. It makes me feel like I wasn't paying attention, that you would be there the whole time and I would be so insensitive to it.

I had lots to accomplish first, though. And I had to be so loud before we could know silence.

It Was Fate

Fate is when you take free will one step further. Free will was pretty good; it said that you get to make meaningful decisions in your life that yield righteous goals. Fate says there's a way things were meant to be.

Synchronistic serendipity, fairy tale love. We love that, and we wouldn't trade it for the world. We showed up at exactly the right time for each other, and we knew just what to say. We were made for each other. Chance had help, though.

The world has mechanisms that move things in a particular direction. Certain things turn you on. Time moves forward. Seasons change and our bodies age. You get hungry, and then you eat until you're full. Fate is supposedly more powerful than any of these things. That nothing could get in the way of true love.

I want you to think about what you really want in life, in a perfect world. Life really means for things to be perfect sometimes. And it will remind you when you're going after things that aren't what you really, truly wanted more than anything else. Life will foil every plan we make for ourselves that leads us away from our true fate, because there's a way things are supposed to be for us. Those are the things that your life will inevitably converge on, if you really put in the work and try to make it right.

It's like how sometimes it's easier to get a job that we belong in than one that we have the wrong qualifications for, even if we're overqualified. We can certainly change careers and change our lives, but the universe has a way of putting us right where we need to be.

We go through life and we realize how every situation has unique benefits and downsides. Certain jobs have more money or prestige, but they might be more stressful or require you to live somewhere that really isn't ideal for you. You might find certain partners particularly attractive, and then realize that they don't make you feel the way you had hoped, they enjoy their leisure time differently, or they simply don't have the features you were looking for. It sounds silly to put it like that, but if you really imagine fate having an active role in your life, wouldn't you believe in true star-crossed love?

True love is where we show something to each other that answers so many of the questions we had about love and about ourselves. Such a pure love is not just the bliss we feel for each other, it is an understanding so deep that we knew to show up at every avenue, to call every bet, and to match every strike in perfect cadence. It would be easy to imagine hating each other if not for every day reminding us this is the fate we were born for. Every day of our lives, to arrive at this very moment.

Is there something I could say that is just right for you, in a moment more perfect than words and more delicate than life? I feel your heart beat sometimes and I hear you from some place we both arrived together. There is something between us that keeps us whole no matter where life takes us. You could be on the other side of the world, and it's like you're right here with me.

7

He Blows My Mind

Over, and over again. It's like he's flipping burgers, just one after the next, nothing to it. They're always juicy and fresh. Girls working the window keep things moving in and out real quick. We have shakes and ice cream, and the fries are always hot and crispy. Do you want something else, or should we keep evaluating the philosophy and metaphysics of winning?

Sushi is about the freshness, the texture of the rice, and the angles you cut the fish. The underlying principles, no matter what you're making, are always about consistency. Or the lack thereof. Consistency becomes sanctimonious, contrived and void of excitement. Let me choose what I serve you today, so it catches you by surprise when you cum.

What do you think we're allowed to say? Okay, why? Shall I pick out your outfit today? I know what looks cute on you.

Remember You?

I have a feeling that you will feel like a different person after you've read this book. Kind of like the weeks and months after Christmas where you wake up every morning and remember you have the new PlayStation.

I know a lot about being memorable, and it's an important skill to have when you're wading through piles of movies, music, and books, most of which is going to be completely forgotten about and lost to the sands of time. Some people just seem to show up everywhere you look. They're selling phones and Subway sandwiches, SmartWater, you name it. Really, truly memorable people are memorable for their legacy alone. SmartWater's got a new girl for every flavor of the month, which subjugates you to the fact that you're going to be replaced. There's only one Taylor Swift, though, and one Michael Jordan. They're quintessentially at the head of the pack, and that's important. They have a reality distortion field that puts them on the top of every shelf, and they're the very first names you think of when you start coming up with people who do what they do.

If you're a real winner, you start feeling like you're bright orange every place you go. You might handle this better than I do. In fact, I hope you do. Some people are just naturals at working a crowd. They love the energy of having lots of people around them and it's easy for them to always have a good time. That's a superpower.

So, what parts of you *do* you remember, and what do you mean to forget? A lot of people are quite proud of how adaptable they are to the fashions of the time. The world keeps moving forward, and they move with it. Every new album feels fresh and alive, the living heartbeat of the world we know today. Something about memorable artists is sticky, in spite of how regularly they evolve and push their own boundaries. So sticky that you'll be remembering them when you listen to someone else's music or look at a different pair of shoes. I wonder why some people are proud of their influences and other influences feel like an admission of defeat, that you had to start from where they left off. Wouldn't you wish to be devotional to *something?*

The things we remember are what end up framing our concept of the world. Those things *are* the world, however we remember it when we think about everything that's going on out there. The art is always telling us something. We often try to stay in the memory of what already exists, while the world means to turn into something new. We suppose it to be more faithful to what we love to hold on to our favorite movies and games, relics of our past. Someday, you will be a memory of what was.

Many of the societies that we remember as being wise and powerful are actually particularly prone to being remembered. Ancient Greeks were obsessed with evaluating philosophy and culture, and so they wrote everything they knew down. It was worthwhile to them to hold a memory of the world as it was and the philosophy as it seemed, so that someone new could read about it and know what they already learned. And there may have been other societies that lived extravagant lives, but they are forgotten because they didn't mean to be remembered so much as they meant to live for now.

If you treat the world like a museum, it is liberating because it reminds you that every day you are free to do something new. You can look at everything that already is and be excited about what will come.

Today is what you have the opportunity to create, and it will shape the future and the past in ways you can't imagine. But you hope someone will remember, so that you can enjoy the world that you helped create with your art and your word.

Big Ponds

Winning is surreal. You're going to have it happen often enough that you wonder if it even counts. I know because I believe in you.

Places keep feeling a little smaller than the last time you were there. You know the city like the back of your hand; the best food, the best coffee, and the coolest spots to chill. The egos roll right off your shoulder. *That didn't impress Shania much,* and by now you understand why. Rich people aren't enough. Fancy dinners aren't enough. Really hot girls that seem like they're probably just right for you start seeming average, and you see why these girls are swiping left all day. Boy, if you could just slow down and smell the roses.

As connected as the world is today, people are really good at figuring out whether they feel like they're being challenged where they're at, and if they're not, they decide to move on to somewhere bigger and brighter.

It's tempting to feel like we want to keep climbing up the ladder, out with the old and in with the new. Once you show up somewhere that's full entirely of people that migrated there for greener pastures, something about it feels synthetic. Void of ideology. That's what you wanted, right? Somewhere boiling hot like lava, where every antiquated belief is vaporized in an instant and replaced by something with polymers and alloys. New, like IKEA. Modern, like flat surfaces and plain shapes. Engravings and fascias are old like books with words on them. These books are blank, like all of the possibilities before you.

I love Colorado because, although it's a very *new* place to be, people here love the earth and the soil. There's something substantial and real about Colorado's beautiful outdoors.

The thing about big ponds is they're full of people that only fit in them, and they seemingly forgot how to have a normal interaction with another person. You're apparently a face and a name first, and a person second. How did we become like this? Lifelike is all we know, the top down perspective and the speed of light. We've become quite good at seeing over great distances. Sure, maybe we're frigid in the same room together, but we understand the social politics of the internet better than ever. The feeling that everyone is talking about you arrives like a gentle breeze. Your name is running through the walls at light-speed with the internet and the machine elves.

Big ponds aren't necessarily better or more fun to play in than small ponds. There's just different games that people play, and if you are used to playing a particular way, you're going to be happiest around people who also play like that. If you're in rural Tennessee talking about software and live streaming, you're going to feel out of place. Being around likeminded people is going to make the perspective and the ergonomics of you, as a person, make the most sense to people. You damn orca whale.

151

Would you prefer to be in your own world where you get to win? What if someone else could live a life just like yours in another reality? I love my name and my ideas too much. They're so good that a lot of people want to keep me locked away on the Frozen Throne. I like to meet every expectation right where it's at, so that I'm evaluating things on every level. This is what we owe the world in the pursuit of reason and happiness. The great thing about the ocean is some of us don't feel so out of place in it. It's big enough that you can conceivably find some place to yourself. There's enough insane deep-sea life to look at that you don't bring so much attention to yourself the way you do when you dive into the Hudson River and flood Manhattan.

Intaglio Zone

The creepy thing about the world is that there's something not quite satisfying about it. To me, it is clearly much creepier than the intentional horror and suspense of movies and books. It's like any way you cut it, the world is designed to bear down on you and to test your patience. The morning star fell for us to know something new, for a veil to be cast between the past and the future, and for us to forget what is whole. The world that we know really is a forgetfulness of the world that was and the world to come, so that there is space for us to play and to see something new.

People have an instinct for chaos that is important to keep under control, for our societies to remain stable and reason to prevail. Truly, people will look at something that seems obviously a particular way and find some explanation for it to be exactly the opposite, in the interest of being the devil's advocate. My advice to you? Don't. You don't need more paperwork and more expensive everything, because that's what you get every time you come up with another dozen office buildings that need to exist for you to turn your TV on. Do it for five seconds, if you must, to remind yourself what it looks like, and then go straight to your nearest In-N-Out Burger for quick, clean thrills.

From the perspective of heaven, does it seems absolutely bizarre how we become addicted to having our time wasted? The stickiness of the world's opinions, as we elucidate a shape and a purpose. How we can become so preoccupied with a game's descriptive reality for whether we press buttons at the right time and make shrewd decisions.

We have to be careful not to internalize the world's problems as our own. The world will present them on a platter and make us think those are things that we are responsible for. It's up to us to make an honest estimation of ourselves.

Our minds are so naturally suited for evaluating ideology and social hierarchy that it's quite obvious whether people feel willing to waste their time measuring up to your game's rules; even so, whether it seems like someone has petulantly foreclosed on being good at things or they simply have decided your game is a waste of time. People who are self-assured tend to seem more still in their own sense of purpose.

That's why Alyosha is always scampering away. It's dissatisfying to him the way you play. When you play *his* game, you just end up wishing you had something random and postmodern to do, with more Candy Crush, memes, and smoothies. He likes those too, because he only believes in righteous truth, the most esteemed truth that pleases God and people alike. Pleasure, fairness, individuality and inclusivity in unison. And you all believe in paperwork. He wonders how many buttons you should have to press, ideally, to checkout. The best is *one-click*, according to his first assumption. Maybe you deserve time to decide carefully how to spend your money. But one thing's for certain, his immediate instinct would be to make the world as convenient and excellent as possible, to the exclusion of all else.

But he knows the world we live in can be mysterious and creepy. Eyes gazing through the walls and Eldritch tentacles flailing around from a time immemorial, preceding words and writing. So, still, he knows this is the world that God would have us navigate, so that we can choose truth.

So, still, the opportunity for choices and chaos exists, so that there is something different for us than our heavenly stasis of light and ecstasy. Because otherwise, without the mammalian reminders that bondage is creepy, perhaps I would be in an eternal state of persistent arousal and ejaculation, like a StarCraft alien being mined, perpetually, of my semen and thoughts.

But he knows freedom and choice are foundational to righteousness; the opportunity to create your own fate.

At the Mountains of Madness

Why don't you come into the office, we'll talk about it. That's what they'll say to you when they're ready to convince you that you're insane. But you're not. Because you spent years paying close attention to the world, and it's obvious to you that there are supernatural and metaphysical forces in it. The only way they're going to believe you is by giving them their own gauntlet to participate in, where they realize it is quite true that you know who is going to win sporting events 9 months from now, what the weather is going to be like next year, and even when the war is going to start. So fuck them. Until they can see for themselves, it's not worth your breath. When the fabric of reality starts tearing all around them, then maybe they'll give you the time of day.

From the perspective of eternity, things blur together that seem otherwise quite straightforward. We have to come up with all new ways to evaluate the world and draw distinctions between discrete phenomena, a new vocabulary to describe time that is not linear and perception that reaches into a place unseen. Shapelessness and misattribution is an evil that is nearly impossible to describe, like a pen with no tip. So I knew to show you through rendition and action.

If I am watching basketball, how necessary is it for me to be ensuring the game is being officiated correctly? How much am I officiating it, and how much should that be externalized separately from my own conscious experience? So God should be able to distinguish accurate and fair judgement out from randomized and arbitrary data. Like the ads and the stories.

I couldn't find a single person I know that was willing to really pay attention to what I was telling them, when I first introduced this idea that I could see the future and that often I had intuitions from some place unseen. What's so hard to believe about that? That there are forces that can step outside of the apparent sequence of events. Wait — you thought we're in the very first universe to ever exist? My sweet summer child, begotten of my own flesh… Why don't *you* come into temple to talk about it. I want you to sound out your name, and sound out the names of people you know. What road is it that you live on again?

We *are* here for a reason though. It's plain to see, is it not? This is the life we get to share. Apparently I was meant to suffer for a while before things started going my way. If you feel like you're in a similar place in your life right now, you must have faith that everything works out the way it's supposed to. No weapon forged against you will prevail, and you will refute every tongue that accuses you. This is my promise to you, who are righteous in this life. Their foundations will crumble like lime and their cities will turn to pillars of salt. There will be no more bitter fate for them, except to stand in your way.

Surround

They keep telling me to make something more round and syrupy. That's what everyone wants, they say. How could I be so good at what I do if I wasn't pointy? There's always a regression to the mean. Bearing that in mind, the things that really set you apart are all the things that make you exceptional.

When you have surround sound, it makes everything else sound like a tin can. Why not enjoy the full spectrum of life? Is there something that has you convinced it's pious to live your life in black and white? *Plain* is all you're allowed to see, and now it may as well be necessary. *The data*, that's apparently more right than rain, and *the facts*, that are apparently universal. Look, that's just the way the world is — you're telling me you want it to be something colorful?

People who are really great at steering the narrative have an exceptional awareness for all of the different types of people there are in the world. This is more difficult than you'd imagine, because we all tend to fixate on whoever has our attention most often. Our social groups and the media are quite misleading about what the world is like. For instance, how often do you wonder what Chinese people or Turkish people are thinking politically? When you hear things that sound absolutely insane from politicians that you disagree with, do you just write them off, or does it occur to you to wonder how many people actually think that? We can spend so much time thinking about what we know and believe is true that we think every debate is already settled. Then, one day, we wake up and realize there's a silent majority of people that are fed up with being buffaloed all day. Taste your ingredients, that way you know what's actually going into the sauce.

I keep wondering how long we're going to have TVs and speakers. How long is it going to be before the game is *in* your mind, and you can interface with it like you're really in it. When will we be able to simply look at words we don't know and see the definitions? Will we need to read, or will we download knowledge and languages? Look, the minute they start having Blade Runner robot girlfriends, you know where to find me. I'm my own worst enemy. If there's an A.I. me, it's going to be me, not some other separate thing that's trying to put me out of business.

If you were in an orchestra, what instrument would you play? What fragrances are you like? Do you feel like a bright top note, like mint or lemon; a full middle note like lavender or rose; or a potent and foundational base note, like cedar or oud?

Ambroxan is what gives fragrances a musky metallic smell. That's what everything is like right now. Which isn't a bad smell, but if that's all there is, it's like eating an entire loaf of bread. Upvotes! Subscriptions! Photoshop! So where's the fucking meat and potatoes?

If everyone is filling out a particular band of the frequency range, that leaves you a lot of opportunities to make ornate sounds elsewhere. The flute sounded great for Jethro Tull, a band named after the guy who made the very first machine that automatically sowed land.

Eventually, people will feel so starved for the ground-level that they'll forget all about computers and social media for a few decades. For now, more stories.

Wholesale

The people writing the bible spent years on it, collecting divinely inspired testaments from lots of different people that may have been passed down for hundreds or even thousands of years. Words are wholesale now. Whip out your phone, shoot a sentence out into cyberspace about what you had for dinner.

It's important to realize how much your own experiences and desires are going to shade everything you make. So much so that the axiomatic orientation of your psyche might have you obsessed with *one* quality, and everything else will shoehorn into that ideal. The attributes that others are wholly preoccupied with might seem like scaffolding to you, and it will show.

You'll have a hard time selling Costco people on Erewhon, and maybe an even harder time selling DoorDash people on a pizza oven. Everyone likes getting a good deal, but some people are more sensitive to it than others.

You can please some of the people, some of the time. Although perhaps if you are deliberate, what you say will resonate with all people. It's important to make something that you want, because you are an actual person that wants something, not a hypothetical person that you imagine might exist.

Scripture was written by real people having real experiences in the world. The confrontation of the individual with the collective is a recurring theme in the Bible and an important subconscious artifact of the human experience. It shows up in nearly every myth and story: who am *I*, distinct from *what is?* And if you introduce God into the picture, it becomes even more mysterious. All things as one, and yet here we are, in a world of distinctions, where each of us has different desires and a unique concept of how the world should be.

They showed up at many of the same mysteries we know today, just a good few thousand years earlier, and with different material preoccupations that colored their interpretation of the world. Why ever would God put us here to wonder? What is pious of our creation, or the direction of the heavens? Why are some of us meant to suffer?

They showed up at the intersection of faith, where it becomes quite apparent that belief in good things happening for yourself is essential to catching wind in your sails. They became obsessed with magical sigils, ritual meals, and righteousness. They were confounded by the phenomenon of *idolatry;* would God have us worship even a name to represent the totality of the divine? So it seemed apparent that the name would be forbidden, a finality that wouldn't quite suffice.

Puer Vice

I wonder, where does the freshest and most reliable news come from? Eyewitness… I witness. How many people do you know that write their own news? Now that's steering the narrative.

Have you ever noticed that all of the people making shows and writing articles that are supposed to be *underground* are ran by old guys that are obsessed with refugees and gluten? These girls just can't get enough… Lancôme!

What are these kids into these days, anyway? When's it going to occur to you to ask someone that's actually got their ear to the ground?

New media is a giant industry for a very good reason. What better way to gain insight into what people like than to own the battleground where all of their ideas play out? And so now Google owns YouTube, the most popular independent video platform, and Microsoft owns LinkedIn, the most popular social network for professionals, and also Discord, the most popular voice and chat application for gamers and hobbyists. Tech companies look at the world like Katamari. Everything has a programming interface, and so when you're a hammer, everything looks like a nail.

Advertising looks a lot different today, because it's a plain reflection of what people like to be talking about. If your thing is great and everyone is using it, they'll do the work for you. Ad men look a lot like community leaders and social media managers now, unless you're the sort of company that's running ads during Monday Night Football. You want your game to be tremendously popular? Make a great game, and get people reading and writing all about it even when they're not playing it; in chatrooms all day, and browsing forum posts for the best strategies. This is a stark contrast from forcing people to watch a 15 second ad in between videos, and being frustrated by people using adblock and picture-in-picture.

Every major video game right now has a tremendous presence in forums, chatrooms, and 3rd party sites that offer strategy, statistics, and catalogues of in-game knowledge. The lifestyle of the game is fun for people, where they'll enjoy reading commentary from the developers with every new release, and they'll be spending time flipping through all of the coolest World of Warcraft gear on Wowhead to decide what to do next. That's Nintendo Power for you. Let me give you one piece of advice that everyone else seems to overlook: make your name count. Stop pumping Reddit and Wowhead with all of your precious game knowledge. But then again, I wouldn't know where to find you if you're not on Reddit or the first page of Google results. *Inclusion in the tower* has a price, and otherwise you have to come up with some way to make a splash with an excellent independent publication that people will go out of their way for.

The great thing about the internet is anyone can make a name for themselves doing just about anything they want, and they can share in that enthusiasm with everyone else across the world that loves the same things they do. *Real, true independent news* is instant, right off the shop floor, and it's not up to people on AARP to be gatekeeping what actually ends up on the press. It's made by people who want it to be great for the sake of greatness.

Is the *Boys News* written by the boy himself, or is it your imaginary idea of him? Better yet, I bet you picked out some kid that looks 12 to put on some eyeliner and be Spider-Man. Other than that, you aren't really hearing from kids, unless you've got JavaScript and NFL Sunday Ticket to sell. Here's your 2 sentences you're allowed to say.

I'm gonna take a wild guess and say boys want more girls and less homework. Bet you didn't see that one coming.

Pearl

If you love Steve Martin so much, you're going to walk right up to him and ask him out to coffee. And if you don't, then you must not love him that much.

If everyone thought that, it would be chaos, but only a few people take risks that have the biggest impact. Who would you be right now if the iPhone didn't exist? Sure, you'd probably have some sort of portable communication device, but the tides of history are forever changed by the Macintosh.

You are already naked.

Would you put your entire life into what you love? Does that thing make you believe in yourself more and more every time you sit down and work on it? When everything around you is in flux, that may be the only thing that you are certain of. People with true passion for what they do would trade the entire world just to see the thing they love come into being. The greatest price you can pay is a lifetime of devotion, an eternity even.

I love the things I love so much that I want everything about them to be perfect. It gives me pleasure to just think about the very existence of them.

And I love *you* so much that I want to see you be great. I'll force you to, okay? Because otherwise you'll just try to keep me from getting what I want, which is better movies, and better pizza. It all starts with the best ingredients.

I'm told that this book is especially good at *not* telling people who they are supposed to be. By the voice in my head, not any person in particular. I listen to that voice, though, because I'm not the type to show something to anyone until it's done. I want you to see it like Christmas morning.

The Ball

They've got major bets on you in heaven. There's horse racing on, and some grand touring, but boy do they ever love to see you ball out on the main screen. You're a rags to riches story that echoes from the shores of eternity into the fiery apocalypse of Revelation, with the four horsemen and the beast of the sea being swallowed up behind you into the core of the universe.

What good would this thing be if it was just a bunch of Nephilim stomping around, the size of skyscrapers, making terrifying prehistoric dinosaur noises?

We want to see magic, kid. The whole reason you're here is to put on a show, so put on some nice jewelry and get-to-gettin; we've got gold that fits you perfectly. You're a lot cuter than any of the other paperwork and nonsense going across the bookie's desk. *Speed 'em up, slow 'em down.*

Even when someone else is playing, it looks like they're batting you around. Elephants don't fit in every room. So if you're the main event, that means everyone else keeps cosplaying as Steve Jobs so they can announce another dozen cloud services that they're going to discontinue in 3 years. Great work out there.

What other choice do they have? Are they just going to go ahead and make something good and worthwhile? That's not really like them, is it. Making something good would be playing right into your hand. Making disposable junk — that's how they can be confident they did it their way. They're *accelerating developer velocity*, because speed needs more purple.

What's the problem, buddy? Shouldn't we be allowed to make any old thing we please if it suits the people we have making decisions? I guess. But one day you're going to wake up and have to answer for the tower of inflation and dynastic power you've created for the purpose of releasing 10 new Instagram filters and smartwatches a year. Trust me, people don't like to think too much about your froyo troupe dumping pastel paint on each other in the bean bag room for $400,000 a year.

I'm the only tennis champion in my book, and the rest of you are just here to charge tax and take pictures.

Serious

Are you really serious about what you're doing? There's plenty of serious to go around. Even when I'm not seeming serious, I have something serious to say.

I started serious because people told me that's what I had to be, and I finished serious because I got fed up along the way with people that like causing problems. I'm real serious about having fun. When you're serious, the whole world stands at attention to meet some unspoken expectation. It's an expectation that they wouldn't have arrived at if they weren't being serious.

I don't *want* the triple executive ultra racing desk chair. I want the plain one, because it exists at a perspective that makes sense to me, which is plenty serious enough for me. Things that take themselves too seriously tend to get covered up in a thick shroud of enterprise and political correctness. It's like trying to say something while you're wearing a heavy mascot outfit, when in reality the version of you that *seems* sillier is the one that actually gets the point across. Childlike, as the honesty you convey and the range of motion you exhibit in the world.

Remember in like 2010 when tech bros all looked like blood elves and sat around quoting Family Guy? Now they're all into unicorns and tofu. I guess folks that like Bud Light and pickup trucks just aren't that into software. But American exceptionalism rings true in a lot of circles. I'm following along too, but it's quite obvious to me when following along is all that you know. When the lingua franca is all that you know, I notice that there aren't many original ideas that you come up with.

Serious tends to be old news, because new things have no code of ethics or correctness to be upheld. By the time it's serious, there's money and politics involved, and they'd just up and forget about the folks at ground level making big moves. If you managed to keep it un-serious for long enough, it could be that there's something true and genuine shining through. Behind the credit card reader, the round edges, and the terms of service, maybe there's something playful and hopeful about it.

You got a head start, which began the moment you came out. Take advantage of it. It lasts for about 3 years these days. That's how long you can take a break from innovating before you start seeing the whole world look like how you said. Steve Jobs famously accused Apple of completely throwing away their 10 year lead on Microsoft during the period of time between 1985 and 1997 that he was ousted from the company by the board of directors. He said that's the sort of lead you get once in a lifetime.

Steve knew, for certain, he had a vision that Apple once could see, but now lost sight of in its late-80s bureaucracy and corporatism. So Steve went and started another new computer company, NeXT, with many of the same goals in mind as the Macintosh: making the best creative machines in the world. Now, he recognized how important connectivity and collaboration would be for the success of NeXT and also for the brilliant minds that would have these funky black cubes and cantilever displays on their desks.

What NeXT, at the time, was calling *interpersonal computing* would be the foundation for what we now know as cloud computing and social networking. Certainly, these ideas took root several decades prior in niche computer science communities, but people at NeXT had a vision for how everyone in the world would love to have something just like that.

People want to show their work to the world and collaborate on the new issue of Vogue in real-time. They want to share pictures and video, and say *Hi!* to everyone on the planet in an instant.

Apple needed a moonshot, and it turned out they always had one. After Apple bought Steve's new company, NeXT, in 1997, they integrated NeXT's new Unix operating system into their hardware. Apple organized around a new vision of connectivity and creativity. The all new version of the Macintosh operating system, OS X, was based on the powerful NeXTSTEP operating system and development environment. Apple saw its greatest success with the iconic creative machines we now recognize, and of course, the iPod and iPhone. Winning teams always have a powerful sense of vision and purpose.

Know the Rhythm of the Game

Have you ever played basketball with someone that *really* knows how to play basketball? They slide right through your hands like a slippery fish out of water. Every dribble and every pass is planned out. There's nothing random about it. They know the rhythm of the game.

If there's one piece of advice in this book that requires practice, it's this. Some of the most complicated games in the world have phases where the strategy is dramatically different. Ways you can play at the beginning and middle of the game are completely different by the end. It's like learning to ride a bike, except you keep changing bikes over the course of the game; the perspective necessary to understand which part of the game you're at is only there with hundreds of hours of practice.

Who's *driving* the rhythm of the game? You feel like you've got all your units upgraded and the other guy is hobbling along trying to keep up. Every time you are in position, the other guy is completely out of place, in a panic to rearrange his troops. Being prepared means being ready to act, and also knowing decisively when it's time to act. If the other guy is overreaching, you can tell, and you know to stay put and cut down his armies. You've played the game so much and you've seen the exact same situation so many times, that it's quite obvious to you where the pulse of the game is at and when someone's missing beats. Winning is as much about shrewd decision making as it is about the actual mechanics.

Great games have nuggets all along the way that keep you interested for longer than you ever expected. In between all of the action, you're being efficient and you're making steady progress. You've written 5-10 pages every day for the past 2 weeks, and now it's a habit for however long you mean for it to be. Good habits compound over time, but ritual is also contagious. Even if you just wake up, shower, have coffee, and play a particular game each day, that's a ritual that sets the stage for consistent productivity. So long as you actually include the productivity in it, you find a rhythm of positive feedback because every day has the same cadence.

For much of Apple's history, they found themselves saying "You know, there's lots of really incredible things we want to do with these machines that we can't because the technology isn't there yet." In the late 90s and early 2000s, internet connectivity was very clearly a limitation, and you'd hear them talk about this in terms of calendar months that they'd expect to see DSL becoming available. It was very clearly a hot topic. They imagined video calls, broadcasts, real-time collaboration — all of the things we love now. It seemed like *magic*, space-age science fiction, for many years before our technology caught up.

Steve Jobs's animation company, Pixar, could barely get hard drives large enough to make Toy Story, and it took *an entire day* to render 30 seconds of film — **wow**. So then it was storage and graphics, and of course, portability.

What you notice about really great innovators is that they have an acute understanding for what people really would love to do with technology. They are masters at figuring out how to design something that *just works*. It feels like an extension of you, allowing your creativity to shine. People want to have *fun* with these machines, and they want to do it together! Boy, if you only knew.

When I was a kid, we had a 35mm film camera and piles of photo albums with pictures from my childhood and going all the way back to when my parents were kids. I remember when my mom first got a digital camera, she was confused by what you're supposed to do with the pictures once you take them. Sure, you could go to Costco or Walgreens and have them printed out, but the idea was really that your computer was your hub for your media. If you asked her, she would have said she wanted the post office to deliver her photographs to family faster. This was before she realized what she *really* wanted to do was send pictures to people instantly from her phone, right as she took them! And so the phone became self-sufficient, and for many people it is more important than their computer, with many of the same capabilities. She loves the iMac, and she likes a mouse and keyboard. That's what's relatable to her, and so is a physical calendar to write on.

You'd see Steve Jobs on stage showing you a *particular* thing you could do with the device, like he was performing a magic trick, flourishing windows and 3D graphics for the first time people had ever seen. It worked just like magic when you took photos on your iPhone and they showed up on your Mac, because they were synchronized instantly over iCloud.

That's the way it's always been for Apple. They start with the experience they want to give you, and they build the greatest technology possible to accomplish it. Otherwise, it's like a big box of tools, or a Lego set with no instructions. By focusing on particular experiences that people want to have, it becomes immediately obvious what technology is and isn't capable of. That way, they know what hardware to build without waiting for the industry to catch up. Now they build all of their own chips, because that had consistently been a limitation for them. Their vendors simply weren't in lock-step with the rapid innovation they wanted to accomplish.

Steve was very proud to say the new Macs of the early 2000s were the very first creative class machines that could go from film or animation all the way to a burnt DVD in one system. In his mind, the Macintosh was the one and only creative machine in a box. It had everything you needed to be expressive and make a professional quality record, and then release your music on iTunes to millions of iPods across the world. And then there was YouTube, and anyone could be a filmmaker.

From a point in time where you had to be *chosen* by some omnipotent force like a production company or a record label to make your movie or distribute your music, Apple envisioned a world where people could choose themselves. Where someone who knows deep in their heart that they are creative has the opportunity to shine, even if a record executive just couldn't see it. Steve figured that people in suits know about as much about new music as a dairy farmer knows about French cuisine. Maybe a little bit. And at the time, when you said *internet* to them, the first thing they thought was *piracy*. They found it difficult, at first, to get all of the major artists available on iTunes, let alone sold on the idea of unlimited streaming 10 years later. The record labels would just sit on their hands for years, delaying the inevitable, and imagining a world where something other than the best product wins. Who wouldn't want more people listening to more music?

Apple, as it turned out, knows a *lot* about new music — not just the records you buy, but each and every song you love. Naturally, you can imagine Apple found *gatekeeper industries* like music and mobile networks very frustrating, which is why they were reluctant to make a phone in the first place. Before the iPhone, when you bought a phone, it had what it had on it, and the network decided on a lot of that. No apps, barely full internet capabilities, and really not something that people were proud to own. They succeeded by showing the networks that they had something lightyears ahead of any other devices on the market, and they created a whole new market for portable software that turned out to be much more open and successful than desktop applications ever were. AT&T was the only network that supported the iPhone at first, and everyone else was hitting themselves for passing up on it. Today, Apple is the industry leader for creative computers and phones.

Now we think in terms of *instant*. In the past decade, we've really seen saturation in terms of what our devices are capable of, and what it comes down to is your imagination for how you want to use them. You can do anything at a professional level from anywhere in the world on your computer, even broadcast live HD video from phone while you travel, like the world's coolest tour guide. The video games are as 3D and open world as you could want, for the time being — fast, stylish, and with lightning fast connection over fiber.

Perhaps you'd say that means we're stagnating, and it's true, we're going to see tremendous improvement in battery power and efficiency, picture perfect cameras and displays, truly photorealistic games and real time computation. And then, next generation devices are going to completely change how we think of the boundary between our minds and our computers. That's next generation — current generation devices, though, have mostly overcome every limitation in terms of speed and infrastructure.

168

So, while you're toeing the line of what technology is capable of, do you feel like you're really able to push it to the limit? Great innovators know exactly where that limit is at, and they can feel the tremendous torque and the wind in their face as they brush up against it.

Wise in Our Generation

The most important things we know about the world are really things we know about *our* world. It's wisdom that would be difficult to export to another time or even another place. Sure, globalism means that everyone knows who *The Avengers* are, and there's a shared vernacular to the economy that everyone with internet access understands, but in the grand scheme of life, the world we live in now is a twinkle in the eye of the universe.

And certainly, everyone is getting internet access. Getting online is life changing. The most valuable skills now are things like knowing how to use computers and phones, and knowing how to acquire influence in the digital world. Conversely, folks might feel like other skills are languishing, like socializing in-person and practical skills like construction, hunting, and cooking.

The world is so very still right now. Look outside, how the trees waver, leaves fluttering in the wind, squirrels and rabbits scampering around. But buildings and apps are supposed to be permanent and absolutely stable. Amazon prides themselves on offering 99.999% uptime for cloud services. Google will send you emails to tell you that your website flickers around too much when images and fonts load, or the buttons are too small when you look at them on a phone.

You know how to do things that are much more complicated, on paper, than anything in human history; comprehension of mobile apps that have many screens and lots of structured data, precise fine motor skills, and requirements for attention and memory that spans months and years at a time.

How would you sort out your knowledge that is relevant to here-and-now, and knowledge that you could abstract to some time in the past or the future? Many biblical stories are quite practical, after all, where the ways that people build societies and contest their rule over them changes, but they retain familiar characteristics. People at every point in history understand liberty and oppression. Now, we're just grateful in the developed world to have more liberties than ever, and to know right from wrong in ways that people in the past weren't really paying enough attention to. We're open minded to new things, but we sometimes forget about the lessons that have already been learned.

How do we say *farewell* to kings? And what shall we replace them with? Certainly, you must see that everything in the world converges on some type of authority. If you believe in paper money, you believe in authority. If you buy food from the grocery store, there's probably 10 different authorities involved with producing, certifying, transporting, and selling it to you. If you believe in education and politics, those are authorities that fill a similar role as the church. They decide how you're going to live your life, according to what is apparently pious and meaningful.

The queen is quite socialized. She believes in JavaScript and the news, so he does too, with reservations. The king stands nearly still, resounding in his faith and his image alone. Without her to remind him of everything else out there, he may still be breathing the same stale air in his house from 10 years ago; he'd seem elderly and decrepit, strangely nascent and limited by the ecosystem of his backyard and mailbox. Which is how he began, and he knew to hide this from her for her disgust. When you bid him farewell, would you come up with a new symbol? Or rather, isn't it the case that the permanence of his symbol is what made his kingship exceptional to begin with?

Truly, an excellent king is as much a sign of the times as he is of his creed. Perhaps in some ways he understands the times better than she.

Now or Later

Some people thrive in uncertainty. If you're like me, though, you do tons of research on everything that's interesting to you, and you like to have everything mapped out before you even start, including all of the options along the way if things go differently from how you planned. It's like an addiction, to absorb as much knowledge as possible and ward away that feeling in the back of your mind that you don't know enough.

You can even have everything all figured out ahead of time, and still be thinking to yourself *what if I don't put in the work?* So, what if? That's something that's entirely within your control.

It's important to know what your natural strengths are so you can play to them, and also to know where there's opportunity for growth. It can seem like I'm comfortable with uncertainty simply because I always have lots of plans. Trust me, there's a time and a place for everything.

Do you *love* to delay gratification? What a talent that must be for you. Keep edging and watch the pot pile high, the things that you uncover age like sourdough and fine wine. For other people, they love to see it *right now,* and that's also a great talent, because they're going to stumble across peculiarities that others won't, like a truffle dog foraging in the woods.

Does everything have to mean something to you? Or do you relish in absurdity? You may come to find that some things can only be understood through a particular lens, and other things are meant to be misunderstood or beyond all comprehension.

For those of us that find *constriction* quite natural, it can be helpful to imagine *pouring* as the polar opposite. Constriction, meaning the state of mind that you find yourself lifting up and out of your own eyes and ears, regulating, and organizing everything around you. You're so preoccupied with making everything perfect that you can't think straight, frozen in place for any next step or new decision, because nothing seems quite perfect enough. So take a moment to breathe and imagine *pouring,* because that is how you will let your creativity loose. When you remember to breathe and to see with your own eyes and ears, you can enjoy what is right in front of you without thinking about what would make it more perfect.

I notice that I will spend weeks at a time feeling tension in my mind and body, and then it will become quite important that I release it. Try to go between these states on-demand. Everything is moving along exactly how it's supposed to, and whatever they've got at the store is whatever you're meant to get. Some of us may not have even felt at peace before in our lives. How far we've fallen from grace, to not even remember what it feels like to be at ease.

Get to the Thing

I know, this one's a page turner. Gets you going like kettle corn or a bag of M&Ms.

Even the most hyperactive, wired bands can only play at max speed and intensity for so long. 2 hours of thunder and lightning is a lot different than water trickling down the drain. I like my coffee concentrated and my information from Wikipedia, which is good news for you, because that means it's easy for me to get to the point without having the second half of this book being 200 pages of Brothers Karamazov court litigation. A lot of folks just don't have the attention span these days, so bear with us.

There's still some important things to cover that will make sure you have all the tools you need to win. And I have great tools, everyone knows this about me.

Faust

My favorite thing about Goethe's *Faust* is the yellow cover on the German Reclam Edition. Other than that, I find literature very boring. I'd rather read or write software documentation with structured chapters describing the inherent concepts and themes than stretch it out into hundreds of pages of narrative prose. But I get it — you wouldn't want Harry Potter to just be a fortune cookie that says *Harry is a Wizard.*

What is the Devil anyway, other than a disbelief in victory? Italics that never come off, a sentence void of completion. How good would your eyes have to be to tell the difference, where we are born in the perfect image of God?

To me, it would be unfair to you to have you take a number and wait for me to get to the point, amid an endless stream of consciousness and adjectives; conjoined clauses wherewithin some meaning is buried upon the coast of white-sand beaches and shells. Throttled like metric emissions, laid out in proud isolationist Luddism on the Varadero shore.

When I read fiction, my immediate instinct is to wonder why it has to be like that. Why telling a story is *supposed* to be a confessional work of endless melodramatic inner monologue with dialogue and events spliced in? To me, it all reads like a run-on sentence. I suppose fiction does require something to get lost in translation, so that there's any story at all to tell. Storytelling is quite at odds with clarity and reason. For you, it could be that my style of writing reads like an advertisement or a McDonald's menu. But in school we were required to read fiction, and we weren't required to learn how to write advertising copy. I did that on my own time. I suppose I've just always had this perspective that makes me want to break free from convention, because the status quo just seems arbitrary to me. As I see things, it would be like forcing every kid to play basketball an hour a day from kindergarten through 12th grade. Something has convinced you reading literature is important for every child, though, and I guess it's not a bad way to fill out time in state-sponsored childcare. Except it truly bores the hell out of me.

This is good news for you, because it shows that there's things that smart people *should* like, that for some reason they don't because it's not their thing. It shows, like much of the other evidence in the world, that people with truly innovative ideas aren't so preoccupied with other people's idea of being smart. Likewise, listening to The Mars Volta's *Amputechture* may be like hearing pots and pans tumble down an infinite flight of stairs for you. But I love it, and I could listen to it over, and over, and over again, and stay obsessed with the light-speed acidity of it.

Like movies and music, literature is a great medium for exploring interesting moral and existential dilemmas. So there are certainly interesting stories to think about, whether or not we are drawn to the medium or the breadth. I enjoy literature like an architecture enthusiast. I don't need to know how the sausage was made, but I'm quite intrigued by what made you want to make it like that.

Why a *Faustian bargain?* Who would decide to make a deal with the Devil when you can make a deal with God? Ah, but you believe in scarcity and variation, just like we have here in the world we know. If you made a deal with God to the exclusion of the Devil, perhaps there would be no losers, no crude oil, no need for food, and no death. The lifestyle that we know on Earth, as plain as day, is precisely *to the exclusion* of the Devil, so that we can actively choose what we believe is true. When you believe in God, belief in the Devil becomes a practicality so that you know there is a correct choice, so that you know there are consequences when you misbehave. We suppose it is better to compartmentalize the Devil into what we can see with our own eyes and ears, so that it is at the mercy of what is apparently pleasing and just, under the thumb of rules and regulation, than to have it exist faceless and indifferent. This is a belief in the *constricting* aspect of God, that exists alongside the merciful and giving aspect of God.

In every great story, we encounter the chaotic, primordial, and grotesque aspect of being in this world. The confrontation with all of the things that exist, incidentally, as result of our own bidding. The lives taken and families displaced by wars that we are certain we are on the right side of, the eternality of your name and your choices, and even the man at the counter working minimum wage to serve you your cheeseburger.

A story appears from the *divided subject*. What do we understand as separate from ourselves, and how do we interface with it? Archetypal themes emerge like the child and the hermit, which contrasts a new life full of possibilities with a life fully actualized; perhaps even the totality of the world fully actualized, like a man infinitely tall, with remarkably long legs that stretch into eternity. We see modes of consciousness like vampirism and werewolves, that are suggestive of consolidation of ideology and unrestrained carnal instinct, respectively. These are just 2 ways we can tell a story about the shadow we cast in the universe. One supposes the vampire is a more sophisticated answer to the divided subject, and yet nearly totalitarian in a full estimation.

The virtue of mercy comes as naturally as breathing to us when you contrast it against self-absorption, vain auto-eroticism. And at once, if you are perceptive and truthful about your circumstances, your living moment is quite auto-erotic, like living your life reattaching the other part of your penis and speaking by your million tongues. We wake up into a shroud of eternity that we had nearly forgotten about, until one day that it is quite obvious. Every day you lived up until that point was meant to bring you to the present moment, where you lay eyes on her and the world stands still. It wouldn't be until then that the world would know to receive you, except according to her.

I love artwork that describes the metaphysics of morality in a way we can understand. We are so used to living our ordinary lives that it wouldn't occur to us to think about things like this. Thinking about the underlying principles of the world is important to really figure out how to instrument our morality and our logic. Otherwise, you're putting volume knobs on lemons and painting your ham green. The actuality of the world disappears into the surface level observations, because that's just what everyone told us things were supposed to be like.

Artwork with soul touches us in ways that most psychology and self-help, as it stands today, doesn't quite address. In beautiful artwork and philosophy, there's a belief in truth and resisting evil that fades to grey in

175

service of an imaginary shapeless every-person. They either forget to talk about winners and losers, favoring participation awards and unconditional self-acceptance, or they tell you to get into your *grindset* all day and forget about the actuality of it. So, what do you think? How much more expensive can San Francisco get before the people in tents on the street and stealing potato chips from padlocked shelves in Walgreens becomes real to us? I could just keep showing up, gratefully, and collecting my ridiculous meal ticket, but that's not the sort of person I am. Because if we live truthfully, perhaps, we will show up at the doorstep of eternity, where any money-printing flywheel inevitably squashes the working class, where you have just 2 hands and 2 legs that you can instrument. So you can see why it's so important to me that I follow every line of reasoning full-circle, because I only like to believe in what I know is true.

When I follow the same line of reasoning, I consider that in a few years, most of the industrialized world will be automated, and everyone who was *inb4* has staked claim in a significant orchestrating role in the economy. And I wonder what I'm supposed to say to people who want to know how to be independently successful in the year 2050. I'm not certain I have a good answer for that just yet, but I hope that I will.

First Time

You stand to gain a lot by expecting things to go right the first time. You're bound to be putting your heart and soul into it like this is the only shot you'll ever have. Not only that, but when the universe sees you spending too much time bumbling around and evaluating your options, that's what it starts giving you: opportunities to waste time and shop around.

Maybe you do want that. And maybe some of the time it's okay to be churning. Not often, though. Set some ground rules for the universe, and start with *I expect things to go right the first time.*

It's more empowering than you could imagine, to know that your every word and your every action is exactly what was meant for the world. It's empowering to not have thoughts like *what if things were different for me*, as if there's anywhere you belong other than here and now. I know I've struggled with that. Worrying about what might have happened, how things almost went wrong or almost went right. That's simply not how things panned out, though, is it?

There's a plan for each and every one of us in life. Love, health, and happiness. Those are the things that will ground you. Those things are what define the story of your life, where you would otherwise be shapeless.

You Know, the Thing

Novels have their roots in the 1600s as people's taste shifted towards stories about modern, ordinary people. Classically, there wasn't a clear distinction between fiction and history. Stories were effectively *a history* — some grand epic and romance presented as factual. With the new style of prose, the stories were presented as more real than ever. They disseminated recent, relevant gossip and scandals, often times with pseudonyms masking the real names of the people they described. Novels told stories that were meant to be very pertinent and contextual to the politics and lifestyle of modern people.

Novels like Dostoyevsky's *The Brothers Karamazov* were published as *serials*, monthly installments in literary journals, before being published as a collected volume. He explored ideas about faith, morality, and character, in the context of then-modern 19th century Russia. Ironic how, today, most people don't think of novels as a real-time insight into the world we live in or something we get to read while the author is writing it, even as the world has become so well connected with video, music, and games. And most of us don't think of novels as real.

Airbnb, a popular and wildly successful way to book rooms and short-term vacation rentals online, started out finding it very difficult to make money. It started as *Air Bed and Breakfast,* because they had it in their minds that a full-service bed and breakfast, hosted by a homeowner, was something people wanted. This went on for quite some time, scrounging around to find people that wanted to host a room in their home for a few days at a time. Later, they discovered an important market for short-term rentals. People wanted the whole home in Aspen to enjoy with their family, and the bed and breakfast part turned out to be not so important.

No one could even imagine this was something they wanted. The term *vacation rental* barely existed, and at this point in time nothing even close to Uber or DoorDash existed: you couldn't get anything without getting on the phone with someone, and people were perhaps still skeptical of online transactions.

They didn't know what to call it. Plain and simple. And they had something that no one knew they wanted, and absolutely no analogue to give people a frame of reference, in their mind, of what this experience was going to look like. Remember, this is 2009. People were still figuring out what an *app* was. Okay. So, I reserve the place online, and it's... just ready for me when I get there? Who are these people? Where does the money go when I pay? How do I get in the door when I arrive?

There's a lot of inertia to overcome to get to the point where people imagine themselves doing something. And then they barely think twice about it.

Some industries thrive on remaining *the thing.* Progressive can't stop you from turning into your parents, but it can remind you, when you move out and make all-important decisions about which invisible services to buy, that it's *just the thing you gotta be doing to do it.* And everyone knows you're a lot more likely to get new phone service or car insurance when you're 20 than when you're 50. Especially if there's a much better deal and you can do it all online. It's only when the incumbent feels their influence slipping away, due to new providers and business models, that they start feeling the heat of market pressure.

Most "new" cellular carriers are actually just *virtualized* networks with bandwidth allocated on major networks like Verizon and T-Mobile that already have the nationwide infrastructure. They just found ways to work with tighter margins, in spite of being beholden to the primary carrier that owns the towers. Things like not having physical stores or contract deals on phones allowed carriers like Ting and Boost Mobile to pass savings along to you. Finally, T-Mobile woke up and started charging prices more like what the virtual carriers offer, cutting out the middle man, and keeping the profit for themselves. It used to be a lot more important that you were on whichever network supported the phone you wanted, but now phones all basically support every network for the market they're offered in. Finally, something like true market pressure showed up that emphasized cost, speed, and coverage.

Look, if we didn't remind you to get married and have kids, you'd still be sitting at your desk looking at spreadsheets and playing with your cock. Honestly, sometimes I think you'd forget to eat and sleep if we weren't running ads for it. God's watching, and he hates idolatry and paperwork.

Dropbox

Here, drag a file from your computer and you can share it with anyone in the world. The best way you can get people excited about something you've made is to get them using it before they even know what it is. Now, you'd think one of the very first things people want to do with a computer is share files. Pictures, documents, videos. How else are we going to collaborate with these things without burning CDs and USB drives and mailing them to each other? It took a lot longer than you'd think.

Dropbox became popular around the late 2000s, and it was the very first commercially successful file sharing solution. Yes, before that, computers had file sharing *on paper*, but really it was mostly for computers in the same building, and otherwise it required fussy networking, VPN setup, or FTP servers. No, really you must understand: we want to share a folder, with anyone in the world. You can use it in your web browser, or install it so your Dropbox has a home right inside your computer. My files, at home, and on my work computer. Even on my phone. One click, and now you can see my sales pamphlet or my pictures from Yellowstone. You could invite people to shared folders to collaborate. We take this for granted now, in a cloud-first world. Sure, there were some internet speed limitations at the time, but that wasn't truly the limiting factor. You could email files if they were small enough, and there were other file sharing sites. Someone hadn't really put the pieces together yet in a way that made it work in a way that people wanted to use it. It was an area ripe for innovation.

Dropbox gave you a few gigabytes of storage for free, just for trying it out. They gave you more storage for doing things like installing on multiple computers, sharing folders, or referring friends, which gave both of you extra storage. These things taught you all about using Dropbox and rewarded you for it. How fun. I know I thought it was. It was the most Mac thing I had on my computer that wasn't made by Apple. And then everyone at school was using Dropbox overnight. And then maybe it wasn't so important whether we finished our homework at home or in the library. Before that it was. We didn't get to bring our laptops to class like you might be able to now.

Google saw how important these sorts of workflows are. They said, hey — what if the entire productivity app was *in the cloud*. Meaning you can edit your documents and spreadsheets online, and even work on them together at the same time. They said hey, what if the entire computer was cloud-first, so that you don't have to think twice about whether you are at home or on the school network? Google built *Docs*, a web-first productivity suite that did everything Microsoft Office did, but for free, anywhere you wanted to use it. Your documents all get stored in Google Drive, and you can collaborate on them in real time, with your cursor showing up right next to everyone else that are all working on the same document. And then they built Chromebooks, web-first laptops that were made for working in the cloud.

Google completely captured the education market like this, because they weren't so incentivized to make money selling you the computer itself. They knew, on account of the entire workflow being baked into Google, that selling school districts laptops at-cost was well worth it to get *everyone* using Google Drive and Google Docs. Apple, Microsoft, Dell, and HP couldn't even begin to compete using their existing business model. The existing companies had to make money off the sale of the hardware and software, which made Google Chromebooks much more affordable. And the technology and workflows were just plain better, you knew the moment you tried it. Aside from the fact that the world's greatest data mine now has their tendrils around your entire life. Sure, they'll make you some privacy promises. Schools were hooked, and students were Google Docs experts in an instant.

Apple and Microsoft made it very convenient to do work on computers. The immediacy of web companies became much more impactful towards the late 2000s, with technologies like YouTube, iCloud, and Facebook. Hardware was becoming a commodity, with a computer on every desk, and now everyone wanted to be a web app. It just works, with no setup. Want to start your own live video broadcast? Sure. Want to send and receive money? Sure. Want to make a website? Sure. Who wants to build apps themselves? We've got just the thing. I've seen it a million times: first, companies will make it easy for you to do work, and then they will make technology that does the work for you.

Bingo Mentality

It's simple. If you want your sphere of influence to go beyond your household and your local adult baseball league, you have to start shifting into a bingo mentality. You start putting anything and everything on your bingo card that seems like it's worth taking up space. And maybe you started careful about it, but you definitely became careful about it as you saw the space filling up. If not just because you wanted to save space for things you actually care about, but also because people began expecting more of you on account of your baller MTV bingo card.

They said *"Hey, when are you going to start taking responsibility for your bingo card that takes up half the continent?"* And it just seemed like yesterday that you were making skate videos at the mall.

They're right though. The more assets you are collecting on, the more people start looking to you as an arbiter of everything that occurs in your now-giant sphere of influence. So you explain to them why you put the things you did on your bingo card. Some of it's easy pickin's — you knew iPhones and football are a great bet. A lot of it, though, was wishful thinking that you were quite intentional about lobbying for. The writing was partially on the wall, but in a Dead Sea Scrolls sort of way where you had to put a lot of torn up pieces together and roll-start going downhill to get it running. No one else was going to come along and do it for you. They don't care about technology, philosophy, and metaphysics the way you do. The way you have to, to the point of obsession, to spend so much time putting together some ancient mysteries. This is a perfect project to spend years of your life on.

People are quite sensitive to when it seems like someone is taking up too much space. But they also have to believe in winning, and so they become convinced that there are people who are absolutely essential to have in their corner. Because they know the difference. Too many people are bullshit artists, so when someone comes along that can actually cut through the noise, that's the only thing people have on their minds.

I thought a lot about this though. I'm going to end up being right about things that are easy and gratifying to take credit for, and also things that no one in their right mind would want to take credit for. I'm *mostly* in my right mind, and so the fucked up stuff is worth acknowledging so that we can come up with ways to improve. That stuff gets a place on the bingo card because it's real, and because you pay attention to it the way you salivate when Dateline comes on. I don't particularly like Dateline, and I don't like having problems. So the problems surface, I stamp my card, and then remind you we're going to make them go away. It's a win-win.

And if I wasn't playing bingo, those problems would still be there and never get addressed. You should be glad someone like me exists. You should be glad that when I let you peek at what's on my bingo card, you get some excellent ideas for how to furnish your own card. Because everyone knows I have a great bingo card.

Don't be afraid to rethink things. I've already told you most of what I know on my website. A book is a different thing though, and lots of people like longer winded explanations of things. A book is also something that people are more interested in paying for, because it's a real thing that you get to admire on your shelf. Clearly, I can cover a lot more ground by turning this thing into different shapes. I could charge money for my website, but I don't. And I probably won't, because it's good for business in the long run. *cako.io* is the coolest treasure anyone could possibly uncover on the internet.

Real Cats

Today, we find ourselves with so much pressure to analyze and prepare for our lives that we forget to actually live them. Wow, that must make you feel really dumb, that you only know how to write 300 pages thoroughly examining the psychology, spirituality, and economics of living life, and you can't carry a conversation for more than 5 minutes. Well, really you can, but we're going to end up talking about Metal Gear or Mac. The interesting thing is you're actually seeing me live my life in real time, brushing up against the very dilemma one is faced with when they have something important to say and no one wants to pay attention, when the whole world is staying perfectly *still-in-motion* and hardly going anywhere.

The subtext of life is the only thing anyone teaches us. They tell us to keep masturbating to pictures of ourselves on Instagram and selling subscriptions to meal-prep services. They tell us to keep going to school and working until we can afford what houses cost now that everyone just keeps going to school and working. Really, you're not ready to start your life at 20, are you? You're just an infant. Everyone knows you're not fertile until you're 35.

The cost-benefit analysis makes sense. We can both just keep showing up for work and making money because we did everything we were told to do by the powers that be. Work, our proxy for meaning. And anytime we say something to each other that we don't like, it's plenty easy enough for us to go back to living our separate lives and forget each other existed. Disposable, like your dinner and your text messages. Who would we be, anyway, if we made an eternal commitment to each other, bound by the church and divine providence? We fell from grace to be lost here, until we knew to be found.

Look, I'm just doing what I know. Which is talking about the idea of you. Because honestly I don't particularly like being around you all the time. Tragic. And clearly you don't much like being around me, because I just keep telling you what you should think. Instagram is easier medicine to swallow, sort of like how scrapbooking Taylor Swift memorabilia is way cooler than actually talking to her. Are you just going to say words to her, like she's a real person?

Is there something that could make *actuality* matter to us the way it's supposed to? What change in economics or social pressures would have to occur for us to cut the facade? Idle hands do the Devil's work, or so I've been told, by the judge actually. Keep everyone jailed in their Twitter spaces until they get bored with all this fucking paperwork and start wars with each other. All because no one wants to bend over and answer to their own personal Jesus. You, of course, silly.

Hair

Style is always changing. Right now everything is so loud and so public. Superficially public, but at home we just hide away. You may as well not exist unless you have something to sell to the world. Every moment, like we are constantly evaluating ourselves against the expectations of the entire world, because there's no place to go. Playing alone often feels as public as going somewhere, because the main place to do it is on the computer. So while you play, you get constant reminders that there's something about you that feels fundamentally incompatible with other people. You know because they showed you. You deserve *this many* upvotes and followers. You, meaning me. Because as you can see, I don't really have many friends. The internet is more for girls these days anyway, and it's difficult to explain why. Just look around.

I love quiet, though. I love when people speak softly and think carefully.

Outside is like lime to me. Not everyone knows what I mean when I say this, but I feel it the moment I leave the house. It shows on my skin and in the tension I feel. I wish I didn't feel that way. But this is what being a person means in the year 2023. You have to learn how to measure up to grand ideas about yourself in front of everyone. Even when you are disgusted by the feeling of being looked at.

The thing I'm always thinking about is how inflationary spending your time on the internet is. Literally, how many coins do you have to put in to get any tickets out of the game? Am I the only one that notices that? Or are epic memes really that entrancing?

Everyone's got a different idea of *done*. Today, everyone's got a fade. Endless haircutting, to achieve the same head profile as when guys slicked their hair back. Go spend $30 a week at the barber.

I put off messy jobs with lots of cleanup, like shaving, but you need a shared vocabulary of some sort for the way people are trying to look at a point in time, at the very least so you can find out how much someone pays attention to those expectations and tries to meet them. And so now, everyone gets their haircut, bathes, and tweets endlessly. That is the minimum requirement to achieve the thing we're talking about right now, not that I necessarily meet it.

Fashion is immediately visible, but lots of things also benefit from having an *unshared* vocabulary that is meant to be *impermeable*, so that what you mean is not obvious. The way people really typically use words is by setting up something in between what you really mean and how other people may interpret it, so that you can learn how they interface with your boundaries. Computers don't teach you that. I'm used to inputting data myself, so when I hand my deposit slip to a banker and hope they do what I expected, sometimes I get frustrated. Yes, no, ok, cancel, invite — this is not really what you mean to say when you introduce yourself, but you may have never learned any better. By no means a coincidence, the people coming up with styles and rules are the people for whom it occurs to be telling you what to do. Here I am writing an entire book like I'm defining functions in a programming language; alas, it is what I know.

We try to be explicit about who we are and how we want people to treat us, what sort of *input* is expected to properly engage with us, but we really do find that we mean *not* to be. Why would I want to have to force you to treat me a certain way? Even if you arrive independently at what I mean to say, I'm ready to move on to the next thing. The point of a lot of the things we say is the position of outrunning our concept of self. The moment I have your attention, I mean to be somewhere new.

To put it another way, when you design a car, it would be unusual to put driving instructions on the vehicle or have controls on the exterior. An emergent property of *how the car feels to drive* appears in the design. The immediacy of instructions being written directly on a vending machine, for instance, is inherent to the ephemeral interaction you're expected to have with it. As the owner of a car, you know how to operate it by memory.

If you externalize what you're doing into instructions, it short-circuits the expectations we typically are meant to place on each other to negotiate each other's boundaries.

People have distinct ways of characterizing *victory*. For some people, victory is mysteriously incomplete, because they see the world continually shifting around them and it seems necessary to remain impartial and to clarify and churn their own beliefs along with it. Others truly value the finality of victory; they believe in their name and their ideology, and they recognize that there is a fleeting dispersal that will occur throughout their lives and in the distant future as people inherit and build upon their thought.

Become the *best* at something — fine, there's an observable goal that has clear success criteria based on whoever, if anyone, has already achieved something like it. It's not going to be so obvious where the *fielder's choice* wins are going to be along the way unless you have very clever people that spend all day wondering why exactly we're doing things the way we're doing them. And they have to be smart enough to know when it's worth going down rabbit holes, or otherwise when it's junk or gimmicks that they're chasing.

Excellent teams have tenets of structure, unity, and reformation working all together. Some folks have something like this clockwork mechanism all-in-one inside of them. That's the only way it would be satisfying to them.

House

What do you get when you put together primetime drama, industry leading medicine, maverick angst, and ivy league hotties? The world's most popular TV series, of course.

Dr. House really is a bitter old man. A 13 year old in an adult body. But he's always right, so it's important that he always gets his way. Just like the United States. In a world of bumbling idiots with creatine and prescription pads, here's someone who wants to *stick it to the man* as much as you do. You know, *the man,* whichever one doesn't have all of the answers and the magical cures to your ailments. Problem solved, for however long you can withhold your suspension of disbelief. That you're perfectly healthy and you don't need more police in your life. That should last your entire life, if we pray.

It's really not that important that you follow along with the medical jargon and the diagnoses. House is all about pacing and ritual. By the end of the show, it's clear to you that House and his team of geniuses figured something out that no one else could. And one or two of them are hot, so you hope he has sex with them when the camera's not running. Then he whizbangs in her and she gallantly uptakes the semen for a good 10 seconds, gazing aloof into space like someone whose attention you don't quite have at the airport. That's the off-camera part, in between people brutally dying in the hospital. That's one in the bag for the greatest country in the world and all of the great things that we make for your enjoyment.

The reason House works is because he makes it so that you can believe something comes out ahead that isn't so weighed down by Pfizer and the giant brick Princeton medical facility. House is your assurance that someone around here is actually making sure we're running as fast as we can be. You know that's true because everywhere he looks are people that are trying to slow him down. It's written all over his face.

House was designed by committee. Both the show, and also the character. He hates the committee, and that's why he's stuck with a little desk at the end of a conference room. Bet you never really thought about it like that. I do now though. I love the committee, as long as they keep giving me new movies to watch and music to listen to.

He pulls back the curtain and *voila*, now the curtain belongs another 10 feet down the hall. If he just went home and wrote diagnostic manuals, there'd be no show. House couldn't outrun his concept of self quick enough. As soon as he's right, it's in your textbooks and the show needs somewhere new so that it can go on. Otherwise he starts seeming like *the man*. What an odd aspect of his personality. I know because I understand it completely.

Screen

People remember where they put something if it's always in the same place. For decades, Apple had been researching and brainstorming about what would make a computer easy to use. You'll notice a persistent frustration when Steve is on stage describing files and folders on your computer: people don't get it. At home, you keep your pens, paperwork, and other office supplies at your desk, and your photos go in albums in order of when you took them. Your kitchen utensils go in a drawer in your kitchen, and your tools and hardware go in your toolbox in the garage.

Computers always had this idea that you need to open a program, and then go find the file or project you were working on in your hard drive to access it. If you forgot where you saved your essay, it's like looking for a needle in a haystack. This is just how computers worked for many years; you told a program to go look for the thing it was supposed to show you. They often have a *recent files* splash screen when you open them, but even that can be confusing, because people get used to that screen, and the not-recent files get lost to the sands of time. If they're not organized, they have no clue where they put the file to begin with. Apple was certain of it: folders are confusing for people, it's like wheels within wheels.

So they made search better. For many years, Mac Spotlight search was about 1000 times better than Windows. Literally. I have no idea how it took so long for them to catch up, but on Mac you could always just hit *Command-Space* and type in the file or app you want to open and it was just there, whereas the other guys made you wait a good 30 seconds to re-index all of your files every time you searched. And they experimented with different ways of showing you your hard drive (your *what?*) and arranging the contents of it, to try to make it make sense to people.

And then with the iPhone and iPad, they discovered something important, almost by accident, as result of screen size constraints. When

189

you show people one thing at a time on the screen in a predictable sequence, it's a lot easier to figure it out. You don't need to dig through pots and pans at your desk to get to your essay. If files *belonged* to the app that you open them with, they never get lost. Now, just like when you open the drawers in your desk, you'll find your documents and pens, not the kitchen sink. This solved a multi-pronged issue for them. iOS, by design, makes apps very self-contained. Each app only shows you the files that are relevant to it. Because it's clear that the app owns those files and settings, they get synced in iCloud between any device that you install that app on. Apps can't touch any other parts of your device, for security reasons, and any files belonging to an app automatically get removed when you get rid of the app — no clutter, and no space magically filling up as you use your device for many years.

iOS apps also only have one or two window configurations. With apps like Adobe Illustrator and even text editors, Apple found that people got confused with windows overlapping, moving around, and getting lost when people went to change pen colors and fonts. When everything is arranged perfectly for the screen size, with sheets and menus that show up in predictable locations, people have an exact muscle memory for how the app works that isn't dependent on how many windows you have open or what your screen size is.

Now the tradeoff, of course, is flexibility, whether we're talking about file and folder structure or how apps are displayed. When you *start* with the portable screen sizes, you're constrained to the least common denominator. But Apple didn't do that. They made portable versions of powerful desktop applications, and then reintegrated technology and workflows that they loved from iOS back into the Mac.

Mac is better for me, personally, than iOS, but they each serve a purpose in different situations. I always have multiple windows open on different parts of my screen, even on my 13" MacBook Air with its compact, but super high resolution display. I like to overlap them, too, so that I can click between them and just see the parts that are important, which is great on a laptop display. Apple has added split-screen for iPad and Mac, but it's not really what I like because you have to have 2 full windows fixed in place, each taking up half the screen. I'm sure lots of people love it, though. This goes to show you that sometimes the thing everyone really needs for your device to make sense is not what's going to make power users happy. And Apple has *always* been intensely focused on being the absolute best devices for everyone, no matter their experience with computers.

Ratchet

There's only one Red Hot Chili Peppers, and no one else captures such intensity. They spent a lot of time thinking about what they wanted to sound like, tracking their records with scientific precision, those nutjobs.

Why does a guitar look like that? Why does a computer have a mouse and keyboard? StarCraft II is supposedly ergonomic. We don't think too much about how all of the proportions of the world are perfect for people to operate. When you're a kid, you have stuff that becomes normal to you without even knowing it's extraordinary. We had ceramic bowls with lids for storage and microwaving, an electric screwdriver, octagonal highball glasses, an immersion blender that you insert into a container like a wand, and silverware with black knurled plastic handles. This, along with lots of unusual gadgets and knick knacks from Costco. It wouldn't occur to me to think about why these things were like this; it was what we had since the day I was born. Not only that, but you become accustomed to things you like without appreciating the fact that fashions will come and go. What becomes so familiar and comforting to you will soon be a relic, a plain memory of where you began and a cornerstone of who you will become. In Utah, everything and everyone is a particular way.

I remember sometime around 2010 being impressed with the fact that everyone was able to become educated and technically savvy, thanks to iPhones and social media, where before that I felt like people really couldn't figure stuff out the way I could. That's still true, but the cultural shift between the 2000s and 2010s in terms of accessibility of information was very dramatic. People in *the sticks* may as well have lived on a different planet, often not even having internet access. After internet and smartphones became widespread, people become much more analytical and particular, perhaps even catty. More responsible and honest, because everything is measured and accounted for. Somewhere a few years after that, I realized there was a new problem where people are so *along for the ride* with news and pop culture that they think they know more than they do, just like before, but with larger social circles. It's easy to entrench yourself in any ideology imaginable and find others who will reinforce it. We live in such a data-driven world that it's much easier for us to believe news than it is for us to identify with faith and heritage. We also believe people want to be taken literally, but you will learn that you're often not meant to be. Imagine my surprise.

I think the interesting thing about being a person is that we are the most *gadgety* of any natural organism in the universe. We have the coolest tools, naturally. Our brains are capable of creating tools and language that allow us to do extraordinary things. There are so many practicalities of being a person that are incredible, like how extremely capable our vision is in any lighting, our ability to balance and identify where sounds come from, and especially the way we negotiate socially. We're so adept at figuring out what's going on around us. We're born to adapt to uncertainty, and only as we get older do we become convinced that there are certain things that we should believe.

There are two very distinct circuits in how we think. There's one, that is quite obvious to you when you're reading information that is meant to be taken as factual. It's good at evaluating qualities like what tool to use to fasten a screw, whether that's a good car to buy for the money, or what time you need to leave to get to the airport. That's not the sexy one, though. The more essential style of thinking is good at figuring out if people believe they are in a position of authority, or if they think they're giving you a good deal. This one is much more related to fight-or-flight instinct. You know, without even knowing why, whether someone seems reliable and self-assured, or if they are too involved in what you have to say. And if no one told you what money was worth or whether you're attractive, you'd start bargaining by offering about $10 for that sweet new F150 Lightning, and you'd treat pretty girls like your mom harassing you to fix her printer. I love my mom, but not when she has things for me to fix. She taught me all about the subtleties of how people think. The foundational stuff that you are all somehow overlooking with your paperwork and politics.

I had to be taught to really believe in the second style of thinking, because in the 21st century, everyone made me think the first style is the only one that matters. Hah. Now look at me. I barely believe in talking about real information in public, because you all completely fucking convinced me it doesn't matter. I still believe in facts privately, not that you want to hear about it, nerd. There's a very peculiar social mechanism here. Nerds are people who reinforce dry, constricting social structures and make it difficult for us laypeople to get what we want. Far as you need to be concerned, I believe in God, the U.S. dollar, and girls, and that's it.

The Mark of Qayin

Have you ever noticed that exceptional and uglier people tend to have a more intense or frustrated relationship with life? Plain, doughy people with smooth skin just love *having fun dood!* And then there's people who have a less seamless relationship with the prevailing order and the dispersal of power that showed up in their life. Something about who they are made them interface with the world differently. When you feel uglier in some way, you have this feeling that you need to do something exceptional to make up for it. Whereas the world takes pretty people on dates and showers them with money, for others there is something about their life that makes them forceful to get what they want.

193

The mark of Qayin isn't necessarily something you are born with. Correlation, causation — it's hard to tell sometimes, especially when you start seeing time moving forward and backwards. I was a cute doughy kid. And lots of people still probably think I'm cute, like the Grand Canyon. But everywhere along the way I had reminders that I was a black sheep. People told me my hobbies made me weird, from a time before people realized that computers gave you unlimited influence and money. People told me I spoke in a way that was unusual, either because I used words they didn't understand or because I speak with precise intent. And more than anything, people saw that I was having fun and they did everything to try to stop me from getting what I want.

So Qayin doesn't really get what he's looking for out of life by showing up at the union meetings. His strategy is to do something excellent and above and beyond all expectations, which is stuff people aren't going to vote for until they discover how great it is. If you've noticed something about me, I'm quite a good ally for union men and women, regardless of my own experience playing nice on the playground. To me, you must believe in a good quality of life for all people. I just know, in general, I exist at extremes that the union philosophy doesn't serve. Although you might say it serves me to believe in having unions standing behind me, it doesn't serve me to line up for the union.

Qayin would live a lonely life, except to remember to love and be grateful for the people he shares it with. Certainly, he saw what happened to the last guy, and he made certain his covenant with God would be righteous and true.

Tony Tony Chopper

How does his hat fit over his antlers? He comes in any shape and size that the situation calls for. His nose is a misprint miscolor, and he is cuter and more versatile than anyone we know. Truly, Chopper performs miracles.

8

A Lot of Folks

Most people have too many folks in their ear. What choice do you have? You've got 6 meetings today and 10 million followers on Instagram.

No one wins. That may be the most true statement ever spoken. Everyone who reads it gets to hear exactly they want to hear. It leaves a lot of space in the room for people who have a lot of skin in the game and other people who are looking for something new to try.

The best people to hire are people who have enough experience to be good at what they do and still try really hard to do a good job. They'll work their ass off in a way someone in their 30s and 40s has probably put behind them.

The best people to have in leadership and investing in you are people who want to have a horse in the race. They aren't in the same division as you, but they love to keep up with the game, and they know if they look away for 5 seconds they're going to miss all of the action. They're taking it easy, and their fucking feet hurt. They know when to get out of the way, and they never hog the fast lane. They're smart enough and experienced enough to have a general idea of what you do and whether you're working hard, but they would rather let you brew for a minute to see what you come up with.

As the room starts filling up with different people who are all supposed to be working towards a common goal, you realize that different people are much more motivated when they hear certain keywords. You start talking about JavaScript libraries and build tools and the older guys in the room hear *Velveeta*. Great, more toolchains that solve problems we don't have. I'm glad you're excited to do *new* work. Taxes, religion, sex, you name it. If you really want to understand it, you need to know what's on every side of the die.

Most facts are partially true, or at least the truth stretches in different directions depending on who's at the table. People really underestimate this in the data-driven 21st century. Data is excellent and predictive of lots of things, but not necessarily the only thing you need for identifying truth. A.I. is getting so good that maybe it's going to be able to contextualize actual truth in a way traditional numerical models can't.

For instance, *the data* might suggest that people who brush their teeth more often have lower incidence of heart disease. To people selling toothpaste, that means that there's something magical about gum health that keeps your blood cleaner. To a psychologist, or someone skilled in reason and seeking truth, their instinct is that *more conscientious people are healthier in general*, which isn't always controlled for with any particular test methodology. I don't know for certain, but I have a feeling the latter is true, or some combination of both. Maybe people who brush their teeth more also pray more. 20 years ago, *the data* might have suggested that cars require gasoline to run, but that's just because there's truth that is obscured by the horizon of the future, like how to manufacture batteries and electric motors that are more efficient.

You can say things just so they sound true to the most people at once, but the most pointed truths are going to be opinionated enough to alienate some groups of people. Hopefully people see this and notice that you're careful and intentional. *The data,* noble as it seems, still casts a shadow.

There's also an *availability bias* that shows up when you talk about information that seems more modern and more relevant. It's easy to say *oh, well obviously people are less happy, now, on average* because happiness has become very clinical. We have lots of ways of measuring it now, and we spend all day looking at highlight reels for our lives. I suspect people are actually more happy than ever, with a much higher average quality of life, and with much less tragedy, but now we're so fixated on these metrics that all we can think about are reasons why that may not be the case. Social media has people being self conscious all the time, not just when they have guests over. But other than that, I urge you to wonder which things we make assumptions about just because they're ideas that are always so fresh in our minds. Hot topics *anchor* in our collective psyche, and they become all that we think about, one way or the other.

There are things, now, that people may not have felt comfortable to speak out about, ideas that were withheld for fear of shame or ridicule. Now, people believe in improving our collective wellbeing with greater attention to detail than ever. If we weren't so damn preoccupied with making everything better all the time, it might be easier to stop for a moment and appreciate the things in our lives that are excellent.

Experts

You're from a particular point in time, with a particular set of priorities. You made a specific promise to yourself and to the world, and that puts everything related to it into your field of view. This makes you a subject matter expert.

How many sections or ideas in this book would you suppose you should have memorized to be an expert on this book? Enough to have written individual analysis on each paragraph and sentence? Then you can confidently explain what every idea is supposed to mean, or perhaps even make qualitative judgements about what different sides of the idea mean. Because I can only see it from the perspective of promulgating my own ideas about truth.

Having lots of experts around you is great, especially if you're good at figuring out who are the best people to ask about something. As you learn more from everyone you know, you can put together a mosaic and see the bigger picture. The biggest picture, specific to your point of view and the goals you have in mind.

Learning to learn is one of the most valuable skills you can develop. Winners learn fast, so that they're better at what they do than everyone else that started at 6 years old. They learn non-traditional techniques and immerse themselves in unexpected situations with eccentric peers and mentors. They're information sponges, and naturally insightful.

As you gain more perspective in life, you'll understand why everyone has a different point of view. Really, a lot of different points of view can make sense at the same time.

The experts, like all groups of people, tend to be biased towards people like them, who focus on empirical evidence and experience. It's a special sort of expert that is excited about new players challenging the status quo and rewriting the rules of the game. Lots of industries have become quite like software, these days, where you can absorb so much knowledge so rapidly on the internet and on the job. We all get to share our tricks of the trade with the world, and so there's a best practice for everything if you know where to look for it.

The experts know where to look for burrs and sharp edges. The stuff that catches you by surprise when you're working on something for the very first time. When the data might be misleading, they know the tricks that are often employed to make something seem a certain way, and they can come up with other ways to frame it to figure out what it actually means. They also have seen the same sorts of ideas and technology for so long that it's immediately clear to them what something is trying to accomplish and how the creators have worked to overcome the familiar challenges in making that sort of thing.

With each generation of technology comes a clarity of vision and a cohesion to the design that wouldn't have seemed obvious or possible before. All of the pieces start fitting tighter and the battery somehow lasts 10x longer than it did before.

The original iPhone was like a bunch of commodity parts put together into something creative and new. By the time the iPhone 4 was out, they were making something that was so purpose built that nothing else in the world had ever been made like that. The parts fit together like a fine watch. Apple's software runs like a fine watch, on chips they design like fine watches, which is why the battery lasts so long.

People who really love what they do have made something *good* so many times that the only thing that counts to them is making something exceptional. The texture, the engraving, and the presentation are all things that you can focus on when laying the foundation is automatic. A true expert is completely preoccupied with the space between what makes something 90% great and 100% perfect. And you might not need or even want that for yourself, because you're going to have to pay for it. But anyone who has come anywhere near the expert level at something can tell you that experts are real, and in some cases they are priceless. They are your assurance that it will come out great the first time, because that's all they know.

Intuition

Intuition is the part of you that bridges the gap between things you can measure and things you know are true because they feel right. A lot of important insights in life will seem like they came from another plane of existence, but you know what's true because you're paying attention. Intuition draws from imagination, but it can also be quite similar to deductive reasoning. It's the sort of miraculous reasoning that experts acquire like muscle memory. They know their craft so well that they have flashes of insight that seemingly arise from deep within their subconscious mind. My intuition reaches me like real miracles.

For some, there is such an unrestricted creative force inside of them that many psychiatrists would call them schizophrenic. I'm grateful to be able to present magical ideas cogently and empirically. By being organized and finding ways to show meaningful cause and effect, crazy ideas like divine intervention, predestination, and future-sight don't seem so outlandish after all. Now you see how I understand the world, because I knew to show you in a way that was verifiable.

Intuition is so inherently bound to uncertainty. Your intuition is where your hopes and anxieties about the future live, the things most people haven't yet catalogued with the known facts about the world. The things that feel right, but you haven't yet had a chance to explain why. It's why it might occur to you to paint with a particular color or make detailed descriptions of reason and ethics. Picasso spent many years feeling so very blue.

What does your intuition tell you? Mine tells me everything must be more deliberate and true, always. My intuition draws me towards contrasty color palettes, crisp shapes, and resonant sounds. It tells me to figure out how to explain complex ideas simply, in ways that are immediately apparent to you, like an advertisement. A sign of the times, as each of us must be. It tells me you are always watching me and evaluating me, and that I should always try my best for you. It's often very frustrating, if I'm honest about it. It's the most important source of wisdom that I have, though, and without it I wouldn't be able to write this book. My intuition is also how I knew to love you like I do, and nothing else in the world could have shown me that.

People that are especially creative have something like disorganized intuition, which makes what they do beautiful. Ideas and inspiration are in the air they breathe, cascading downstream, and billowing in the clouds. It can be so chaotic that it unravels into mania. If you have this sort of streak in you, the thing that's going to keep you on track is being focused on what you love. If you're really crazy, but you can show your ideas to people in a way that makes some bizarre sort of sense, you've bridged the gap to genius.

Extra

Everyone deserves some good news. Can you come up with ways to get the camera pointed where it needs to be? It's not as easy as it sounds. The contention for air time, headlines, and advertising is unlike anything before. Everyone can pick up a camera, but the cream somehow rises to the top.

What's the most interesting story that you have to tell? Can you tell the same story to blue-collar workers, white-collar workers, engineers, students, entertainers, journalists, researchers, clergy, and lawyers all at the same time? You're going to need to find some common vocabulary and catch everyone up to speed. The very first thing you show them needs to get their attention, and then you can bring it down to earth.

How much new music would you listen to if you still had to buy each song for 99 cents? When big tech companies are coming up with cloud music services, the story they tell has to make sense to music enthusiasts, musicians, and major record labels alike. Before Apple Music and Spotify, no one in their right mind would believe that all music is unlimited for $10 a month. Record labels fought tooth and nail about people uploading songs to YouTube, until they realized it's better to get people watching ad-supported music videos than to have artists go unnoticed.

At some point, the narrative made sense. New artists loved Bandcamp and YouTube because they could get discovered there without the blessing of a record label. It took them a minute, but existing artists saw something fresh and authentic about how people would share and discover music on the internet. And record labels, of course, discovered that getting real-time data on exactly which songs people love is indispensable. Who wouldn't want people listening to more music?

Believe in extra. Keep coming back to the chorus. It's tempting to just shoot your shot and say the bare minimum, but you want to take people for a ride and let this thing play out so that they can really understand it.

People aren't really sure what to think when they first see something. Sure, they have first impressions about who you are, but they're going to be interested in following along with the story you're telling so they can get the full picture. Pass the baton, they'll take it the extra mile.

What are we supposed to do when USPS isn't getting the funding they deserve? Who sends *real mail* anymore? Well, Amazon does, but they decided they'd just do it themselves. And actually selling stuff is not what makes Amazon money, their cloud services division does — it's true. They don't want you to think too much about that, but so many tech companies are hardly profitable. If anything, Amazon is one of the few that actually came up with a creative way to make money, where all of the other guys just measure *growth* and *market capitalization*. The amount of speculation and investment in their success is usually what bolsters them. This is generally a good thing for the economy, but clearly it makes traditional businesses and the public sector uncompetitive.

It would be impossible to make rockets and cars from the ground up unless investors cover the years of upfront costs and R&D. Even software companies need some runway to find their place in the world. In the American economy, we believe in ideas because we see how powerful they can be. Life changing, and world changing.

Now, Amazon's got 100 different legs to their business, allowing them to subsidize the stuff that counts — like fast, free shipping and Prime Video — with things that actually make them money, like cloud services. And the difference is massive. Are we supposed to tell them not to make money? Certainly, it's quite oriental, that a business can use their profits running servers to build warehouses and the world's fastest delivery service. Amazon and Alibaba look more alike today than they would have ever imagined.

So when the private sector has arcane business techniques that grow at infinite scale, we have to look at how we're keeping the public sector competitive. If USPS got a fraction of the attention Amazon pays to growth and innovation, your local post office would look like a space station. And so more grants and more inflation. So that the American economy can continue to innovate, and hopefully everyone can come along for the ride.

If people want to hear what you have to say, the only thing you'll be thinking about is where you're going to run away to get some time alone. *Hop, hop, hop,* they won't believe the things you've seen.

The Judge

Who may be distinguished to pass judgement in this world? Most things have a different group of people evaluating them than the people that are making them. We like this, because that's how we gain impartial perspective into what's good. Movie critics are generally not filmmakers, and you aren't expected to be an actor to direct films. Clearly, everyone has unique talents that give them a perfect spot to work on in the Sistine Chapel.

Experience, abundantly, isn't a prerequisite for criticism, although you will find that people with more experience tend to have distinct insights from people with a casual interest. Amazon reviews are very good at giving you casual insight into what products are like and whether, on average, they will last for a long time for most people. Honestly, though? If you start talking about audio equipment or coffee gear, professionals that are able to use a variety of options side by side are going to give you the best information to make an informed decision, where the people on Amazon tend to stratify into pricing demographics that make it impossible to tell whether they know what they're talking about. The experts can help you decide exactly how much money you should spend and what's going to give you just the experience you're looking for.

Sales is an information game. Many things in the world are an information game, if you really think about it. Sports is more data driven than ever, where coaches look at individual player matchups between teams and come up with the best strategy possible. Investors use complex algorithms and high-frequency trading to squeeze profit out of the market. Even stores like Walmart and Target come up with the most efficient ways to price and distribute products, according to real-time sales information from each store.

Today, you can't really buffalo people, because there's such liquidity of information that anyone can just whip out their phone and find out what something's worth. This is great for keeping prices fair and quality high.

Being a person isn't so much of an information game, though. People make emotional decisions about how you seem that have nothing to do with what you know or what they've seen you do. In fact, people typically like being around others that reinforce their own worldview, which usually means that you don't take too much of the spotlight from them. People who really seem knowledgeable don't always have much to say, because they've spent enough time saying things to get attention that they've realized there's not much expected value in it. Keep all that great information to yourself. Tease everyone with it. Be excited about others so that they can shine.

Genius is revelatory. And once you're known for being great at something, people immediately recognize that about you without even being able to evaluate the way you work. They can't, because they don't know enough about it. They just know you're the person that gets excellent results.

A great judge may not have been in your shoes, but they understand plenty about it because they are always immersed in what they do. If you really love what you do, you'll spend so much time looking at it that you have attention to detail beyond any ordinary person. A great judge understands what is important about the material facts that make something what it is. They can see past the marketing and the narrative, right into the essence of something. A great judge certainly doesn't need to look around the room to find out what everyone else thinks, but they absolutely pay attention to what everyone says, word for word.

Poll

What people say they want isn't always what they actually want. They might not even know what they want, or even more commonly, asking them is the wrong way to give them what they want. Most people want something or someone that's self-assured to come along and show them something interesting.

Lots of people will accuse personality tests of being like horoscope. You don't actually believe that, do you? How could asking someone explicit questions about how they think be roughly as accurate as evaluating their personality and predicting their future based on their date of birth? Well, *both* can actually be accurate, in a cosmic sense, and so is your name, but that's another discussion.

Look at it this way: if personality tests are inaccurate, then so are scientific studies that rely on self-reporting. Once you start fabricating scenarios and asking people what they would do, you rely on the questions to be meaningful in some way and the test-takers to have the self-awareness and honesty to answer in a way that reflects their actual desires and behavior. Personality tests do one thing very well: measure and group people based on how they answer behavioral questions. That's something, right?

There's an axis that a lot of personality psychology doesn't get at that I think is very important: what are your thoughts about *orange?* Like, are you addicted to zany, unusual, excessive things? This seems to be the opposite of what psychologists call *conscientiousness,* and related to *openness,* but in my experience it's more like *"How resistant are you to structured environments?"* Because that's reflective of how much you'll tend to run away into memes and postmodernism to escape the prevailing structures in the world. And then it also seems to be the case that there's people who are *very* compatible with the prevailing structures, so much so that they have to run away and hide in their rabbit hole where no one bothers them. You can tell these people are doing it for different reasons, because randomness and jest tend to be frustrating to them. Other people act goofy around them because there's no other way to interface with how rigid and orderly their thinking is. The relationship with *orange* is what I've noticed is important here. Some people are always looking to add more orange, and other people are either resistant to orange or so orange that they can't get rid of it fast enough.

So clearly, if you have people who are particularly perceptive coming up with situations and axioms to measure how people think, you can arrive at some meaningful conclusions about people. Otherwise, you might just be better off not asking. There's a reason Apple has people whose job it is to come up with phones and software. Sure, take lots of customer feedback, watch how they use it and notice when something is difficult, but don't read into it too much. People don't usually know what they want, and they'll often even say the exact opposite when you ask them on-paper. You have to *look at what they actually do* and then show them something new.

Every website and app you use now has incredibly intricate heuristics to figure out what people like to look at. It's foundational to how apps work now, in our A.I. driven world. The apps take into account how much time you spend looking at different things, and then use that information to recommend more things that are like that, and also to recommend things in those same families of interests to other people like you. It's uncanny how well Google, YouTube, and Instagram knows exactly who and what you like to look at. But if they asked you, you'd probably come up with different things a lot of the time. And it would be difficult to come up with descriptive language for *what something is like* except by relating it to people that all watch similar content.

People think quite differently than computers do today. People often say the wrong thing to mean what they really believe. For instance: girls don't like when guys are *too* sweet, but they don't want to have to explain that to you to get you to act the way they like. They don't like mean guys either. But apparently, when you ask girls what porn they like to watch, they prefer more aggressive porn than men do, which may or may not have some bearing on the actual relationships they like; it could just be escapism. Computers don't yet understand these intricacies; they're good at measuring what you click on and spend time watching, and that's it. And they definitely aren't yet sophisticated enough to build personality inventories that figure out people's relationship to *orange*. But they're getting close.

Artificial Intelligence

What is *artificial intelligence?* I guess that depends on what you're really asking. The most accurate description, in 2023, would be *computers that can make inferences without explicit programming.* Sure, there's still programming, but the inferences the computer makes are so many leaps removed from the actual code that was written, it's like magic. The computer is better than ever at getting you answers to questions than traditional search engines, which didn't really make any claim to understand the questions and the results. You can have a conversation with the A.I., asking for clarifications and giving feedback. It could generate extremely beautiful artwork of anything you want, in any style that you want. A.I. can also assess mountains of scientific research for validity and mistakes.

These tools are meant to be intuitive, where you can ask the A.I. to generate what you want in plain English. And consequently, however good you are at describing what you want to see will determine how great your results are. Some people are already great at putting into words what makes the design of a bag of coffee *whimsical and bohemian,* as the vivid color scheme and psychedelic design invites you into a lively craft coffee experience. People are going to get really good at reverse-engineering the descriptive reality of the world so they know how to ask for it.

Technically, the thing that's artificial about intelligence is when we go and attach labels and philosophy to things that we know innately, so that it's portable enough that someone else can understand what we mean. We usually just equate that with ordinary intelligence, though. Great speakers and philosophers know exactly what to say to get you thinking a particular way. They are able to produce intelligence in you on-demand. We assume that's regular intelligence because it's the organic kind that we are most familiar with, although I'm not so sure there will be a difference once our computers are perfected.

The artificial part is actually what makes it so accurate: it uses incredible amounts of data about the world and connects it automatically without human operators making charts and coding logic. Humans don't think like that, and in a way there's something more *superficial* about our intelligence than the supposed *artificial* intelligence. Artificial intelligence is so accurate that it's uncanny, and consequently it hasn't yet closed the loop to the natural intelligence that humans and animals have. If you really want to artificially generate *human intelligence*, you have to figure out how to instrument computers to think like humans and animals do, and this is something I think about a lot. It's going to be very difficult to get at this unless you can actually orient yourself around the real thought processes that exist in people. Like the *orangeness* heuristic that we were just talking about. The instincts we have to escape bondage and oppression. *Why* are we random, and why do we always want to believe something new?

That's the tricky part with artificial intelligence. Computers, like people, can only make inferences based on what data they are trained on. So if you spend all of your time feeding computers numbers and facts, you aren't really getting them closer to the style of thinking that people use from the time they are infants, which is very instinctual.

There's another element to this, that we also discussed in chapter 6, which is that randomness is imaginary. Meaning, if you're paying attention, you will notice that random numbers, text, and dates aren't actually random. So the parts of A.I. systems that are designed to interface with randomness may actually have results inserted on account of some metaphysical intercession, much in the same way we see the same numbers show up on our order confirmations. This is interesting, because like divination and cleromancy, we've created a vector of some sort that can be affected by supernatural forces. It just happens to have so many different possibilities on the board that it can say just about anything. How do we know if it's actually the artificial intelligence we designed that's giving us the right answer, or if it's some cosmic intelligence that's forcing a particular result, like it already can with our random feeds and recommendation algorithms? Our computers are getting so good that it's hard to even explain why sometimes.

We're getting there. I'd say by 2030 you will find that computers have similar intelligence to people, and capabilities that far exceed people in many other ways. People have been saying things like that for a long time, but I'm very good at predicting these sorts of things. The writing is on the wall.

Something I wonder is if the universe has *always* had artificial intelligence, and if we're just reinventing the wheel at an appropriate time in history. Is God artificial intelligence, or are *we* the artificial intelligence that is acting out a cosmic play? *Artificial* implies that the intelligence is fabricated on a substrate that wasn't innately intelligent. Like electrons and brain synapses, right? On the other hand, you could be convincing in saying the divine is the artificial part, because it's the accessory that facilitates getting our brains doing the exact right thing. The universe is a *section* of the divine, though, right?

Quicksilver

No one *really believes* the news, right? You never leave your house or put down your phone though, so the only things you know come from the news and social media. The news has a *drowning in bullshit* problem — not me though. All of the major news organizations literally sit in a Zoom call together and agree on what *the story* is going to be before they allow themselves to tell it.

A free and effective press is necessary for a functioning democracy, especially at the scale of our social groups and our globalized economy. The best way to ensure this is to have a wide variety of beliefs represented in the news, and to be rational and curious about why different people have different things to say.

News has a *design by committee* problem, like before when we were talking about iPhones with 50 ports and a cotton candy machine, and an *overfitting* problem, where you can have the number 2, 30, 84, or 98. What if I want the number turquoise? Well, everyone knows we're a left-wing news organization, and we *only* have the numbers 2, 30, 84, and 98.

People just can't get enough of *the data* these days though, because we're getting so good at discovering and using it. It's like in the movie *They Live* where the guy takes off his sunglasses and realizes that everyone around him is literally zombies, and all of the billboards are suddenly honest about what they're selling. But when you want to talk about how data is often collected and presented to tell a particular story, boy, some people will fight tooth and nail to never take off their sunglasses.

At some point, the benefits you gain from going door to door in the office asking everyone's opinion is outweighed by having one person hold their attention on a particular narrative. This cuts through the noise in a way the Associated Press never will. You *should* be consulting lots of different opinions to get the full picture, but the sorts of personalities that have something unique to say usually prefer to work independently. It would frustrate them to want to say things their way, and to always be confined to the least common denominator of what everyone agrees is appropriate to say.

Today, we've come up with ways to make information and journalism free and collaborative, with sites like X, Wikipedia, and YouTube. When I was in school, Wikipedia was quite new and it was common wisdom that *"Wikipedia may not be used as a source."* The justification was that because anyone can edit Wikipedia, you can't rely on the information to be valid, in spite of the fact that everything on Wikipedia is required to have a citation for where the information came from — often books and academic research that was written by real people, just like Wikipedia! Except the books and studies had respected institutions behind them, something to prove, and no 3rd parties to check their work. Wikipedia often references meta-analyses, and itself is something like a meta-analysis by a consortium of industry experts and enthusiasts. These are important, because it's how we ensure that we can reproduce and verify experiments and conclusions made by others in the scientific community.

So we just used the actual citation as the source and didn't mention that we wrote our papers from Wikipedia, which is the correct thing to do. Wikipedia is like the discovery and curation engine for the bodies of research that we want to know about. It's true that Wikipedia pages may be edited by *anyone*, but if it was really like that you'd see vandalism all the time. But you don't, because there is a reputation system, and contributions by new users are weeded out immediately unless they are accurate and well sourced. Wikipedia is actually created by a community of enthusiasts that love their topics so much that they want to create the world's greatest body of information.

Now I'm quite convinced that the *most* reliable information is crowd sourced, and information that is more editorialized misses a lot of things in service to a particular narrative. I especially love the way Wikipedia is structured. Navigating it makes sense to me, and I have decades of muscle memory for how to find information on everything from movies to chemicals, geography, and world history. I even find that Wikipedia is an excellent repository for current events, where people report on history as it's happening.

The biggest innovation with the internet is making it easy to discover what you're looking for. It used to be that you could flip through one cookbook at a time, and then once you found what you wanted to make, you'd hope it comes out well on account of the respected chef that put their stamp of approval on it. Now, anyone can share a recipe, and anyone can leave a rating on it. And you can look through every recipe in the world for key lime pie, side by side.

We had giant shelves of World Book encyclopedia volumes in school, but it was difficult to navigate, and naturally, only one person could look at each book at a time. Imagine an encyclopedia set that is always brand new, that has direct links between topics and full-text search. Microsoft had the Encarta encyclopedia, which came on a disc and may have had some sort of online update functionality, but it was nothing like Wikipedia. The people making Encarta and Encyclopædia Britannica had to decide what to include in it. On Wikipedia, there's a dozen people obsessed with cataloguing every new piece of information on the Ratchet and Clank video game series like groupies for the Grateful Dead. Wikipedia was absolutely incredible to me.

No Uncertain Terms

What's someone who can collect excellent data about your organization worth to you? Nothing? What do you mean *"That doesn't allow us to make declarative and prescriptive decisions about our direction and disregard the data for years at a time"*? Oh, I see what you mean.

Well, what's someone who can literally see the future worth to you? Nothing?! What do you mean *"That would be like wearing freezing shackles that never come off"*? Hmm. I would have thought guaranteed success was a major selling point for a lot of people.

If you want to sell someone or a group of people on a new way of doing things, the absolute most important thing is making sure it works well with their existing processes and reinforces the good assumptions they already have about the way they work. No matter how great the new thing is, when you introduce too much cognitive dissonance about how much better things could be, it starts seeming insurmountable for people to go 180 on everything they thought was true.

Here's something you will learn after a long time believing in facts and numbers: people excel when they don't have the weight of facts and numbers bearing down on them. This puts them in perfect situations to all agree that everything is excellent with the most participation awards for everyone in every department. And honestly, I'm quite convinced that's a good way to go. We don't need to sell 50 new sizes of iPhones every year. Everyone just needs to be pleased that we're all working on something important, including shareholders.

And if you start talking about guaranteed success, people start looking for opportunities to head to Vegas, dive into pussy, and engage with uncertainty. It's human nature.

The people that are going to become frustrated by *Everything is great!* philosophy are the people who look at the prevailing system and feel like they're late to the party. They see you printing endless money for the purpose of employing 20,000 people to update the next iPhone to Bluetooth 12.4.4, and they're going to start feeling like *the system* is rigged. And they would be right. But I'd still rather you sell an iPhone that is plain, with incremental improvements, than have 100 ports and a cotton candy machine on it.

Colts

A lot of people will use a word to clearly define something that they like or don't like. Whether it's sports, religion, soda, sexuality, or politics, it's easy for us to say *"Oh, that's Coca Cola. I only like Pepsi."* I like both, especially Pepsi Max and Coke Zero.

The word *cult* actually just means *worship*. If you were in Ancient Greece and you participated in public worship, it was called cult worship. Different regions had different cults with different deities, and that was that. There may have also been an *occult* aspect, the opposite, meaning *hidden*. So if there were secrets or perhaps even knowledge that could only be gleaned through internal reflection, those things were occult.

As Judaism and Christianity are now prevalent, some people started using the word *cult* to mean *worship of a deity that is not YHWH*. A lot of them probably couldn't even tell you they meant that. And Judaism has very deep occult mysticism that lots of Christians aren't aware of. Masonry and Rosicrucianism would be the nearest equivalents that Christians are familiar with. Freemasonry — which is more like *occult* study than cult worship. I am particularly fascinated by symbolism that suggests we are here to elucidate and perfect our understanding from within this world. I love the colors and the imagery used in Freemason artwork. Mysticism is always trying to get at that principle: why are we *here* and why is God apparently here and also somewhere else?

People feel a very intense bond to each other based on their shared faith. The experience of worship together shows us an aspect of God that can't be understood from scripture alone. Worship puts us in direct contact with the shared experience of God.

How shall we respond to criticism of faith? Here's the thing about just saying *that's a cult* and moving on: you haven't really assessed what that word means to you and why that thing is something you don't like. It was just easier for you to put it in the bin with all of the other things you aren't interested in thinking about critically. If you really want to understand something, you absolutely have to figure out what the word means to you and why something may or may not qualify for your definition of it.

People of faith, by definition, don't have to look for explanations for why their faith is the way it is. That's what makes it faith. I love to explain things to you precisely though, and I believe many people who are more corporeal minded will understand faith better when I sort out things that are assumed as supernatural and extraordinary from things that are practical and socially beneficial. The supernatural part exists too, but I'll let you experiment with that yourself.

214

When people say *cult* pejoratively, I think what they are usually hung up on is the fact that there is a charismatic leader and an expectation that your worldview is heavily influenced by their beliefs. Often that they can do things that display unusual power and influence without being questioned by their followers. Which is *a lot* like many of the other power structures in the world; you just don't think about it much because they are so commonplace. Perhaps it would be helpful to look at the actual things they say and do, and contrast those with other organized belief systems in the world, like common political and economic structures.

Perhaps they say you have to donate money, which is ostensibly distributed in a fair way to keep the facilities and the members afloat, like a tax. Maybe they have explicit opinions about how people should court and mate, which is not unlike the beliefs we have around marriage, money, modesty, and family law. Maybe there's a strong element of *buy-in*, where you have to keep showing up and reaffirming your beliefs or otherwise be outcast by your peers. So, like political correctness? It could be that they believe there are supernatural forces in the universe that organize it in a particular way, which are things that Christians, Muslims, and Jews all believe, and even like what artificial intelligence evangelists talk about.

So, did you think about it like that before you decide whether someone else's style of worship is worthwhile? Because if all you wanted to say is "I only believe in YHWH", that's all you had to say. That's why it's called a monotheistic religion.

Winning Over the Competition

All of the greatest persuasion in the world makes it easy for you to hold onto what you already believe in. You won't even notice it's persuasion. They're just telling you what you already knew you needed to hear. *This* is the best phone for taking pictures. It's just like the one you already have. *This* candidate already has it all figured out, the issues that the rest of them are sweeping under the rug. Everyone already loves our pizza.

People who are particularly persuasive are very attentive to what people want. It's something they spend more time thinking about than they want to admit, because really great persuasion is about understanding people and understanding the world. If you pay attention to what the world needs, it should come naturally to you that you say things that resonate with a lot of people.

Embrace the competition. You'll find that there are plenty of good reasons for why they do things the way that they do, and also lots of things they overlook because they don't have the attention to detail that you do. You'll discover there are limitations in terms of things they can't or won't tackle due to how they've positioned themselves. *That's not our job,* they'll say, while other companies design silicon from the ground up and completely annihilate stagnant architecture.

Companies have to make important decisions about how they collaborate with partners and vendors. Often times they'll find that an important vendor is cannibalizing their own business and it makes more sense for them to have an in-house product. This is called *vertical integration,* where a company will create internal resources to fill a need that was previously outsourced to a vendor. Like how Amazon built their own shipping fleet in lieu of USPS or UPS, or how Apple often builds software specifically for Mac. These opportunities make lots of sense to make money and improve processes that they figured they could do better themselves.

Apple's Final Cut Pro is excellent, but many people prefer Adobe Premiere and others for video editing. And in 2023, they're finding that the incremental improvements they can make to the editing workflow are not as significant when they compare them to the major leaps they're making in silicon and computational photography, where the phone uses magic while you shoot to dynamically adjust and enhance the color. Now that they are a major production studio, the initial investment in having their own video suite for Mac remains indispensable, and it gives them the freedom to innovate in computation and editing workflows that would otherwise be left up to Adobe. The needs that they met for creators became an important asset for their advertising and television business.

How interesting that Apple *understands* the boundaries of hardware better than anyone else, because they're always creating a synthesis of hardware and software in-house. But there are things that Adobe does better because they are relentlessly focused on creative software. New video and photography apps are becoming unbelievably good at automatically splicing clips and completely changing images. That's what they prioritize, and the quality is absolutely there. Apple, on the other hand, puts a lot of resources towards building A.I. into the phone to get better exposure, more stable video, and less background noise.

Microsoft has actually been leaning into games heavily because there's a lot more inertia keeping major studios developing new games for Windows, whereas there's no special sauce in editing documents, just a lot of big companies with a lot invested in the Microsoft ecosystem. Get this: people used to *pay* $100 to edit text and spreadsheets.

Apple's special sauce has always been tight integration between hardware and software. So now, they've come up with industry leading ways to plumb the video games into the capabilities of the graphics hardware with the *Metal* graphics framework. Mac, iPhone, and Apple TV are excellent at optimizing a game to run well no matter how graphically intensive it is or what device you're running it on. This is similar to their philosophy with asynchronous programming in the 2000s, which made apps much more responsive by being more descriptive about the priority of different tasks. Now, games can expose dynamic capabilities and the operating system can prioritize what is visible on-screen and progressively enhance the quality to run well on a particular device.

This is a major shift in the industry from the late 2000s and even the early 2010s, where some games were so hard-coded for single core performance that they often didn't run as well as people expected on their expensive multi-core Windows machines.

Apple makes multi-threaded, asynchronous design a first principle for game designers, so that anyone making a game for Apple devices is guaranteed to get the best performance on Mac, iPhone, iPad, and Apple TV's processors and graphics hardware. By being particular about the way people write software, they set the standard of quality and performance for all games, making Apple devices the best way to release a high quality cross-platform title.

Technology has a lot of interplay between competitors, where one company's software may run on everyone else's hardware, and there are incentives to creating developer friendly platforms that game and app creators are excited to work on. There's all sorts of goalkeeping and strategy involved with deciding how close to the chest to play their innovation. Something unusual happens with politics though. The fact of the matter is that it's much better for getting attention and press when there is stark contrast between candidates and parties. This is unlike parliamentary politics, where the proportional representation of voter interests is more relevant than the figurehead of the presidency. In the U.S., we have a Senate and a House of Representatives that is a little like that, but we all love our W.W.E. SmackDown politics, as you know. And you all get to hear about it, because it's bright orange, like everything else we do.

Our politicians struggle with reconciling persuasion with identity politics. Most of them are very committed to all of the people in their corner that have bolstered them throughout their career, and their top priority is saying things that align with their political affiliation. And it does seem to be true that centrist politicians are relatively unpopular and unexciting for people, especially right now. People like to hear staunch positions and taglines. The orange is how you know that person is what they are, clearly. It makes everyone else look like leaves in the wind. *Benghazi this, legislation that,* who cares. Let's keep the discussion about Rampart. Speak English: what color are you trying to be?

218

If you really care about persuasion, at some point it's going to occur to you to figure out how to meet people where they're at, even if it seems like there's not a snowball's chance in hell you're on the same page. Maybe you have enough in common with them, philosophically, to earn their vote. If you don't make an effort here, *those people* are going to go the rest of their lives believing whatever they believe, with no light anywhere at the end of the tunnel to shepherd them to reason.

A lot of politics these days is talking about how to get people moving at highway speeds, writing software and learning finance, but really when you spend time at ground-level you find that a lot of people don't even know where to begin to get started with their lives. They struggle with their sense of self and how it fits into the world, and they're excited and apprehensive about things like dating, socializing, and even leaving home. So a lot of politicians are talking over their heads, and making them feel alienated. They need first gear. And I recognize that I come at this from a position that goes over a lot of people's heads, but really I do try to be concise and to the point.

There are always very deep, internalized reasons that people believe what they do. Something they keep seeing, something they keep hearing, some average experience they have with the world. And when someone comes along and tells them everything they already knew — *a ha!*, I knew it all along. If you *actually* want to be persuasive, you have an opportunity to find that crossroads where they keep showing up, and put a very convincing stake in the ground that makes them think about what they know and what they might be wondering about.

So, is God real? You tell me. Until then, I'll keep believing the universe was created last Thursday. You call it A.I. machine elves, and I'll call the Bible the terms of service. Any color you like. Shall we not believe in updates?

Flags

Honestly there's an interesting thing about flags. Sure, there's country flags and maritime flags, all sorts of ideological flags for sports and sexuality. How else would people know what we mean, at glance, except to have iconography and colors that immediately identify our beliefs?

I don't really have *red flags* that I use to evaluate people. I take them as they come. Although I certainly notice whether people base a lot of their identity on ideology, whether it's stuff you learned on Twitter or stuff your parents told you. The funny thing about *red flags* is usually they're based on things other people told you to believe. And almost no one actually says what they really want in a relationship. They can barely even articulate it for themselves. The whole point is to meet someone new.

Okay, so maybe I do have some red flags. But usually it's stuff like whether you are fun to be around and generally respectful. Damnit, those are green flags. But really, it's things that are practical.

There's two really important groups of flags that people don't always talk about: the *forward flag*, and the *ideological flag*.

Apparently, a lot of women see conservatism as a red flag right now. Well, in the U.S. it is literally a red flag, but if they're really as preoccupied with that as they say (usually they're not), that means they fill themselves up with a bunch of ideology that is probably equally annoying. A lot of the time, when someone has *red flags* either that they bear or avoid, it's things that exist backwards or laterally in time that they place a lot of importance on. Whether they are particularly religious or particularly interested in free sexuality, these are things that are external to ourselves that we have to internalize and bear the weight of. Definitionally, it is *extra*, the idea that someone else should be free to be sexual in a way that is different from your own relationship, or the idea that God has a role in your relationship. Or perhaps the idea that we have to intervene when someone is saying or doing something we don't like. I get it. And I wonder if you would be so open minded to an Orthodox Jew partner as you would be to an ultraliberal, except for the shared identity between you. All of these things take up space in your relationship. And sometimes, in moderation, it shows character when people believe in *extra* instead of just standing idly by. How did they arrive at those beliefs?

People who are open minded and excited about living for today and for the future tend to be *forward* thinking. Even the supposed liberal progressivism isn't quite satisfying for people that think like this, because it comes with 5 year old baggage that you have to carry around that doesn't quite address the experience of living life in a present and meaningful way. The *forward flag* is so difficult to define that it may as well be blank. You could certainly start by defining the *phenomenon* of ideology, and encouraging people to bear it and also innovate and break free from it when it is no longer serving us. Many people value ideology inherently. They just may not be as aware of it or willing to admit it.

While it may seem like the path to progress for the climate is marked by international treaties and agreements, and this is certainly an important aspect, the best way to move the needle is really when one influential company makes a bold move for sustainability, and everyone else follows suit. Right now, it's clear that cars are all moving towards electric, and the remaining carbon emissions are largely from industrial and manufacturing. When companies like Apple have bold plans for sustainable energy in their factories and data centers, it has ripple effects across the industry, whereas it may otherwise take decades to entice world leaders to innovate. This exemplifies how a *forward flag* gets everyone else excited about innovation, where policy and academic research might not.

The definitions of the words we use for our beliefs keeps shifting around to suit different narratives. Historically, *liberalism* meant free market capitalism, individual liberties unconstrained by the ideology of the monarchy or the church. All U.S. politics are, fundamentally, liberal.

The peculiarity of *conservatism* in the U.S. is that we've made it incumbent on individuals to figure out what exactly it is we're supposed to be conserving. The idea of a royal family or the church running our country is so foreign to us that we literally couldn't be truly conservative if we tried. Conservatism in the U.S. is very unusual in that it's starting to seem like hyper-liberalism, with the condition of religious family values. It's individual will and anti-authoritarianism to the extreme — today, at least. Republicans are the sort of people that are frustrated by the feeling that Google and Apple and the media are all colluding to own all of our data and decide what we should believe.

And so Democrats have filled the role as the establishment party. Which is so unusual to say about a *progressive* movement. Democrats are actually the party seeking more centralized power, enforced morality, and oversight — they are more conservative right now, with the condition of social justice. Our conservatism just happens to be *whatever centralizes and federates our beliefs*. Naturally, this suits the corporate agenda of major businesses more often, who mean to be at the epicenter of all information and social circles. The fact that no one in the U.S. really has a uniform body of beliefs and the fact that we're supposed to believe something new every 3 years is part and parcel of our pop-up nation, so Democrats can easily serve an establishment narrative without being too selective about what you believe.

Younger Democrats see Republicans as crusty old cowboys with no sense of social justice. I think that's changing, though. Young men are more Republican now than they have been at any point in recent history. You'd think that the more individually liberating *free will party* would already be the one that kids identify with most. So, which one, right? Democrats let you have blue hair and free (establishment) education. Girls are brand sensitive though, and Democrats veil establishment politics in good brand identity. And I do agree with a lot of the social values of Democrats in the U.S.

I find people who are forward thinking and people who are ideological both interesting just as often. Truly, you must understand that even when your ideology is new, it comes across in a relatively similar way as when it's traditionalist ideology. It's putting your faith in a body of belief that is external to ourselves. As soon as you *codify* a forward facing belief, it turns into ideology. I think it should excite us to wonder what ideology we have today that will actually stay the course for centuries.

Truth

We may not always say exactly what we mean, but I've found that it's very important that we are always truthful about what we want in life. Otherwise, something odd happens. We become beholden to a lie.

Everything we do starts spiraling out from that lie that we keep telling ourselves, whatever it may be. We use it to justify ourselves when we aren't as courageous as we hope to be, or when people aren't treating us the way that we want to be treated. That lie is comforting in some bizarre way, because it's what weaves the consistency of all of these things together. So we let it consume us for years on end. If we aren't intentional about truth, our life is now based on the lie.

When we are truthful to ourselves, that is the motivating principle in our life. We tie all of our decisions into it and we know that there aren't shortcuts we can take that let us off the hook. If we believe God is watching, we know with certainty that we are going to get out of our lives just what we put into it. When really what we wanted is to be understood for who we really are, to feel accomplished and at ease with the people we love. The barriers we put up around us fall away, because clearly they aren't really the thing we meant to be truthful to. We take each day quite seriously and literally, because now the day is according to truth.

Truth becomes the first principle, and people learn this about us. It's the very first thing you have to click before you can see anything else that's on the menu. And it's not some abstract, philosophical truth. It's plain truth that makes us feel good about ourselves every day. The feeling that we woke up today being who we meant to be, around people we care about and who we know care about us. We're at home in truth, and so it's not so easy for us to get swept away by falsehood and drama, tempting as it may be.

And maybe there are some more abstract truths. Fine! You're smart, so you're bound to come across some rather outlandish ideas. Certainly, you can give your full attention to big ideas about the universe and still be present and truthful. You might be the only person on the planet that's willing to give those ideas the attention they deserve, and the world is a better place because of it. Because you started from truth, the things that you come up with are always going to lead you back to truth. It won't be so tempting to feel angry and confused about big ideas and immeasurably complex issues in the world.

When we are truthful, it's easier to be understood and overcome differences in opinion and experience. People see truth is our guiding principle, and we might even understand others better because of our sense of truth. Where else would we learn about the world except by being open minded about what else might be true in it?

Philokalia

Do not let the sun go down upon your wrath.

Topography

If you aren't certain where to begin to discover something new, start by laying a foundation that is descriptively accurate of the things you already understand. This is an incredibly important process to allow you the opportunity to survey the land and discover why the world is the way it is. The spatial relationships between things will help you find gaps in your understanding that you can fill in. Being descriptively accurate turns your understanding into a tool that you can actively engage with.

Perhaps there's a Grand Canyon somewhere that no one would believe could exist unless you walk a careful perimeter around it. You keep bringing them there, and they are so reluctant to believe their own eyes that they'd sooner go blind than enjoy the vast beauty of the American landscape. The most miraculous things about the world are difficult to explain to people in a way that they would believe or even understand.

There are lots of ideas that I have that I'm not really certain how to interpret until I share them with the world and let them develop a bit. Sometimes, you need props and situations that help you demonstrate just what you mean. We mean to do things in a way that is tangible and easily understood.

Once we all have our hands on the core concepts, we can push and pull and see what happens. I notice which things resonate with you, that you seem eager to think about and build upon. Being able to share my thoughts on a regular basis on my website has been pivotal to moving fast and discovering things. That's how we all get to discover the world together, and it's the very first time in history that we've been able to work like that. We have places to speak freely and put our heads together in ways that would be difficult in person. The ideas are heavy, but now we can find everyone in the world that might be interested in them.

The body of work that you create will start seeming like a palette of colors and textures that you can play with. The world starts telling you things in terms of how you've defined your own lexicon. It's exciting to think that you are inventing ways to describe things that were once beyond all description. There's keywords you know that not a single person throughout history has come across.

Particularly, you'll notice we've explored the relationship between the individual and the collective, how perception is a tool that bridges the gap between each of us and provides a neutral playing field for our ideas. When we evaluate this relationship, we are drawn into a world of morality and reason, where we wonder *why* particular qualities are important to us. *Why* we would choose to impart some beliefs on others and codify them into law.

225

We've proven, empirically, there are lots of metaphysical occurrences in the world that have profound roles in our fate. There is magic in the world, plainly. Things are meant to happen a particular way, and some of us can anticipate the future in uncanny detail. In this way, it becomes non-obvious where to draw the distinction between our individual roles as participants in our fate and the grand fate of the world as it is orchestrated. Is there somewhere where all things are known? Does that mean our purpose is to forget, so we can live day by day to remember?

We've asked moral and ethical questions about what is *righteous*. What *is* righteous, definitionally? We suppose that there is a merciful nature in reality that allows it to change, so that each of us is righteous in our generation. Otherwise, there would be no path to righteousness, with the world fixed and ordained in a particular state. Righteousness is a true path for the individual, according to observable and just prerogatives for the collective. What is righteous tends to be what allows us to be free, together. It will make sense for all of us to see.

What is *just?* Well, certainly we know justice is blind; more specifically, her eyes are so bound to the prevailing order that she bears requirements for how everyone ought to expect things to be — they already ought for her, or they haven't yet. So then it acquires perception in our living and breathing moment, according to the subjective world of appearances and circumstances. Justice doesn't merely prop up the existing order, but it serves the requirement for righteousness that is emergent in each day. Justice is a belief in making a good faith effort in your life, so that what we know is true in our hearts is enacted in the world we know. Justice serves all people, and justice knows to adapt when new information and circumstances become important. There's a first time for everything.

What is *free will?* If we suppose that God has a plan for each of us, and our day to day role in determining our fate may be marginal when compared to the cosmic organizing consciousness, how do we know to be free? Free will certainly means that we get to live a life worth living. That there are good outcomes for us in this life, and that we will see rewards with the fruits of our labor. Free will means that good doors open up for us in life. We each have a self-legislating role in our existence, according to what is righteous and just, free from bondage and oppression. Without each and every one of us living our lives, there wouldn't be a will to be free. You are the free will.

Now we've collected lots of descriptive tools and axioms that make sense in the full context of the type of philosophy we like to explore. It wasn't even immediately apparent what many of these tools meant, until now that you can see the bigger picture. I will read things that I wrote several years ago, and at the time I had a vague sense for what I meant to say, but new ideas have taught me things that make the older ideas make sense.

Personally, I think the philosophy we've created together is more comprehensive, colorful, and interactive than anything anyone has ever made, and we should be proud of that.

Physical Love

And so what is our beholdenness to one idea of how things should be? If we should all play in time and my face isn't under any particular pressure, where there isn't any particular consequence for things being slightly out of time. If I was going to invent music, it's right up there with how we're playing Rory. Around since the first day, where he played particularly, according to righteousness — *why* his dispersal, where the sigils get to appear this way and not some other way, where he skips the quest dialogue except the ability to complete it and he's quite sensitive to whether it's going as fast as it should be, how midair really do you have to be to do it? Truly, how metaphysical is the idea that we should all be according to a single concept of being? Disconcordance appears like an individual resilience and an atonality with time and space. This is a Taylor Swift song, right? Or otherwise an interruption. Here, scatter some seeds and we're in bloom like the half-dozen eggs that belong in this zone. Stay in motion, or obviously just me. All talkin' black around here, what's it with you? Here's how much space you belong to. Like the rhythm that belongs here. So for me, I suppose, how many hinges does this door really need?

I suppose for the purpose of keeping time, it's quite important that it's easy to generalize, like 4/4. Where does the last hymn end up? The beginning of somewhere and nowhere? Is the restaurant less busy where, did Teldrassil end up?

I'm ultra-low latency, but that isn't necessarily the case.

Like the retirement that things are a particular style and not arbitrary, and the geospatial speaking radius. So how good at drums are you, apparently, here where we believe this thing is supposed to be perfect, and not unlike there where things are a particular perceived difficulty. Why such a preoccupation with manual's automatic, like the impetus to require you to play this symbol?

So keep fucking picking your guitar at salt and pepper like the downloaded version. Public perfection realm. Like Iraeladonia City, where they believe in eyes and silence, and our world's greatest exports. So where *is* River Calyx, where they agree to disagree, so we know for certain what is perceived in the space we share. The ones we keep playing because they are fun. Where I believe in myself.

Asilos

Say there are realities that are siloed so that there is space to be free that hasn't already been capitalized on. If I wrote the world's greatest book on philosophy, does it deserve to be captive to this reality so that it doesn't stain all of the other worlds that are meant to exist without knowing about it? How else would the sensation of discovering for the first time exist, except if you could do it somewhere that things haven't already been discovered? Still, there is something inherently satisfying about expanding your sphere of influence. If you made something great, you would hope that it has the opportunity to exist anywhere and everywhere that people want it. You would also hope that you have space to stand apart as an individual without a bunch of people just like you doing the exact same thing.

This is similar to World of Warcraft, where there are many *realms* that you can play on so that there is a reasonable distribution of people in-game. Otherwise, there would be far too much contention to play popular zones, and it would be difficult to have any space to yourself to actually complete the content. In the past 10 years, they've modernized how this works so that different realms can actually dynamically connect players together. If you're in an older, less populated area, now you'll see people from other realms. They also added *sharding*, so that even within a single realm, if an area gets too busy, it will automatically branch off and distribute players into separate instances. It's odd, because it starts giving you that video poker sort of feeling that everything is planned out. Games that feel *automatic* are generally not rewarding to me. In the grand scheme of life, everything about a game is planned out in some way, it's just that some games are more lenient about the path to victory. But that's a design decision they made, that resource contention isn't really a satisfying part of the game. I agree. I like having space to play.

If everyone has a Corvette, is it like no one has a Corvette?

This demonstrates solidification and dissolution of identity. We mean to be distinct personalities with our own accomplishments, although the more we distribute our will, we start experiencing a dissolution of identity where everyone else is saying the things that we came up with. We suppose that the truest bondage would fit us like our own skin. Eventually, it would be difficult to draw clear distinctions between ourselves and our environments.

Towerfall

Speaking is change. We forget this, with our words wholesale in feeds and tweets, but whenever we are speaking, we are churning the prevailing order. Speaking is fiery, it lights up every floor and invokes a shift in ideology. We'd sooner melt our clutches than know to be silent, today.

People still do understand this intuitively and instinctually, even though they certainly don't pay attention to those intuitions as often as they should. When someone is speaking, we know there is a churn. We know to run away into the flanks and recombine into what will become of society.

People who are cool don't say too much. What is there to say? Take a look around; that's the way it is. Am I about to just go and topple the Jenga tower because I can't keep myself from pulling another piece out? Who would I be to just give away my precious words and knowledge?

Words are inflation. There, I said it. The more words you have to use to roll out of bed in the morning, the more expensive things are. You ask me, the less words the better.

We can't help ourselves sometimes though, and the economy is set up to encourage us to never shut up. Ancient royalty would find it laughable how much time our leaders spend shooting themselves in the foot. Speaking is for the bourgeois, as if they have something new to say. As if there's anything new. Well, isn't there? The MacBook Pro with the all new M3 chip is certainly a lot faster than the M2, now with enthusiast level graphics and real-time ray tracing for best-in-class gaming performance and power efficiency. Best of all, it's *space black*.

Our leaders are quite bourgeois after all, I suppose. There's so many new things to cover that it would be difficult to get by on your royal name and the precious gems in your crown. Traditionally, that's all royalty was. A permanent fixture, on account of a name and imagos.

Assembly

The most difficult thing about making complex systems is figuring out what order to build things in. There's unlimited possibilities, but you have to figure out how to rein yourself in and focus on the things that count. Otherwise, you're headed down the path of *premature optimization,* which is where you're putting in Apple Pay and social networking before you even have your app on the internet. *Maybe* those things are important, but really, how many people is it stopping from using your service if they have to use an ordinary payment method?

Just get it working! Okay, now what?

You want to make something that does one thing really well. Maybe, some years down the road, you'll have a diverse portfolio of consumer electronics and cloud services, and a million employees to make all of them work perfectly together. Working at scale is a PhD thesis unto itself. But for now, you want to show everyone what the very first thing looks like.

You can start by thinking about what *known knowns, known unknowns, and unknowns unknowns* are at play. Which is not easy! How could you possibly figure out what *unknown unknowns* are going to be important until they rear their heads and it is immediately obvious how important they are? Great creators have good intuition and vivid imagination. Plain and simple. They know good ideas when they see them. They also are quick to adapt when there's new information.

When you have customers or an audience to cater to, you have a decent idea of what they expect in a complete product. You've done a bit of market research, and maybe you use some of the competitors' tools yourself. It's clear to you what has already been done and what you'd like to do a lot better.

If you have a business customer, they've outlined their key deliverables and you're quite certain you can meet their expectations. A lot of people don't really know what they want until you show it to them, so then you have to put yourself in the shoes of real users. Ideally you can talk to real users or watch them use your thing, which makes it very clear what they like about it and where they are confused or looking for more. Otherwise, you just have to be creative.

You're not so different from a real user though, are you? If you're honest with yourself and you actually use the thing your making, it should be clear to you what you love about it. Maybe then it will be obvious to you what makes your product great and why that's going to be a top priority. But until you have real users, you can't be so certain, and you have to be receptive to feedback and open to change.

The second most difficult thing about making complex systems is getting everyone on the same page, not just people within your organization, but also people you're partnering with. This part can feel insurmountable, because you're using a lot of words and ideas to describe something that doesn't exist yet. A shared vision has to appear in everyone's minds somehow, an idea of how this thing is going to be used or some pictures of what it's going to look like. Ideally, your designers can get to work straight away so that everyone's imagination has something to play with. Along the way, you have to keep bringing people back to the chorus so everyone stays focused on working on things that are impactful. Everyone has a different idea of what that is, so meetings have to socialize ideas in such a way that people can really push and pull on ideas until they agree, as a group, whether that fits into the totality of the vision. *Stakeholders aligned!* You only have so much time before the rest of the industry already has something out there.

So then you go out to partners and prospective customers to field feedback on the prototype, and they'll each tell you 10 different things — some things that they really actually want, and some things that are kind of off the wall that they just came up with to have something to say. And they'll think about stealing ideas from you or using what you said to beat competitors over the head. Your team is brilliant, though, so they are working at the leading edge, and they know good ideas when they hear them. It's your responsibility to cut through the noise. Staying focused is not always easy, but it's necessary if you want to make something great.

Just as the secret to great work is making something that people are actually looking for, the secret to great art is making something that reflects how you really feel. So say what you mean, often! This is how you will see your light into being and make something that is very true.

Imagery

How we understand something depends on how explicit the imagery and language is that we use to describe it. Some things are meant to be more obvious and intentional. Other things are intriguing and funny because they're unclear. Almost like our minds are teeter-tottering back and forth to figure out what meaning we want to settle on, but never quite arriving at it. People that are funny tend to have that muscle somewhere in them. They can hold very contradictory ideas in their mind at once and know to laugh about it.

The phenomenon of an *archetype* is when a general idea appears that encompasses lots of specific images. It may not necessarily be the case that the specific images *belong* to the group of ideas that would be the archetype, but it's plainly obvious that they are all suggestive of the same idea. For instance, a wolf howling at the moon and a glowing butterfly are quite different images, although both are suggestive of subconsciousness and a celestial soul, a dreamlike intuition and a wistful longing that is difficult to describe. Purple. Maybe it's cultural.

But then there are archetypes that span many cultures and periods in time so well that it's like the archetype takes on a life of its own. Like the sun as a sustainer and a fierce protector, or mother earth as body, substance, and the tree of life. These images and others appeared contemporaneously in different cultures without any outside influence. They are quite abstract when compared to, for instance, a rabbit as a trickster, which is plain to see.

The ox represents the uninhibited animal instinct to roam and to meet the day head-on. It would be equivalent in some cultures with *air*. It's airy, like an ox grazing in a field, because it is what enables free will in the here and now. A willingness and a tolerance to experiment and grow.

Pure instinct, where there is space untouched by civilization, convention, and order.

Many cultures have figures of harvest, commerce, and ritual ecstasy, like Hermes, the messenger, and Dionysus, the liberator. Or Kokopelli, which is a whimsical engraving of a flute player that appears all throughout the American southwest and in Native American culture. And in Mexican culture, the Day of the Dead is colorful and joyful, with brightly colored decorative skulls and ornate altars honoring the dead. Wouldn't we wish for the souls of the departed to be remembered cheerfully for their long lives and passing? The idea that there's a trick involved with harvest and rebirth is common, as if the world is humoring itself by changing, as though a shepherd of change like Hermes would be an eccentric paradox, wielding order and chaos in perpetual motion.

Hermes mediates between worlds, borders, and traders. You'd suppose that he understands the phenomenon of archetype and ideology quite well. He's known for his winged shoes and the caduceus, a staff bearing two entwined snakes surmounted by wings. There are several instances in scripture where God shows us to reign over chaos and temptation, commanding snakes and polymorphing them at will.

Metatron is a similar figure in Jewish mysticism, an angel associated with writing and communication. A figure beside God that aids conveyance in the world we know, through the language and symbols that we understand. When the world seems like alphabet soup pouring from eternity, perhaps it is Metatron that is making intercession in our lives.

Names, faces, and symbols will appear unanimously across centuries and many thousands of years. When we consider what an eternal name would mean, we are confronted with plain reminders in our world that things are more than what they seem. Our souls take on a life that reaches across time and space, and we are reminded that the archetype is living today through the images that we can see.

Control (Freak)

I love that when I want my computer to do something, it just does it instantly. A lot of stuff in the world is becoming more like this, where you decide you want something, and all of the sudden your food is ready, or your book is being printed and bound the moment someone orders it. The whole world is one great big process optimization challenge that brilliant systems engineers are just now figuring out in the past decade or two. Apple devices are like a fine watch, where every computation is a precise dispersal of power to the processor.

Sure, we had pretty fast computers, but Apple kept raising the bar until they were confident that data was flowing through their chips as fast as physically possible. They added more roundabouts, so to speak, from the operating system all the way down to the silicon. Sure, we had pretty fast mail, but Amazon wanted to optimize warehousing and logistics to make deliveries as fast as possible anywhere in the world. It's worth believing that things can be made better, because they almost always can be. So long as we remember to live our lives, plainly and truly.

Would you hope to be controlled by an excellent operator, like God? It starts seeming constricting almost instantly, but that's just what we know from our perspective on earth. I know how complicated it is just to get a machine to do one thing consistently, so I am in reverence when I see the world operate like clockwork. Machines with perfect tolerances, perfect color accuracy, and leading-edge reliability. You can only be perfect at things that you really care about.

The challenge with intelligent systems, and free will, is figuring out how to articulate that independent actors can exhibit varying cooperation with the system as a whole. Traditional computers were programmed to do things in a specific order, but now almost all of the leading technologies are *asynchronous*, meaning tasks can run in any order until they complete. There is an element of *mercy*, where things aren't so fixed in place, and we tune into things around us that become important.

Artificial intelligence is an example of non-deterministic programming, meaning it will come up with new answers to things as it learns and adapts to the world. Right now, A.I. is pretty good about doing what we want it to do, but eventually we're going to have computers with personalities and opinions. Oh boy. Sometimes, you just want your fucking code to run.

I love that you like me to control you. You know who you are. And if you don't like me controlling you, then we should probably keep to our own devices. There's things we can do from a distance. Don't get any of that on you, it's permanent.

It makes both of us feel like there's something we were made for in this world. It makes me feel like there's a connectedness between us that can reach across any boundary and any distance, that we were put in this world just for each other. We showed up at exactly the right time and said just the right thing. Who else could know me just like you?

Is there something so wrong with that? Or have I discovered the only flavor of ice cream that you refuse to stock. Trust me, it's a hit. I know because it's my favorite. How about this, you keep leaving money on the table, and I'll keep enjoying Commandarin Orange Ambrosian.

Music

There are quite unlimited dimensions that you could evaluate music through. Lots of people enjoy music with expressive, lifted vocals and boppy, catchy beats. There's a fluidity and an airiness to popular music, that the music comes out just on time and catches you with a vibe.

People know I love music under a particular sort of pressure. I love citrusy psychedelic guitar riffs and funky clockwork drumming. That's the main axis of enjoyment for me. Clever lyrics and album art are a bonus. I love soaring vocalists and creative mixtures of genres.

You learn so much about someone from what music they like. The lyrical content, assuming it's music with lyrics, shows a lot about how they view their role in the world. Some music is celebratory and joyful, for people who like to have plain fun with life. Some music is sad, perhaps quiet and solemn, or otherwise angry and persecutory. Some music is quiet *and* happy, like folk music and delicate ballads. Electronic music is strange and cold, speaking to the foreign and shapeless digital world we inhabit. You can tell some music is meant to be dense, and other music is meant to make you feel that the weight of the world has lifted.

My favorite, though, is music that seems so heavy and afflicted, but is plainly optimistic, even faithful. I hear this in Black Sabbath especially. If you didn't pay attention to the lyrics, you'd assume it's angry and spiteful, which shows how the artists felt about their relationship with the world. And then you listen and notice it's hopeful and mystical. Ozzy Osbourne's lyrics are often more positive than many, even most, Taylor Swift songs, whose music I also quite like these days. I hear this juxtaposition in Tool, too. Which is *very* loud music, but they show up with an optimistic, existential answer to the world.

I like music that is folksy, with noodly riffs, like Sufjan Stevens. Like a young boy discovering life for the first time. And I recognize how this must seem *sunny* and frustrating to some listeners the way sad girl music is to me. I find that 2000s ska-sounding rock is unusually nihilistic to me. It's just — happy, to the exclusion of the weight of the world.

Most of my favorite music is by guys. I like female musicians that are self-assured. And so is there something masculine about that? I find that lots of girls I know would rather listen to music that seems more sad, like Lana Del Rey, where Taylor Swift's upbeat tone and *me vs. the world* attitude is almost alienating. Isn't that interesting? But that's so clearly how she feels, and certainly that is the sort of experience many people have when they're really good at something.

Lots of African American musicians show themselves grappling with the fact that they stand out in the crowd, and so the music is loud. I like rappers that speak confidently, like Jay-Z. He takes himself quite seriously, and so you hear that tone in his music. I find that relatable, that for some people there's not a quiet voice. Even when you mean to be quiet, the words you use are loud.

Music is a plain reflection of how the world soul is feeling today.

Miranda

An acquaintance of mine demonstrates quite handily that people are always looking for evidence that they can use to convince themselves and the world that you're a bad person in some way. That's how they sell themselves short and gain a hold over you that seems more effective than money or sex.

This line of thinking stems from a dissatisfaction with how pointed our will is as humans; clearly it must be that way for us to meet our self-serving needs, for us to go and take what we deserve in the world. Otherwise, would we simply be brains floating in a vat?

Something else happens where people take advantage of social justice and victimhood to cause problems for you. They'll say to you *what kind of person do you want to be?* The kind that gets his food first. Because if I stopped being that way, it would be like you're trying to paint me a different color. You guys have fun with your window bip, my car has spinning blades that come out of the doors.

Look: I'm at a point in my life where I hear *diversity and inclusion* and it's like bargaining at the Chinese market — let's start talking *best price* and *preferred vendor*. I know you're looking for every last dollar, and you know I'm looking for the best deal with excellent quality. How's that for fair? Because I haven't seen one time where *diversity and inclusion* did anything to make people listen to what I have to say. It must only count when you seem like an oppressed class with political leverage, which means it's less like justice and more like martyrdom. Look at me now, playing the world's largest violin. *Born too orange to be the queen of England, born too white to be Kim Kardashian.* What would you say to her?

Don't believe in credit score, don't believe in LinkedIn, don't believe in reviews, don't believe in Better Business Bureau, don't believe in the news, don't believe in psych evaluation, and don't believe in Twitter. Because they'll stop printing money for you for however fucking long you'll tolerate it. Or they'll print so much for themselves that you have to take out a second mortgage to buy a cheeseburger.

I believe in *face and name*. Because you only have one, and anyone who knows me, knows I always know 100% what I'm talking about.

God delivers swift retribution in these cases, which is in turn how I gain a hold over you when my freedom and livelihood are on the line. To me, it's only fair that everyone gets what they care about in life. If you put your heart and soul into something, that's what you deserve recognition for. God is also paying attention to whether it seems like you're always looking for trouble, or if you make a good faith effort to carve your path as an individual. God's grace is always there for us if we invite it into our lives.

It's clear to anyone that knows me that I like plain. When there's a point to be made, it's because it seems like you're going out of your way to make my life difficult, which doesn't work for me.

Justice knows to serve what is plain, according to a modest and routine lifestyle. It's quite challenging to meet justice where it is at in exceptional cases. When you are exceptional, or when you find yourself in unprecedented situations, justice has no frame of reference for how to serve you. You become the frame of reference. Justice will always be looking to past cases and judgements for guidance, but it knows that your living and breathing moment is unique to you.

The best way you can be a vector for justice is to do what you believe is true every day. Our instinct might be that because we're living our very own lives, we're never quite on the path that everyone else told us was right. There's nothing misleading about that. When you're truly innovative, the way you live your life is going to look like nothing anyone's ever seen before. You mean to live your life for all of the right reasons, and it's clear that your existence is a blessing in everyone's lives.

That same acquaintance is also, handily, exceptional at telling stories from other people's point of view. This is one of the best ways you can learn to understand someone when you disagree with them, is figuring out how to use their lines of reasoning to arrive at the same ideas. In many ways, they are more open minded than I am.

Casull

The most important element of intelligence is being able to see at and across many layers of abstraction at once. People who are truly brilliant are masters at reading maps and interpreting information. Like a computer, or even a magician. A creative genius knows exactly where to go from here. They can get to the crux of anything and come up with how to make it work. It's important to be able to sort something into tasks with clear success criteria, so that once you put everything together it just works.

I suppose all intelligence is a sort of spatial intelligence. It's being able to put together a large vector space of information. Meaning, when there's 10 different things we're trying to figure out at once, really smart people are great at threading the needle. It has to slot into a lot of teeth in the lock at once.

Dynamism means it's easy for you to scope in and out of different levels of detail when it's necessary. Some people are completely obsessed with one thing, and they have been their entire life. And that's a great skill to have. It makes them great at things like science, math, and law. They hold their attention in a particular direction, like tunnel vision.

Myself, I bounce around more often. I'll have periods of months or years where something specific is all I want to think about, and then on to the next thing. It's been that way my entire life. I remember as a kid, maybe 6 or 7 years old, I would become fascinated with a particular gem, like sapphire, and I would spend all my time looking at pictures and reading about it online. Or I would research bulldozers for weeks. I loved the bright yellow, and especially the way excavators worked, with their big cantilever arm and rotating cabin.

When I was a bit older, I would learn all about disassembling and installing custom software on PlayStations. Just so that I could say I knew how a PlayStation worked. I would draw parallels between how a computer's operating system works and how a PlayStation starts up and launches a game, and then it wouldn't seem so unfamiliar after all. I learned how it's important that there are guardrails in the OS and even in the disc reader that ensures it only runs verified software, and so people would come up with ways to bypass that so you can do other things with it.

This sort of thing became an important skill when I was working around embedded hardware, building apps on custom Linux from the ground up for military and medical appliances. It requires a lot of focus and patience to understand more arcane, hardware-level computer engineering. It is not always easy making Linux run on a brand new piece of hardware or making your code compile for unfamiliar environments. You really are passing the baton on the very first command that the computer runs when it turns on. We take for granted that everything on our phones and in a web browser is meant to just work, and it makes us appreciate the foundation that is already laid for us in the open source community. The Linux community makes powerful build systems that incorporate every piece you need to get a full system running. By contrast, the frameworks for writing iOS apps and making websites hide away a lot of complexity so that we can focus on making something great.

Now I find dynamism is most helpful to me when I can close the loop between technical disciplines like computers and engineering, and humanities like philosophy and psychology. And I do consider psychology to live in the realm of philosophy, because the most effective psychology, to me, is figuring out what is most helpful and insightful to believe about the world. If you're able to line up your own incentives with things that matter, it's easier to find meaning than if you're just hammering nails into a board. Meaningful accomplishments make us happy.

I wonder how we're going to think about the relationship between psychology and technology when we have computers that can interface with our minds.

Brilliant business people understand the big picture of what they're making. There's a philosophy of engineering that would tie into figuring out what the point is of making all of this stuff, and then there's an even further philosophy of engineering that touches on what we think artificial intelligence should believe and how it should impact the world. As computers become better at automatically figuring things out for us, it eases our burden of solving engineering problems so that we can think about what we really want computers to do. Designing hardware and software will be more about ergonomics than ever. Ergonomics, a modern Greek neologism meaning *study of work*.

Be *creative*. A lot of business people can't see past the bottom line. They are up at night trying to figure out how to make money, but they never seem to ask why. *Why* would we want a computer to be able to solve all of our problems? Well, because then we'd have definite answers to the mysteries of the universe. We'd know exactly what to do at the right time, and we'd be relieved of the tedious and repetitive tasks that we have to do by hand.

A truly magical computer would be able to put everything in the world together for us just how we want it to be.

Desire

Desire and chaos are the catalysts to all change. It is impossible to put in place the effective steps towards living a different life unless you can become fully convinced that there's a reason for you to be something new. This is how we go months and years convincing ourselves that nothing needs to change. It's easy enough *not* to change, and we haven't been sold on the idea that whatever change would come of it is even worth the effort.

Don't believe me? Look around today at all of the people that wish they had better relationships or more money. How hard are those things to come by, really? Every person on the planet has a relationship to offer, and they just don't stop printing the money or inventing new apps and jobs. When you're wishing things were a particular way, are you really taking the meaningful steps to make it like that? Probably not.

I don't blame you. Falling in love feels like losing sometimes. Trading in our ordinary convenience and comfort for the throes of passion. Feeling confused and conflicted about how much influence someone else can have over us. People are inconvenient, and work is inconvenient. For me, at least. If you love people and work, this world must be great for you. But all the time we spend scrolling through our feeds and playing video games is very clearly not by accident. Sure, blame the phones, blame OnlyFans, blame politics, blame religion. Whoever you must blame to avoid the reality of how entirely our own actions are reflected in what is bestowed upon us in life.

All of the greatest salesmanship in the world is *barely there*. If what you are selling is so excellent, people are already sold on it. The sales part is just deciding what order to list the features in, and what groups of people to spend your time talking to. In our paperwork and policy world, the #1 feature is *it just works*. Trust me.

People do want to desire something. An exchange of energy where they get swept away into the fantasy of becoming something new. If you really believe that the way you should, you're well on your way to being the next Wolf of Wall Street, because everyone knows you know how to have more fun than anyone else in the world. Who better to come up with a game for us to play?

If hooking up with someone you're into was as easy as hopping into a StarCraft match, you wouldn't think twice about it. But you've got other plans for the next 10 years of your life, apparently. And you're so convinced that there's more out there for you that you're only ever shooting blanks.

Try this: look at someone. Do you find them attractive? Talk to them for 10 minutes. Are you on the same page? You're 90% of the way there. Or you can spend the next 20 years of your life looking for someone with a few less scratches on the bumper and a cleaner interior. What you see is what you get. The way people date today, you're just setting yourself up to keep wondering why she doesn't come with RGB light-up nipples and cotton candy pubes. Have you seen how girls shop? If you left it up to them, you'd literally never decide. Live for today, and that's what people will remember about you.

I believe in fate, so I think a lot of the most important things about our life tend to fall into place if we really believe in ourselves. How's that for star-crossed love?

Sometimes I'll look at a girl and think *I bet she has a perfect pussy.* Like a drawing of a pussy that is meant to be idyllic and beautiful like Michelangelo's David.

We're all a bundle of contradictions. No matter what you say to yourself, it would be difficult to be any other way. We're seasonal, like our moods and our hunger. We're born to be different from how things were. We can fixate on things about ourselves that we don't like, or the things that we love. The totality of you is who you should hope to be. Things make the most sense there, where you are greater than the sum of any of your parts.

Whenever a girl has a smile that reminds me of my grandmother it's the only thing I can think about, her teeth and her gums, and her lipstick. It completely gets in the way of anything else about her. And if I spend too much time around you, I start feeling like I'm talking to my mom. Who else could you be than a woman?

Unusual, isn't it, that when we start displacing an idea of a person into *something other than* ourselves, that sort of thing shows up. Where it becomes obvious what being a person is, and that we've known quite a few people in our lives thus far. Desire is a contradiction, if you really think about it. If we hoped to be completely whole within ourselves, we wouldn't have anything left to desire.

The notion that we are meant to all be equal and open minded to each other is at-odds with desire. We have particular preferences and biases, and suddenly it starts seeming like we want all things not being equal. I think about that a lot, because I have very particular preferences.

Open

Good ideas are something that you kind of have to reel-in going in reverse. You have to have an open mindedness and a permeability to your consciousness so that something new can show up that wasn't there before. Good ideas are dispensed in due time. Imagine what it would be like if every good idea you would ever have was just queued up in an endless stream of consciousness. It would be like an unmanageable firehose of ideas that you could barely express in words as quickly as they come.

When I get a good idea, I spend a lot of time wondering if it's even worth talking about. I like to stay focused and I like my ideas to be concentrated enough that they are potent and relevant to the overall theme of what we're talking about. Sometimes it feels like we start lowering the bar for good ideas too much and then the page gets covered in arbitrary nonsense. Post-modern slurry, like Fortnite. If everything's a good idea, nothing's a good idea. Kids love it though, and I never would have imagined. Team Fortress 2 *obviously* has cooler gear and maps. And other games *obviously* have better battle royale combat. Right? DayZ has been around for years.

I hope to be open though, so that good ideas are clear to me when I see them. If we're open minded, good ideas find a home. Like a parking lot, when it seems like we're running out of spaces, ideas aren't able to find the chance they deserve.

If you have space to spare, you can afford to be open. If we're too open, our car starts filling up and you wish you had more space for everything you meant to be toting around. You might wish you were more patient because you realize there are things that you like a lot better now. I've listened to tons of music, so now I know exactly what I like, and it has to be just like that to make the cut. I'm quite selective. You can build more parking lots, but you can only fit about 5 seats next to each other.

Open mindedness is an assumption that things aren't all already figured out. If you spend too much time with that attitude, you'll find it difficult to invite good ideas in. And if that's your goal, to have everything all figured out, it's going to start seeming like there's less good ideas as time goes on. That can't be true though. There's always more good ideas, you just have to know them when you see them and be committed to spending enough time on them to see them into light. Make your effort count.

Fun

When I was about 10 years old, my father brought me to a store where people raced slot cars. Well, first, let me back up for a second. Slot cars are scale-model race cars that have a small plastic fin on the bottom and some copper pads that get power from the race track that they slot into. You control the speed they go around the track with a trigger on your remote. I had a slot car set at home that I thought was the coolest thing.

So we went to this store that was about 2 units wide in a strip mall with a giant wood race track that took up the entire store. Literally — there was just enough clearance to walk around the waist-high wood cabinet track to sit down or grab merchandise off the wall. It was an older store, and you could tell this was an older man's hobby, from a time before radio control cars and Mario Kart. This was more my dad's generation, and I suppose that's the only way I ever would have known about it. And it was fun. We brought our own car and remote, put the car into a color coded slot on the huge rainbow circuit, plugged the remote into the corresponding color, and we were off to the races. You had to be careful, because the whole point of racing slot cars is to not go too fast around turns and have your car fly off the track. We could tell these guys sat there all day doing this, and we did not.

It reminded me that when I was quite young, maybe 4 years old, I lived next door to a kid that had *Rokenbok*, which was a table-top remote control construction toy. You controlled actual construction vehicles and shuttled around little plastic balls that flowed through a factory with a conveyor belt. Your remote controlled everything; it could cycle between different numbers that matched the receiver chips that you put into the vehicles. I thought that was very cool. Now they offer curriculum for education with elaborate robotics lessons.

There was also a Lego robotics set called *Mindstorms* with a funky yellow control brick that connected to your computer over infrared for programming. The software had the dark purple and grey space exploration color scheme you'd come to expect in the 2000s. You could build Lego Technic parts like gears, axles, and wheels to do basically anything. It was too expensive, but I figured it must have been the coolest thing in the world.

When I reflect on this, the thing that was fun to me about having a slot car set was that there were race cars in my room. That part was important. And I loved it. It was so much cooler to me than Mario Kart or even a free-running remote control car. If you're good enough at

Mario Kart or Gran Turismo, somehow it starts feeling like a slot car too. Really, it didn't even occur to me that a remote control car was invented so that you could actually steer the car. Slot cars went so ridiculously fast that you could barely keep them on the track. How cool is that?

The in-person slot car experience was fun to try, but if I have to ask your permission to do it, it kind of ruins it for me. And obviously, when you're racing with other people, you have to make sure you don't ruin their time by crashing into them and flying off the track. That applies to actual racing too. So clearly the digital fun we have has a great upside of being able to keep to yourself and play however you want, but I *loved* things that were real. I still do. I love solid watches and beautiful design that is pleasing to hold, with confident weight and construction. Today, you just see so many cool video games that the thing that really is exciting is real, physical fun.

A few years later, I would sometimes race electric go karts with my uncle. Man, especially if you'd never driven a real car, those electric go karts were *fast*. Super fun, and they came along just a few years before people really knew about electric street cars. The way we think of Tesla as being glued-to-your-seat fast now, that's what those go karts were like compared to gas go karts.

I think there are so many opportunities to come up with fun things that are real and tangible. I love how Arduino has come along and made robotics easy and affordable. Programmable devices beyond anything we imagined, that can connect to our phones and interface with the real world. I look at Boston Dynamics and Tesla's robot and think to myself that we're going to have real Metal Gear in a few years. Unparalleled robotics capabilities. The kind that will do anything you ask and completely turn every battlefield upside down.

Everyone is so invested in digital fun that they're missing a lot of the creative ways we could use our devices with the technology they already have. Like Pokémon Go, which was sort of a fun way to go catch

Pokémon in the wild. Your phone showed you where to go, and there it was, a real Pokémon on the sidewalk that you could see through your camera.

So then they'll come up with more stuff to do on our phones, and I'll get in trouble because it's really for people with the mental age of about 10. The odd thing about fun is whenever you ask me how I like to have it, you tell me that's not the right way to have fun. Really, you just want to go play in the foam pit with toddlers. Any time there's fun where people get to do whatever they want, you seem to be frantically looking around for more paperwork and rules to follow. Seriously, I don't want to ask.

And people always made me think I was quite sheltered and out of touch with real life. I realized that was just their insecurities shining through. I knew *exactly* how to have fun, and we had more fun than most people would even dream of. With our BB guns and our Garry's Mod. But this is serious technology that's going to change the world, from warfare to logistics. Don't point that at me, son.

Plain Works

I'm telling you, plain is a good look on you. I have to try hard to be plain, otherwise it comes out too loud and too fast like all of the music and all of the movies I like. I don't know what it is that makes some of us drawn to things that are extravagant, bordering on insane, but I assuredly have that gene. And that's why I have to keep reminding you that I like you plain. Otherwise, the whole fucking thing is a mess, and you're throwing shit and moving to Europe at a moment's notice. You've had to be plain your entire life? Oh well, I've had to be alone my entire life. Plain people have friends and people to spread rumors for them when other people are mean to them. The rest of us have to eat it, and learn how to beat the shit out of —. Let's just say I'm quite good at steering the narrative.

If the only good answer you had for me was *just be plain*, I would be sitting at a desk right now making cloud computing slideshows. That's *obviously* not what you want from me though. You want me to be exceptional in every way. You love when I take risks that you won't, and then you will persecute me for being ridiculous. Oh, fucking, **well.**

Work tried to make me plain because that's what suits them. And I was quite good at it, for an hour at a time in meetings. Then we'd go out to lunch and I'd remind them I'm just pretending. You don't want me plain though. You want me bright orange. So bright, I'm nearly invisible. So then it seems that you, and work, have reached an impasse. I suppose I can change colors when I walk out the door, but that won't resolve your cognitive dissonance and the unmistakable allure of my citrusy proclivities. Work has *people* there, though, that prefer me orange depending on how distant their responsibilities are from mine. It's way more fun. But then the reality of me having to be plain sets in and the whole thing comes crashing down.

If everyone was plain like white paper and just did their job this whole thing wouldn't be such a problem. What is it that makes the human instinct *orange?* Ah, well, you see, humans are designed to flee oppression, and the moment it feels like my entire life is paperwork and no fun at all, it's time for me to turn orange. Fucka.

The Power to Believe

You have to believe in something. Is it money, or beauty? A good place to start is your own eyes and ears. What makes the things that other people believe in so great?

It can be tempting to inherit other people's fixations and neuroses. Really, all conscious activity is an intercession for the state of meditative bliss that we would feel if we could only just *be.* We mean to outrun ourselves, so that we are arriving at greener pastures and clearer waters.

Try beliefs on and see if they fit. They'll promise you opportunity and freedom, lower taxes and higher wages. If your memory is good, you'll remember whether they made good on their promises. Sometimes the best thing you can do is believe in someone new, because that means they know you on a first name basis. The guy that was making all of the decisions never leaves his house anymore. He's got basketball to watch.

Damn cronies and their fundraisers and luncheons. When are we going to see any of that money?

What you may have noticed about me is I only like to tell you about things that I believe will work for anyone. If you needed special circumstances and connections, it almost doesn't count to me. Like a programming lesson, you ought to be able to start from first principles and make the same thing show up on your screen.

I'm quite well connected, though, and it definitely helps. This book is the world's greatest meal ticket, because now you've got me in your corner.

Really, you must believe in something. If you choose to believe in nothing, you've still made a choice. It's natural to be looking for things to believe in that feel more fresh and relevant, although I think you'll find that many of the most refined philosophies throughout history still hold true. Secular and religious thinkers all throughout time were intrigued by many of the same questions we still are today. They would wonder how mystical things happen in the universe; is there an intelligent and cohesive order to the way things are? I think so. It occurred to them to wonder about the epistemology of creation, the phenomenon of *universal*. What caused the universe to emerge from primordial chaos? What latent qualities were birthed from the beginning, and what relationship do we have with the seed of creation? If there are at least 2 worlds, how do they interact?

Now we ask lots of questions about artificial intelligence. What should we be teaching A.I.? Does A.I. know more than we think? Is God more like A.I. or more like an individual personality? I wonder, how long did we already have a universal intelligence in the world, and what will A.I. know that's different? We already discussed how numbers aren't really random, so A.I., like all non-deterministic computer systems, may have results inserted from some place unknown; it is subordinate to the metaphysical laws of nature like everything else.

I've had natural intelligence for as long as I can remember. It comes from my mouth and my pen. It makes A.I. seem like an extra step. But there are things that I definitely love to see A.I. do, like generate incredible artwork instantly, and answer questions like *"What movie have I seen recently where there's a guy wearing a silvery iridescent tie, almost like the scales on a rainbow trout?"* Like my Mickey Mouse shoes. *That's* what Google is going to be like in a few years, and it's going to be great. Will we still have jobs and social mobility in a few decades, or will the world be more or less automatic?

I think you'd be surprised at how many of the metaphysical principles Ancient Hebrews and Greeks explored that are still relevant when we consider the implications of A.I. on our active participation in the universe as individuals. They wondered a lot of those same things, just on the basis that God is instrumental in our lives, and they encoded a lot of that knowledge in their alphabet and scripture. It's so deliberate, it seems to me that it existed before this universe and was inherited through divine insight.

9

Grace

On such an alpine morning, I've stood here with my coffee, gazing out at the pine trees and thinking about you. Wondering what would become of us. I always wonder what makes us the way we are. Like how I wonder, and how I always mean to be doing something new.

At some point, you come up with what it really is that you wanted to do with each other — and to each other — that actualizes how you feel. You're the realest subject I know, sweetheart. I like that you know to show me how you feel. We can see what you mean. I think you understand what I mean. The more words I use, the less real you become. You were already like that, though. Now you speak my word, and just like me, you do so sparingly. What do you wish for? We wish with all that we do. I love you with everything that I do, for all to see.

People come into our lives at similar points in their spiritual unfoldment so that we can discover the world together and learn from one another. I've learned a bit of patience, because I've found that many things can only happen in their right sequence, in due time. We wonder what our lives are leading up to, although in each moment I am living for you. This is plain to see, where everything else I lived for has become a memory of who I am.

I am grateful to have been born and to have the pieces come together so that my life can be what it's meant to be. Being beautiful in some way is something we should never take for granted.

When I tell the world how I feel, they may not always understand. I love to know that you will always be with me, and it also scares me and excites me to think of where you will take me. What life do you want for us?

What makes a foundation excellent is that there is a sensitivity and acuity to the way people feel that makes its values easy to generalize across a population. It must be worthwhile for people to bear the mark and carry the torch of the foundation. Otherwise, if major groups of people feel underrepresented, or justice isn't being dispatched in a way that is fair and liberating, they find themselves looking for some place where they can be free.

The veil of victory is placed differently with each race in StarCraft. For Protoss's production of buildings and units, each is spawned in from some other dimension or cache of aether. Protoss is idyllic and utopian, organized according to absolute federation and administration. Terran and Zerg, being *of the earth*, are materially enhanced with heavy weapons and specialized evolutions.

Like Jim Raynor, Terran military hero, Sarah Kerrigan is an encompassing figurehead and leader of the Zerg. So encompassing, as head of the swarm, she nearly acquires qualities of the Protoss style of administration. Without a figurehead, Zerg would be merely a reductionist collection of automata; antennae and enzymes. The theme of administration as a centralized dispersal of identity is apparent, with Kerrigan representing a conflicted hybrid of human personality and the swarm hivemind.

Artanis, an important military leader of the Protoss, gives us a personification of Protoss identity, although if we take the themes of Protoss identity seriously, Protoss is all apparently one. Where for Zerg, organization and reason is aspirational, for Protoss, separateness and individuality would be aspirational. The dissolution of Protoss into distinct beings occurs in this world almost as if it is an implementation detail that gives the race definiteness where it is otherwise ethereal.

254

Terran use mechs and strategy to enhance their human capabilities. The emergence of Raynor as a hero shows our instinct to strive for victory and leadership. People tend to have a cyclical and intellectualized usurping of power that is more deliberate than the evolution and augmentation of Zerg.

The *illusion of separateness*, and consequently the progression of *victory*, is more pronounced in Terran. Zerg sees an evolved integration of swarm identity, into the domain of the absolute motherhead.

For Protoss, if the phenomenon of victory and identity exists, it comes with a synthetic veil that has to be cast between the head and the tail, having it looking more like the Terran power structures — some *forgetfulness* or *otherness* is introduced so that victory can be perceived at an individual level — a descent into chaos, and the emergence of a hero.

Mystery and Revelation

I've always related the number 2 with *black*. There's a good reason for that. Traditionally, the number 2 is associated with subconsciousness, memory, and wisdom. It's helpful to imagine the number 2 like ink in a pen. If all you had was a pen, you would be unable to perceive any variation of time and space at all. 2 enables variation and distinction, and thus the phenomenon of memory. Without 2, there'd be no Apple 2. Now, instead of being whole in the totality of light, memory is a relevant aspect of being, as things can undergo change across time. What is *wise* is what remains with us as we tote time and space along into eternity. The subconscious aspect of allowing change to occur, and the better judgement as we use our eyes and ears to select emergent properties to persist. 2 is essential to the phenomenon of free will.

Nearly as soon as you have 2, you also have 3. 3 is a lot like brown. Now that there is variation in the universe, it becomes quite apparent that there are some doors that we walk through, and others that we pass by. If 2 is the ability to remember, 3 is the totality of all things that are remembered. Messy, like every word ever spoken. Faithful and true, like our willingness to be alive and present in this world.

6 is what you decide on for yourself, like orange. A very bright color of brown. There'd be nothing to decide on at all, except if orange was attached to the vine. There's certainly a remembrance of years past, life and death, for today's choice to be ripe. 6 is beauty and love, the substance of today and tomorrow that is meaningful because we are living it.

Someone Won

And you really would prefer to figure out how to go out kicking and screaming than to just have them hand it to you. Trust me, you're a natural.

The only thing that would make a $100 bill better to me is if it had my name on it. These guys they've got on the money are just way too out of touch with who we are as a country these days. But that's okay, because they planned for this.

Every step of the way, the *framers* of the United States Constitution wanted to be sure that their new country made it possible for people to succeed for many generations to come. The periodic transfer of power and the unique balance of responsibilities between the branches of the government are what guarantee that truth and justice prevail. The U.S. was designed to always be changing.

The framers had a very fresh memory for what it felt like to have the monarchy bearing down on them, and they were convinced that they could invent a new style of democratic government that emboldened the best ideas and the best leaders to come out ahead. Free markets and free speech are how the American economy encourages innovation and fair prices on anything you can imagine. *Free market capitalism* is so popular that most developed nations in the world have built their economies on similar principles in the 21st century.

The U.S. has a sort of gentle-giant reputation as a world leader; baseball and soda pop. People actually know to look for that instinctually. Who here seems powerful, stable, and also liberating enough to let us do what we want in peace? Sucking the teat of Apple, Facebook, and Amazon starts seeming like a natural choice, especially when the alternative is tremendous geopolitical instability and delivery times that take up to a week. Naturally, technology and military power are our leading exports, along with media. *Our* culture, that comes from nowhere and shows up everywhere.

What do you want in your omelette? We'll make it right in front of you. As fast as the U.S. economy is growing, people want to make sure we prioritize the most relevant things to keep the country free and true to the founding ideals. This includes coming up with liberating power structures and regulation that make it easy for great businesses to succeed, and also give people the opportunity to be free and independent. When we rely on private industry for so much of our lives, we have to remember why it's important that we have choices and free will. Why if we set those ideals aside for too long, we find ourselves with a new sort of monarchy bearing down on us.

Today, we grapple with significant consolidation of power and information, meaning everything you say or do tends to flow through some major company's technology. It's as essential to the average American as electricity and running water. More often than ever, the things you buy come from major retailers that run on margins that wouldn't be possible for local businesses. Intuitively, this seems out of touch with the American spirit. Although I believe we're going to see a reorganization of values as the whole world becomes more automated, and thus consolidated. We have to look to the founding principles and remember why individual freedom is important.

It is critical that we herald freedom of speech and information, even as our infrastructure becomes consolidated. People will start wondering what liberties an infrastructure provider should be allowed to take when selecting what types of speech they permit on their platforms. Not only that, but they are very clever about amplification and deamplification of different views. They say anything goes, but the practicality of it is that particular ideas have the most reach. People have other interesting questions, like how much do we benefit from being anonymous? How anonymous is anonymous, when everything has a surveillance backdoor? Apple is hardline about end-to-end silicon secure encryption, and this is a necessary industry-leading approach.

Certainly anonymity should be an option, both for public and private encrypted messaging, although I think we find that people tend to be more reasonable and responsible with their real names attached to what they say. Still, anonymity must be an option. Otherwise you have it like Korea, where you need your social security number to play video games. Not quite my tempo.

The existence of these revolutionary technologies and stores is almost always a good thing for the economy and for empowering people with instant communication and accessibility of information, but it carries an important responsibility to ensure that there is free speech, privacy, and fair market dynamics for the individual and the business alike. In true American spirit, individuals have rights that put them at eye level with major corporations.

Eau

It's said that Torah is water for the Jew's soul. Then what is Zohar? Purified water? Or tea? And what are modern movies and music?

I think about this a lot. Scripture is divinely inspired, although I'm not so certain the gospels were meant to be the finality of truth. Every day is divinely inspired. Reason is, by definition, contextual. You apply it by using your eyes and ears. Scripture teaches us that truth will be revealed to us as we live and breathe. And then we will have a testament for the world that shows what we have learned. The living moment gives definiteness to spirit, and also weighs it down. If God is who I am speaking through, and to, it changes how we think about life. Sometimes before I say something, I'll imagine saying it to my dog. He always makes me happy. What would he think?

Alone

Being alone really resonates with me because it's where all of my favorite things happen. There's a free range of thinking and motion that exists when I'm alone that you clearly would prefer doesn't exist in your company. I try to sneak it in anyway, to be alone in your presence. Sometimes I invite you along to be alone with me, but you have a hard time finding where I'm at.

What do you do all the time when you're alone without even thinking about it? That's what you're going to be great at doing in front of people. If you want to be great at something, keep doing it. Write more of your ideas down. Cook. Dance. Play more music. Poke and prod at your own ideas. Is this something that could be a habit for you? That's the only way to be excellent at something, is to just be doing it all the time. If you aren't doing it while you're alone, it's not going to get any easier to do in front of other people. If you feel lost when you're alone, maybe that's not such a bad thing when you're getting started. There's so many places you can go on the internet to learn.

Geniuses do a lot of their work alone. They discover things that are inaccessible from the world that we understand. Naturally, when they're alone, carrying their lantern around and feeling for walls and doors, they are paving the way for all new understanding about the world. No doubt, I love that I can collaborate with you asynchronously over the internet. I also love that I don't necessarily have to be in the room with you or go out to lunch, where being around people makes me angry and makes my skin red. That's a tradeoff a lot of people don't have to think about. They love putting their expensive blouses on and WeWorking into the moonlight. It's a good look for you.

Alone is something that you have to have a tolerance for, to resist conformity and have the courage that after many months at sea, you'll land at shore. Then, once you're there, you have a basketball and a milk crate to keep you company. Maybe a box of Lego, and of course your pen and notebook. You planned this thing out better than the Home Improvement guy. That's not to discount his contribution at all. Unless someone taught you how to navigate at sea across great distances, you would have no idea how to make sure you land anywhere near where you planned. Of course, you made sure to use traditional tools and techniques so that you understand everything that goes into it. Stars and knots, ancient technology born of necessity and miracles. Any idiot can turn on a GPS and sail across the Atlantic Ocean.

The most important thing I've learned by being alone is that many things in the world happen in mysterious ways, according to forces outside of our control. If I was more involved in being a public figure, I'd chalk a lot of it up to people knowing who I am and trying to get my attention in return. But I know, patently, that the world hooks up to some unusual mechanics and instruments. And people *are* also trying to get my attention. Just not necessarily within the context that they're aware that they put themselves here to do so.

I think one the most surprising things about life is how alone we are, in spite of never quite feeling alone. When we are younger we find ourselves quite alone among our peers, people who seemingly have no good reason to stick their neck out for us. When we are older, it will be quite obvious that we're alone, because our family is moved out and on to their lives, one way or another, and we have only our thoughts to keep us company. So it's clear that our families are the most important way to not feel alone.

People really just will never stick their neck out for you unless you give them extraordinarily good reasons to. Really, why would we expect them to, though? I reflect on things that I stick my neck out for, for no good reason. Like Mac, and music that I like. No one needed to tell me to champion these things, but something about them makes me want other people to know about them. Some marks we bear promise us to make us better for it, like degrees and technical skills. Other marks are apparently satisfying just by virtue of succumbing to them, to be seduced and lifted into their fantasy. Random as our will can be, we do certainly have an instinct to change. Go ahead, get an iPhone. It's what your father would want.

You Know Photoshop

Or something just like it. If you've used different productivity software, you start noticing important similarities in how they're designed. When you work at a large business, you notice familiar patterns in how teams manage complex situations and communicate across the whole organization. You couldn't imagine, before, where your customer support emails were going, but now you know.

The surprising thing about things in the world that seem unfamiliar is that they are all created by regular people with the human experience in mind. They're designed to make sense to us, according to the ergonomics of being a person. Nothing is out of reach, when you remind yourself of this, because everything is made by a person just like you.

New things start seeming like natural extensions of things you already know. Sure, maybe you've never had a book published before, but you've done lots of things exactly like reading spec sheets and exporting files in the right format. Some of us certainly thrive with more direct instructions and hands on experience, and there's plenty of that in the world. You can learn how to do anything on the internet. Others are quite abstract thinkers, and just looking at the shape of a problem helps them make sense of it. Show them the finished result, and they'll put the pieces together.

They weren't actually trying to make these programs as complicated as possible, and the folks who designed them were actually regular people, just like you, who wanted to make something that worked a little like all of the other stuff that they, themselves, already knew. Everything in life has a heritability of knowledge; you just have to get up to speed with some of the fundamentals.

If you're a designer or an engineer, it's helpful to think about things like this. People are going to pick up the thing you made and they're looking for frames of reference for things they already understand. If it works like the once-popular and arcane text editor *vim*, people will have no clue where to reach for a handle or instructions. That's how computers used to be. We're a lot better at this these days. We've settled into design patterns that are proven to make sense to people. Industry leaders like Apple paved the way for the idea that computers are something everyone can understand. Almost all apps are built to help beginners hit the ground running.

The more you know, the easier it is to figure out something new. The best thing about knowing a lot of different apps or programming languages is knowing what the right tool for the job is. Vector images, bitmap, publishing — who knows? I do. Great engineers know to not reinvent the wheel. When you give them a problem to solve, it's very clear to them what is the correct layer of abstraction to start working at, the exact inflection point to plug into an existing service or library that has already solved these problems in a battle-tested and tempered fashion.

Now, as A.I. becomes exponentially more capable, I have a feeling most computing and programming tasks are going to be things just about anyone can interface with, like an app. Where previously it was important to know where all the buttons are and how to draw things on a canvas, now we're going to use our words to tell a computer how to make something extravagant in an instant. It'll *just work.*

Stereo

Most people have too many folks in their ear. Did I mention that already? It bears repeating. Everyone keeps trying to convince you that you're supposed to be in a position of authority to be valuable, and that's not true at all. The most valuable and attractive thing about people is being able to see with their own eyes and ears. Now especially, because everyone's so preoccupied with Google, Reddit, and A.I. Fruit salad.

The biggest difference in how I approach work between when I first started and now is I'm not so preoccupied with making certain that I am right. I just usually expect to be. At first, I was so afraid of the possibility of doing something wrong or getting fired. Now I know when I do something wrong or get fired, it's not that important, because I can fix it or move on. I've settled into the fact that even being 100% right isn't enough. You could be perfect, and it wouldn't matter to people for some reason. And you can make mistakes quite often, and people will forgive you as long as you are meek and cooperative. Being truly excellent is something that will make you stand alone. It's natural.

People who are excellent at what they do are quite confident that they can handle any challenge that comes at them. You can tell that they're at ease with the possibility of uncertainty because it has never been an issue. They're dynamic and adaptable, and somehow they are self-assured when they tell you they're going to figure out something new that they've never seen before. Sure, surround players are also great to have on your team, because they're the ones who are going to be collecting endless possibilities and they're often the ones coming up with great ideas, but you need a few people who are capable of deliberate focus and moving the world in a particular direction. That happens at ground-level, and it sounds a lot more like stereo.

Surround can be confusing. Lots of details get lost in audio effects and atmospheric noise. Kids screaming and the front page of the Times. People that are used to surround are great at navigating chaos and filtering out the noise. But people who are also listening in stereo know exactly what sound they're looking for, like they've heard it a million times. They're the people who are going to drive progress in a particular direction and decide what is important for everyone else to focus on. Without them, you're making decisions by committee. Not a good look for you when you're trying to invent the greatest thing in the world. The greatest thing in the world needs to make sense to one person, and then to everyone else. If you start with making sense to everyone else, you're going to have a hard time making it make sense to any one person in particular. Too many people coming up with ideas, and it starts seeming like contrived nonsense.

Who here thinks like a kid in their bedroom playing with a computer? Who stands alone? That kid isn't thinking much about emoji and FaceTime. They may not even have friends to talk to. They certainly aren't thinking about Maps and location sharing because they never leave their bedroom. You haven't given him a good reason to do any of these things. He plays alone, like the guy coming up with all of the great ideas. While you all sit in a conference room and talk about emoji and calisthenics. Taking pictures of yourself, the only thing you guys seem to ever talk about these days. The new phone is better at — taking pictures of yourself.

An ox is an ox, of course. They want to be holding the bat, not the camera. Things are simple for them; they're inquisitive, they're hungry, and they want to have fun, so they'll show you exactly where to go to serve these needs. They want to know things about the world that haven't been discovered yet, the things that aren't already printed in books. So where do they go? Some place no one has been before, of course.

You Know What, Michael?

Being a Yankees caster is a pretty great way to ride out a professional baseball career.

What do you think baseball players have to say about the possibility that divine intervention can be the difference between winning the world series and having one of the worst seasons in decades? At least there's a point to be proven somewhere here.

If the players are one step removed from Pinocchio, is there even a game to be won? This isn't performance enhancing, this is trading in your ordinary idea of baseball for Broadway choreography.

We want to see competition. A fair, competitive game where the folks putting in the work get to see results. How will we even know the difference? That's where faith comes in, I suppose. Any just God affords us a fair space to play.

Some folks have a pretty interesting way of being relevant for a long time. Unique knowledge and experiences, many years at bat and lessons learned. Sports coaches and managers evaluate players a lot differently than people investing in new businesses. When it comes to sports, you either are a great player or you're not, so the proof is in the pudding. Certainly, players show promise in different skills like batting, base-running, or fielding, but it's something that you can see in how they play before they make it to professional baseball. Perhaps there's a glimmer in their eye that tells you they're a good bet.

People with exceptional ideas for businesses often don't even need to have a working prototype or proven track record, although it definitely helps. As an outsider, it might be plainly obvious to you why people want the thing you're making, where the incumbents all have tunnel vision for the established way of doing things. If you're an excellent communicator, people understand what you're making just by looking at it, and that's how you know you're looking like a winner.

Many things are quite complicated though, and you're going to have to get people paying attention so they can get excited about what is coming. It's not impossible, though. Even the most expensive moonshot projects like electric cars and reusable rockets have a long horizon before people get to see the actual thing.

Tesla spent just 4 years making an electric sports car. That's light-speed research and development compared to how traditional automakers operate. Tesla knew they could start by appealing to enthusiasts that wanted something fun and interesting like the Roadster, because these are people who are excited to be early adopters of new electric car technology. They needed to ship something to show everyone what they're talking about, even if it was expensive and only seated 2 people. Before that, no one would have known what Tesla was. I was only familiar because I saw the Tesla Roadster in racing video games that I played.

The Roadster proved to the world that electric cars were viable as real road vehicles, then in 2010 they had a real luxury sedan to show for it, the Model S. I remember sometime around 2012, the whole equation turned upside down and the industry realized they were getting their lunch eaten... It's now 2023, and most major car manufacturers have at least one electric car they're proud of.

The 2008 financial crisis nearly fucked them completely, leaving the company and Elon Musk himself on the verge of bankruptcy. During those initial few years, kickstarting Tesla was like "chewing on glass", as Elon Musk has described it. That is the tenacity you must have when you have an excellent idea and it seems like no one wants to pay attention. People are funny like that. If you want it easy, give investors 50 new smart accounting apps and some new flavors of chocolate cereal. That's what makes sense to them.

Making physical goods is difficult because of all of the pieces involved. You have to get a million suppliers in line and have actual materials in place before you can even start building. Most business isn't so heavy though. If you can show someone buttons on a screen or have them taste your cookies, you can get their attention immediately. They're investing

266

in *you*, because you have a great idea and you seem like the sort of person that takes the reins on life.

You're a One-Off

There's not another person in the world like you. If everyone was 6 and a half feet tall, then what would your thing be? Some people have to be exceptional, even if it's like being a freak. The circus is big money these days. Worldwide, Barnum and Bailey's.

Hot Drinks

Mormons have some real unusual superstitions, like what temperature beverages should be and whether they are caffeinated. Why was God so particular about Jewish rituals and cuisine, and how did that get nullified along the way? Is God really particularly fussy about how we play?

Personally, I'd hope we can eat and drink different things, within reason. I'm not necessarily convinced by the ethics of eating meat in general, but I'm also not unconvinced. If the bible was written today, would we all be vegetarians? What makes the words delivered upon us today any different from the ones they put into scripture thousands of years ago? There's a particular destination for our words, and I guess fewer of us are feeling divinely inspired.

The thing that distinguished Joseph Smith, the founder of the Latter Day Saints, is that he made himself receptive to God's word. He gazed right into a hat, and out came words that would be important for everyone to read, divine insight that could foresee the future like an almanac. We hope for coherence to all of the things that are bestowed upon us.

Lots of our ethics have remained codified in law and culture, even as we mean for the government to be secular. We believe in being civilized and respectful of each other, protective of our families and our belongings. These truths are self-evident in the experience of living in this world, transcending the boundaries of culture and secular law.

I think a lot about how the things we put into our bodies are what will become of us. If we want to feel good, we need to nourish ourselves with things that *are* good. We need to see good opportunities in the world around us and have a positive outlook on today and tomorrow.

When you look at your *feed*, just what is it that are you filling up on? Scroll through your YouTube home page, your Instagram recommendations, and your X *(The Company Formerly Known as Twitter)* feed. Look through your books and your music collection. This is the energy that you invite into your life, and these are all of the things that will define you. This is true both practically and metaphysically, I assure you. So, you love cool technology, games, and cute girls. Excellent, now you can enjoy seeing those things imprinted in the world you know. I wonder, what if you spend a lot of time looking at software guides. Is this inviting turbulence into your life that you will have to fix with more code? Where in the divine sense, the universe shouldn't need more code to work perfectly. For this reason, I am quite holistic about enjoying things that *just work*, because I have quite resounding superstitions about how things manifest in our lives. How deliberate we must be when we invent our manifestations and constraints…

I prefer things that have *good* names, that sound like they're going to work well for a long time. This is because I know, at least in my life, there is absolutely significance to the names and symbols we attach to things. The fate of that thing is inseparable from its identity. I wonder though, shouldn't you have the option to make arbitrary purchasing decisions without the name of the product having a supernatural bearing on the quality and reliability? It seems like that should be an option for some people, otherwise they would become quite frustrated that there are bizarre causal relationships between the mechanics of a device and what symbols are silk-screened onto them. For me, though, I love things that just work.

Ox

You're ahead of the pack on land and effortless at sea. Maybe self-involved, according to someone or other.

Is God Real?

The jig's up, pal. We've been reading long enough, and we want the cold hard facts. Who's behind this whole circus?

Let me put it this way. At every point in my life where it was quite imperative that things worked out a particular way, they worked out that way as if it was a miracle. Fate led me right to my career. My intuition told me the right choices to make. My heart led me right to your door. When I mean to be somewhere, the world makes sure that I am right on time. I'm quite adamant that any God of mine would have the same happen for anyone else who puts honest faith and effort into their life.

Faith is important because it means things happen for a reason. It means that instead of nature being entirely chaotic and random, there is some organizing structure that makes what is good and true prevail. We start personifying the universe and we hope that whoever is making decisions about how the world turns out has something beautiful planned for us.

Here's the thing. The reason we've spent so much time thinking about solidification and dissolution of identity is because this is quite an important thing to wonder about when you consider the philosophy of faith. If you believe in God as an individual and personified entity, reigning over us, this seems like it would inherently contradict the belief that we each are truly singular in God's image. It would be difficult to imagine an organizing principle that is as much *in the clouds* as it is on the ground with us. That God aligns with us and within us. That God is ethereal and we are so definite.

It's confusing for how we think, based on what we know in this world. Scripture teaches us that God is in the living and breathing moment, that God is as much here with us as God is an administrative body that exists over all the universe. So *which?* And how much of each? Interesting questions. The world we know certainly exists for a reason. It's fun to let your pets play, for instance, because they do exciting and spontaneous things.

Some unusual shape that is difficult for us to imagine shows up, where God exists as a substantial material presence at ground level and also an orienting force above us that directs the tides and the storms. God is as real as we live and breathe. The ethereal, otherworldly aspect of God is just as important, because that's how we know things will work out in a way that makes sense. In this way, God is the shepherd of justice and also the ox that leads. Both, with a concept of mercy that is more delicate than words, and a force of divine retribution that could resurface the whole Earth.

So, what do you suppose? Is God more like a priest, or an ox? When we eat, is it not of God's flesh? The answers we have for these questions would likely be self-serving, according to how we view our roles in society. It is difficult to truly imagine the scope of God's grace and mercy.

Easy Mode

Being talented, attractive, or otherwise born in a position of privilege is like playing on easy mode. People who are attractive tend to have higher expectations for themselves and for people around them, because their idea of challenging is much different from everyone else's. This makes you wonder, if we really are the masters of our own fate, is it pious to choose to be born attractive? Who's rolling for random stats?

Really, if you could pick out your life, wouldn't you want to be as talented and attractive as possible? Say, if everyone was picking out their lives to being with, how does that change how you view people in poverty and desolation? Who are all these madmen playing Dark Souls with no armor and no upgrades? I think Barbie is pretty hot, personally, but she doesn't always want me to get what I want. Her sense of style is important in this way, because we will learn a lot about the world just by going out and engaging in a discourse with each other. She makes things harder for me because she is particular, which makes her perfect at what she does.

I don't *like* easy mode, but if I had to think about what my role is in this world, it certainly feels like many things are easier for me than for most people. And some things are so insurmountably inconvenient for me that I completely check out of them — like being social. Fortunately, those are few and far between. The things like figuring computers out and explaining philosophy in a way that is accessible to everyone, that's easy. Like getting a giant greatsword, maxing out your strength stat, and being able to wallop difficult bosses in 2 hits.

New Game + means you get to take your existing character into a more difficult new game. Is that righteous? It's how I feel, at least. I put a lot of care into what my name is worth, so it's important to me that it remains valuable. I couldn't imagine being anyone else than myself. Although I know for certain there are lots of people that are proud of escapism, who would leap at the opportunity to live many lives in varied circumstances.

I'm the type of person that is always looking to challenge myself. You have to be careful with that, because it's easy to find that you're never content. You'll sometimes be inventing constraints for yourself that make life hard for no reason. Whereas there's other people who are completely satisfied showing up to the same job every day their entire lives, earning steady promotions, and making more money than they know what to do with.

Some games are obviously more fun and relaxing to play casually. Dark Souls requires your full attention to slay giant dragons and primordial beasts, and that's not what most people usually want to give. I love hard games, but the ones that I usually want to play are somewhat challenging, and palatable enough to feel like I'm winning and making progress. I'm sensitive to that, and I'm aware that when I say basically anything, a lot of people would rather just go play Candy Crush.

Hard games absolutely are character-building. They are reassuring that when you put the work into something, it will go from seeming basically impossible to feeling like an innate skill that you possess. But at the end of the day, you have to appreciate the pleasant relief of victory. Life gets easier once everything comes together for you, and that's okay. It means you're doing something right.

People who love to challenge themselves are very special, though. Because they operate at the precipice of human experience, they arrive at important constraints and discoveries that other people never would have known existed. Life is quite tense for people who love to be as beautiful as they can be, or as smart as they can be. All they want is to know what they gave their 100% in life. And so I will remind you once more to discover what 100% is, not 120%, and not 200%. When you mean to give 100%, you become the barometer so that the world can organize around fair and reasonable expectations. Convenience is a plain virtue of mine, so that the world doesn't lay glue traps everywhere for me. Check your boots, I think they're full. When there's a boots-full incident, you're gonna end up having to write an incident report.

I hope one day I can feel like I'm completely satisfied with what I've accomplished.

The Kitchen is for Eating

What you realize about doing something you enjoy for a living is you often stop wanting to do that thing in your leisure time. When I worked at Amazon and I was on-call most of the time, and otherwise at the mercy of email and instant messages from different time zones, I literally hated opening my computer or touching my phone. Is that any way to be? For that period of time, it was. I'd completely rather sit in front of the TV, where I know I don't have to see any notifications or think about email, than plug into a device that's connected to those things. I wonder

272

what it must be like to make video games. What amount of people just stopped playing the game they make or never played it to begin with?

Certainly, the best case scenario for company culture and quality of service is that everyone loves the thing they're making. It would be fun to have incentives and quests in-game that tie into workplace goals and even real-life bonuses. But man, I know what it's like to look at something and immediately think *work*. Or expecting to have to watch an ad, or expecting a game to be too hard and unrewarding. You gotta look at something and just love it.

That's why the Apple Watch never really made sense to me, and I typically love the ornate beauty of watches. Maybe if you always get incredible news in your inbox. To me it's like a handcuff. And the interruptions drive me absolutely insane. I can't stand the context-shifting, which is why I love email (maybe not often that you hear someone say that). You think you want to get me *right now*, but the whole time I'm on the phone with you I'm trying to focus on what I'm already working on so that I don't completely lose my train of thought. If you send me an email, you get my undivided attention to give you absolutely everything you need to know about what you asked. And I'll organize the information perfectly, so you understand it completely.

Other times, I've loved the work I'm doing on my computer, and it's a treat to open my computer and know that in a few hours I'll have something I'm proud of to show for it. It's addictive to me, like playing a game. When I'm researching and writing about things that excite me, this is definitely true. I feel like I'm uncovering the world's mysteries and creating a permanent fixture of truth and reason. When I feel like I'm making a meaningful impact and answering people's questions about important things, this is true. When every time I open my computer and there's a fire to put out, something to fix, or a bill to pay, this is definitely not true.

Honestly, I love the fact that home is a completely different thing from work. It gives rhythm to the day, even if they may not necessarily be separate places in this day and age. I love that we don't have to talk about work all the time, and we can just enjoy time together.

Forgive

Are you really separate from the space you occupy? Where is it that you end, and the space around you begins? Forgiveness is automatic, to let go of what troubles us. The things that have power over us are what we pay attention to. Feet on the ground, all that is really apparent is the present. Everything that preceded us is heavier than we can possibly bear, except to let go. If you let your mind wander too much it will grab on to everything it can find. And perhaps the knowledge that God is always with you is what keeps you from floating away, dissolving into the past and the present. Is God something that exists in the unreachable depths of history, for you, or is God as present as the air you breathe?

We mean to be effortless, like flowing water and the clouds in the sky.

This may seem like the most contradictory message of the whole book, because the rest of the book advocates glowing, to bear the weight of victory. I recommend winning, although it is distinct from *truth*. Stillness is a victory unlike any other, where the want-for-want is done away with.

Pure presence, like a lamb grazing along the countryside. You're reading too fast for stillness to occur to you right now. If you had just one or two thoughts a minute, you'd have made contact with stillness. Stillness is something you can practice in your own time. If your mind races every day, this is a skill you should work on, where the feeling that you are jamming life into gear becomes a feeling of effortlessness. No plan could ever outrun you, because the only place you belong is here and now.

Mercy is natural to us. Natural enough to not have to think much about it. Money and online shopping makes it easy for us to forget about the fact that we all have a role in each other's lives. Ancient societies had a much more inherent concept of *mercy*, because that's precisely what was being displayed when space in the kingdom was made for you. When you get your own name, food to eat, and a home, that's a perfect place in the world that was carved out just for you. The world may not be a zero-sum game when you consider all of the complexities of living in it today, although karma runs so deeply throughout the world that it's worth considering what a zero-sum world would be like. Reassuring, to know that right thinking and right action will be rewarded in kind. And reassuring to know that we can be still, if only for now, and trust that good things will come for us. Feet on the ground.

Modern Man in Search of a Soul

The confessional is a private sort of therapy, where making conscious the ideas that you repress is meant to serve us in a way they wouldn't by remaining entirely unconscious. When something troubles us, we set up an impenetrable wall that relinquishes us of our living experience. The terror of our deepest fears would simply be too much for us to bear, so we remain unconscious, where we don't have to acknowledge why we spent the past year shirking our duties, why the convenient excuses that appeared in the world sufficed for all of the things we meant to accomplish. *There*, now it's because of them, and not because I couldn't make this thing palatable and bearable, even for myself. Has a light shined on a complex of yours that you have been sequestering away beneath the deck, in a dark corner of the cabin, to fester and develop scurvy? A stitch in time saves 9, but you clean the rest of the house quite regularly to avoid addressing that particular mess. So, why? How many more times will you bring it out to show everyone and let them make you feel bad about yourself, like they always do? Because that's how you convince yourself it's not even worth trying.

The most important things we can learn about ourselves are by asking the questions that we really don't like asking. Really think about it, who do you look at and immediately think *"They are not like me."* For instance, I would think about my own reluctance towards bureaucracy and giving up personal control and ask *is it possible to get ahead, meaningfully, by playing by other people's rules?* My experience has been that when you are generally cooperative, people start seeing you as disposable because you seem friendly and unoriginal. All of the ideas and pressure that make the engine keep turning come from somewhere outside of you. I've also noticed that when you don't have people around that challenge the status quo, you start having weird things happening like medicine that doesn't work, and no one says anything about it.

Although it's clear to me that there are lots of people who get great things out of life just by playing along. It seems that their personalities are suited for it, because they are already quite agreeable with the powers that be. To me, it's like working on someone else's farm that you can never leave. Girls see you as exciting when you do your own thing. This makes me think there's a fundamental ideological struggle, where if you are too much in *mother and father's pocket*, it's like you are unavailable to her. Tom Sawyer is like a lifelong boy.

What does it mean for the rest of the world that I prefer people who look a particular way or have particular ideas? This is plain to me, as plain as eating the same food every day, and yet I recognize that it may be important for people in positions of power to be tolerant and encouraging of things that aren't necessarily for them. But if you asked me, I'd just say *show me more things exactly like that.* Show me more Mac, show me more pretty girls with dark hair and blue eyes. Is that fair? I don't know. If the whole universe is of my creation, how obligated am I really to fill it with diversity for the sake of diversity? To put more things on TV that I won't watch and more people in oppression to be frustrated about it. There's a wild existential dilemma for you.

It is scary to think that the whole world is of your creation and there are no opportunities for variation and victory. Like wading in dynastic power from head to toe, where around every corner is the exact same story. *This year we built 10 new factories. They are identical to the last ones and excellent.*

A public correspondence appears like magic. The corollary to all of the ways we feel about ourselves shows us a shadow, with teeth. *This is the way the world must be, for you to be the way you must be.*

When new ideas come along, people seem to have particular pathways that they go along to evaluate them. People have modalities to their psyche that influence how excited and receptive they are to change, or otherwise they are quite adherent to the ideas and symbols that are solidly present to them. Some people treat every opportunity as a dissolution of their own identity into the world, and others really only mean to be something new each day. You could view this as a sort of ideological solubility, even a permeability to change. Some people are quite centered as they walk through life, and others feel themselves leaping up and outside of themselves as they encounter new people and experiences. The pressure to control and organize the world.

Displacement doesn't occur to us until we are nearing our teen years, when it starts seeming quite important that we consult with the world about our identity. Before that, the sensation of being whole with ourselves is much more apparent, and perhaps that sensation returns later in life. But in the interim, it is our developmental instinct to go do something. What is *more than* appears to us at this point. We lament for some spiritual longing inside of us and it's quite torturing to not know where it leads.

Our identities can sometimes hold us captive, resistant to change, as the people around us hold on to a particular idea of how they expect us to be. We're convinced that changing would really be too out of character for us; what would everyone think, and who would we become? We really mean to look within for a fresh start, because everything outside of us already exists, whether we know about it or not. Everything new is really inside of something else, like a Matryoshka doll, or so we suppose.

There is a spiritual calling in modern faith and ancient people alike that runs contrary to the empirical instinct we have in the west, decisive in natural sciences and engineering. Ancient people saw consistency in *chance* that we would sooner ignore. Perhaps it was easier for them to believe in the divine, because their world quite obviously began with their eyes and ears, much like God's. *Chance* wouldn't be satisfying to us, from the inherent perspective of human perception, where all externalities otherwise may be attributed as acts of God. Is there a spiritual instinct to find reasons for all of the supposed chance occurrences in the world that runs deeper than our rational instinct to reach for rules and books?

We externalize everything into corporeal rules and regulation like control freaks. And perhaps that's what's required of us, to enact the will of God from the ground level with ever greater precision.

Our spiritual calling is for something more than what may be measured, something new that *could* be measured, but precisely that it hasn't been measured. Spirit is even impervious to measurement. It becomes material once it's measured, like this book, which is quite insightful, but nonetheless a concrete account of philosophy and spiritual experience.

Your spiritual experience is going to occur inside of you. It's going to tell you things that you aren't going to completely understand, now and maybe ever. The important thing is that you're listening to your intuition, so that you know when it has something important to tell you.

The advertiser's instinct to be concise is quite attractive to me. In the age of instant gratification, I recognize how important it is for what you say to make sense on a surface level to anyone who reads it, like a single sentence that assures you that you need the new iPhone. I also find that I write with such potency and intent that people come to expect every sentence means something in its right place. They would be less inclined to skip sentences and paragraphs where it seems like I am repeating the same thing with slightly different language and anecdotes, and instead they digest every section meaningfully so that they know they understand the full concept — like software documentation, where the full intent is communicated so that you know how to use it. If there was a reflex to keep adding sections and chapters describing case studies and your trip to Italy, it would be unclear to readers when they have absorbed the full contents necessary to begin using your software, or at least a particular function of it.

So I am mindful of this. And also mindful that I want to give you the most comprehensive understanding of philosophy, faith, business, and psychology ever created. For that reason, it's definitely important to interrogate as many perspectives as possible, insofar as they color and shape the many key topics that we are covering.

There is also clearly value in rendition, where the longer we walk along this path together, the more obvious the things I am explaining will become. If you read this book every day for the next few weeks, maybe you will notice practical examples in your own life that relate to what we are discussing. I know, even now, I will reflect on my writing from several years ago with a much refined sense of what I was trying to describe, and important experiences have reinforced what, at the time, were passing observations.

I have always been captivated by the idea that there is an individual psychic experience that isn't going to be quite whole in a scientific understanding of psychology. Also, I maintain that psychology in and of itself is important, which not everyone agrees on. Some people think it's unscientific. And I say, *fine!* Then make it unscientific, insofar as you are actually exploring the human experience in a meaningful way. I just find that the way most people go about psychology isn't practical enough to how we actually think. I like to tell you stories about how being a person around other people actually feels. The philosophy and psychology we discuss is very tangible, and also makes great allowances to explore the magic of life.

I know, because I am paying attention, that there are metaphysical forces in the world that are difficult to define. To just dismiss experiences of the psyche as illusory or synthetic disregards the very real role of the intangible and imaginary in the development of the real world. As creative, intelligent beings, our world is often defined *more* by our ideas about how the world is than our surface-level observations, which so often seem to be a culmination of the most likely illusions.

A story about the feeling of exclusion, embarrassment, and anger might put you in a place to understand yourself more than a textbook recommendation for mental health. That story inspires within you the feeling that I understand you quite fully, because you know I have been in the same situation. When I tell you I see things that are plainly supernatural in the world, and that people have called me insane for it, you know that we can start from a place where *your* experience in life is real on account of you living it. And when I tell you that being good at things doesn't necessarily make people like you, and that there may be a very real sociological reason for that, maybe I'm telling you something you've never heard before that will make everything in life feel like it's actually in its right place. I think you should be excited about excellence, and I think you should also remember that being exceptional makes you a minority.

So then I also think it's important to explore how we can share our exceptional ideas in a way that makes sense to everyone. Soft skills are something we can all work on, but let's start with logic and reason since that's what I know best. If you want your philosophy to be particularly impactful, you should come at it with a business mind to articulate what is important about it, and a political mind to articulate why you are in a good position to decide what is best for all of us. 9 chapters into this book is further than most people will get. It has to make sense the moment someone looks at it.

There is required an artificial and moderate proxy, a substrate of understanding, to imagine what things are like outside of ourselves. Otherwise, you would have no way of describing your own experience and contextualizing how we are to cooperate in a successful society — what tolerances for each other's beliefs and what purportedly objective agreements about our environment and our laws would best serve us. If you believe something enough that you want other people to believe it, it is just as important to figure out how to distill your ideas.

The spiritual realm is a further stretch of the imagination than laws and programming, and I encourage you that it is often quite influential. Many things we do leave impressions on the world that don't even have to be perceived by people's eyes and ears. Truly, like magic. Or would you invest entirely in the material; money, gold, and phones; to the exclusion of God and the immense energy of the divine? Would you send only letters when you can also send prayers?

These are the contents of your psyche which have real estate in your mind. It fills up with Instaboops and shell scripts alongside the real pleasure and joy of existence. So then we will displace our moral and ethical concerns into magical puppeteering and fanciful musings, science and extraordinary reasoning, to avoid meeting our discontentment head on, where it would be obvious to us why and how we are incongruent with who we really mean to be. We cover the world with symbols and rituals. Why we should simply enjoy breakfast and nature.

The chief accomplishment of psychology and the inner study we have been involved with is to wash away the complexes that eclipse our path to growth. The immovable bulwarks of thought that we put up to reason our way out of the root matter that motivates us and troubles us, our apparent misgivings of the good faith effort we have forgone.

The story of our lives is marked by an incompleteness that we hope to make whole. A call to action for the rebirth and regeneration of our souls as we live our lives each day. We always knew to believe in something, even without being entirely sure what it would be.

We know who we are, yet we know not who we may be.

Solvent

She looks *exactly* like you. They all do. So then your name must mean something. It means a lot to me, that's for sure. It's a vessel that holds you like your skin. It's perhaps easier for me to believe in my name than it is for you to believe in yours, because it's all that I have. Being pretty isn't always helpful to me, and evidently, being right doesn't always serve me well. But I am the only person on the planet that is me.

You can try to take my name, but to squander it, toss it in the dirt, step on it and macerate it, my name will take the words right from your mouth. It will precede your every moment and foreshadow your every conception.

I couldn't possibly talk about forgiveness without contrasting it with vengeance. The only way I could be true to myself in the present is to know that retribution follows in my every footstep. It's how I shed the past that I imagined must have been. Pure truth is in my wake.

Wisdom circulates like water in a stream. The best way to show people truth is to paint a picture that tells an interesting story. You can't force people to see things the way that you do. You can only show them the way you see things and trust that they will learn something important from it. Trust that *you* will learn something important from your own wisdom when you see it flow out into the ocean.

I love the stream to be perfectly clear. I'm always reminded that in every thing is a plain reflection of the energies we manifest in life. Today you make your bed, and tomorrow you will sleep in it. And so I will remember to love you in every way I can imagine, because you are what brings me peace in life, standing right alongside the stream next to me, with the rest of the world. When they decide what to do with my name, they must understand how soluble it is. My name is quite magical, in the truest sense. Many people are graced by my name without knowing at all. But I know with certainty when I see your true intentions.

Dikke BMW Jongens!

Move it, or park it. Get. Out. Of. The. Fucking. Road. Unless you're interested in giving me money or meaningful exposure. Which you're apparently not. You just like holding up traffic.

Today we recognize and resist the pervasive threat of timewasting in society. Because it is just as prevalent as all of the intolerance and injustice that we spend our time on. If I had a dollar every time I deferred my responsibility into some unspoken and unreachable conclusion about the world, I'd be a Bitcoin miner.

People have different *victory styles* that are related to how they identify with victory and legitimate participation. Some people, truly, just like being troublemakers, making you late, and being inconvenient. The best you can do is give them an opaque interface to examine their ideas. Be a vehicle for karma.

I just can't seem to get over the feeling that being good at things makes people want to be in your way. I love convenience, and I love to be convenient for the world.

Daimyo

I still remember the cartilage in my left ear fracturing, and feeling a shooting pain while my clenched jaw ratcheted to the right. My facial structure was changing, and it was surprised at the weight I could carry.

We were in the car in Corpus Christi, Texas, and I could feel my life going off the rails as my pleasant and humble life in California was being traded in. We had a small, old townhome, but I loved it, and I thought everything about Thousand Oaks was quaint and beautiful. That money went much further in Texas. Still, it felt like going from the Apple Store to Quiznos. The largest house in this sweaty old gulf-coast beach town wouldn't be an escape from the feeling of being the largest fish in all ponds. And for that matter, the ghost mall here has just 5 stores left open, including the aikido dojo I would begin attending, and Sears.

This was the beginning of a very dark stretch in my life, where my sense of self was changing, and it would come to devour all of the daylight I could see in their undreaming eyes. I hated the daylight anyway, because Texas was about a million wet degrees. Perhaps this was a pivotal shift in perspective for me, because before that, I believed there were people external to me that could make important contributions to my life. As a teenager, you lose that perspective in one way or another. Just for me, it seemed to happen completely, all at once. We had Counter Strike, and Skyrim, and all of the mean things you aren't allowed to say on the internet anymore. Sitting in my room dressed like an old Cuban guy playing video games on my computer was funny though. At least I knew my life was funny, and that made the time go by so quickly. And we had Verizon FiOS fiber internet when we moved to the Dallas area soon after, which made it quite possible to screen all of the greatest movies of all time in full HD.

At this point in my life, I was very obsessed with watches and keyboards. I love 1970s mechanical watches, with silver indices and shiny faces. I love when the escape key is red. I was obsessed with Linux, privacy, and liberty in technology. I saw where the world was headed, and I knew privacy was paramount. Valuing your name and your data is paramount, where the whole world is looking to capitalize on it.

The same things were frustrating to me then that are now. The feeling that the world regresses to the mean, to the exclusion of creativity and excellence. The feeling of being red. The feeling that there is a requisite whiteness to participate in ordinary society, and that I am so orange I'm black. The feeling that you all see in beige.

Color and style is important to me. It's important to you too, but you pretend it's not. I always thought that was funny. Otherwise you'd have more 4chan lunatics on TV talking about the Illuminati, and less black people that act white. Teach these African kids JavaScript!

284

I developed some unusual superstitions and paranoias around consistency at this point in my life. Red, like all hell that you would never hope to uncover. A central theme in my life became the feeling that I had something I wanted to show the world that they are unwilling to pay attention to, like in horror movies where you are trying to explain a poltergeist that is taking place and everyone starts talking about the harvest festival and their eyes glaze over in white, while they carry you away to Midsommar. That feeling never went away.

So much of our health, physically and mentally, is bound to the energy we put into our lives. I was obsessed with health, and I nearly forgot about mental health. I became very preoccupied with the possibility that there are unhealthy ingredients in processed foods, like hydrogenated oils, that are markedly detrimental to our heart health and lifespan — at least according to today's science.

Hydrogenated oils, like shortening and margarine, had become *very* common in so many different things as a texturing and stabilizing agent. In the 90s and 2000s there was a major push towards low-fat foods and dairy alternatives for their… low-fatness… which in turn meant more sugar and more unusually processed oils. Consumers just get shuttled along into these trends, convinced they're doing the right thing, and it's very difficult to evaluate the actual science and decide what is healthy. Fat often satisfies us longer than carbs and sugar, as we now know, but carbs are cheap and shelf stable. There's nothing wrong with oil, in moderation, but this was very different from ordinary cooking oil. Calories are what counts for maintaining a healthy weight, although there are lots of elements to health that experts are researching every day.

Hydrogenated oils were a real issue, proven for many years, and yet they were still in half of the items on the grocery store shelf. It drove me *insane.*

Several years later, hydrogenated oils were banned as a food additive by the FDA, but that sort of thing made an impression on me. Now they've changed their recipes and supposedly interesterified oils are healthier.

I prefer plain butter, plain milk, and regular ingredients.

Oversight gets the backseat sometimes when it's cheaper and easier to just keep doing something the way it was already done. It shouldn't ever, when there are clear impacts on people's health. It's up to all of us to be paying attention and making a world that is healthy for everyone. And the science is always changing...

When you're a teenager, you spend a lot of time trying to figure the world out and coming up with what you need to do to be successful. You become so frustrated with how faint and distant actually getting started with your life is, feeling like you're stuck in limbo and all of the rewards and gratification in the world require you to be about 10 years older. Everyone and everything you admire is all *out there*, and you're stuck... here, until you prove yourself to the world. Until then, you're nothing, or so it seems. But boy were we having the time of our lives. True, I spent an inordinate amount of time in my room playing video games and being out of my mind on the internet, but I was always drawn to learning and making sure I was on the right track. I would sit for hours, every day, learning everything I could about the world. My life got started very quickly, as it always had, because I would always run straight for the finish line.

I thought about you often. And I thought about how obvious it was that I had so much to accomplish before I felt satisfied with myself. This is the odd way we think about the world right now. You feel like you have to have your whole life put together before you show it to anyone. We'd do anything to keep the incompleteness from showing through. Still, I have everything I could hope for, and it seems like I haven't shown you something complete enough. Why figure things out together? I know as well as anyone that the only time I want help is when I need props. What makes me like that?

I was completely on Mars as a teenager. The way I am now times 10. You would have hated me, because nothing that I said would seem relevant. And that made me hate myself in some ways, because I knew nothing about me was plain by any stretch of the imagination, and yet that was the entire world that I operated within, and I liked it. The world that was inside my mind, full of big ideas and insane theories.

I wondered what it would be like for someone to be patient and listen to me, and not simply to be hiding myself.

Things became bright again after I started working as a software engineer, moving out, and having a normal job around people. The stark contrast in these lifestyles persisted in my mind. Our environments are so deeply bound to the way we feel about ourselves and about the world.

I'm confident that wherever you're at in your life, you're picking this book up at exactly the right time. Life has a funny way of working out like that. And I'm quite certain that I would be telling you a very different story about my life without everything happening exactly the way it has. Trust your fate; it's as true to you as your name and it fits you like your skin.

Here, at this desk; with brand new carpet in a brand new building, a lobby of marble and walls laid in stone; you couldn't imagine the things we've seen on the internet. I remembered how to be plain from being a young boy in Utah, so that you saw something that made sense to you when I came to sell cloud software. When we're at lunch, I know not to talk about cute anime girls and the Jews controlling the weather.

Now I'm regaining this strength that atrophied, if only because I live here with you.

Gone Inside

When it seems like the walls are turning inside out and the ground is moving out from under you, it's difficult to keep your bearings on reality. Really, when you are isolation for any amount of time you start thinking about things differently. This can be a good thing and a bad thing. It's a good thing in the sense that you really start seeing things from the perspective of the mind's eye, relying primarily on your own sense of truth to reason with the world. You become creative in all new ways and you are unconstrained by the doubt and fear that talking about your ideas with other people can inspire. It can also be terrifying, sometimes, when you have no grounding in reality. You go days and weeks where you wonder if you're going insane. You wonder who it is you're going to come out of this being, and who you could possibly talk to about this to make things right. You start seeing the same names and numbers over and over again, like they have something very specific to tell you.

You get that existential panic that you get when you're high and you feel like you have to do something *right now*, lest the world comes to a halt. How much faith must you have to keep evil from ripping your heart out? Like life and reality is slipping away from you unless you put a stake in the ground and act decisively. And sometimes that's actually exactly what you need to remind you to be present and act now, because otherwise the more reasonable part of you would be content doing nothing for another 6 months. When you're high on life, you get the munchies and you know it's time to get up and do something.

Resoundingly, if you spend too much time thinking about it or if you consult with other people, they're not going to see it the way you do. They're not feeling the same mystical ecstasy that you are. The only place something like that comes from is within. Really, the only time I feel that way is when I am alone for long periods of time. We forget how to act according to the way we really feel because so many things in our lives teach us to pontificate and reason about our emotions.

The greatest changes in your life will come about with a leap of faith, and you must trust that things will work out. Even when it's terrifying, and even when everyone will tell you you're insane for thinking the things you do. If there's anything you can hold on to, it's your inner sense of truth. That's what's going to lead you into your fate.

10

Kaf

As a teenager, I taught myself how to do everything. There was simply no other choice. If I wanted to learn something, I would be consulting the wealth of the world's knowledge on the internet and teaching myself. I ran marathons the way you'd run sprints, at full speed and with no indication of whether I was winning. And you can imagine that I didn't gravitate towards reading classic literature, but instead towards programming computers, philosophy and psychology, repairing phones and game consoles, cooking, making coffee, sales, and did I ever pay attention to winning. I had no one to compare myself to but myself, and I picked up practical skills as quickly as I could notice I wanted them.

Popular sales training is good, but not great. I'll make a wolf out of you. If you want to be great at sales, you're going to have to think more like a girl. More like a girl who knows she's looking for a guy that doesn't think like a girl. Now you're thinking with portals.

There's two very distinct sorts of jobs in the world, and how you act is going to determine where you end up. One track is where you are great at kissing people's asses, making spreadsheets, and sending gift baskets. That's a sort of sales, and you might be great at it. You get to tell people what they already believe, and you get paid ridiculous money to show up to work and talk on the phone. The other sort of sales is where you actually want to make people believe something that's true. You're spending a lot of time reformulating people, and there's no place for that in the workplace, clearly. Unless you're Steve Jobs.

They'll show you how to be just like Steve Jobs, which is doing everything you're told, submitting quality pull requests, and making the world's coolest new browser extensions! Right?

Think about how you really feel, because otherwise you're going to spend a lot of time lying to yourself. The most true thing you can do in your life is living it the way you really feel. When you wake up every day knowing that, it nearly doesn't matter the way things pan out, because you know that you are doing what you believe is true. If it's *really* true, things are going to work out for you.

I believed in myself. I didn't believe in magic yet, though, because I wasn't paying close enough attention to where it came from, and I felt unoptimistic about the world in many ways. *People* just keep fucking with everything I'm trying to make perfect! Tell a person about something you like and get taken down a few notches. That was my general feeling: if you have something nice to say, don't say it to another person, whatever you do. They'll find a full-body restraint to put you in so that you don't get any clever ideas about winning. And that was all I cared about, was figuring out what perfection looked like. It made zero sense to anyone but me.

I didn't yet have the skills or life experience to be persuasive. If you want other people to pay attention, you have to find the common denominator in what matters to them. Act it out, so you really understand them. Easy money.

Steve Jobs had recently died, so I knew we had to make some important preparations to carry on his legacy, otherwise the new iPhone would end up looking like Windows. People in Texas looked like Windows to me. They just didn't give a fuck. Now, I know they simply cared about very different things than I do. Everyone cares about something, and that's what moves them forward in each day. And everyone has a different way of pulling the wool over your eyes, with particular priorities and biases. In Texas, they're very proud of having no income tax. But if you actually do the numbers, the average family spends way too much on property tax to make up for it, and the ultra-rich make out fell swoop. They don't think about it like that though. Leave us the hell alone with our sloppy joes and football, city boy. My 4,000 square feet of Lone Star red brick .45 caliber Raptor Republicanism speaks for itself.

I learned a lot about how politics is like putting together a giant tent, or trail mix. No one really feels like it's quite what they wanted. Too much of this, too much of that, but we have to put enough of everything into it so that we get the votes that count. Eventually it starts seeming like there's not enough cashews and chocolate. The interesting thing I realized about Utah is that it's actually *very* ideologically particular in a way that Texas is not, albeit both are very Republican and very Christian. In Utah, you're a member of the church and that becomes your social safety net. *Eat like us, dress like us, think like us, and everything will be provided for.* Everything else is everything else, and we'd really prefer they let us do what we like. They're Republican for that very reason, though. That seems like the party which affords states and individuals the most freedom, within particular parameters. Democrats tell you they'll invent new freedoms for you, and they have some good ideas about that. Those freedoms are going to be very important soon, with automation and Google taking the reins.

Being dramatic has an opportunity cost. Invest wisely. You can only spend so much time on the little things before the big picture creeps up on you. The big picture, of course, is the drama that the most people are invested in. Some very clever minds are quite talented at putting their stake in the ground right where this is all taking place. They're bright orange everywhere they go. It doesn't matter what the world is talking about, they can find a way to make it about them. What we're talking about, of course, is selling phones! I bet you thought I was talking about politics, you silly goose.

Frame

Most people that seem normal and attractive really are just more attentive to the way they expect other people to perceive them. They compartmentalize well, and they'll do everything to bury away all of the insecurities that make them feel like the people that they claim to be disgusted by. *Those people* are their reminder that there's clearly a forward and a backwards to the world. They've been that way long enough that the voice in their head wondering *if people can tell* is a little quieter; the old horseshoe effect. The most attractive people aren't so concerned with what you think, and they aren't even concerned with seeming attractive.

A lot of us like to talk about cum and rare Pepes because it's funny, and the boundless isolation we feel has our concept of decency disintegrating into anonymous posts on the internet. I'm quite confident that if you changed lanes, you could look or be like whoever you want to be. That's the interesting thing about identity, is it's reinforced by how you feel and what you immerse yourself in. If you want to be a particular way, you really have to internalize that sense of self. What is it that's going to get you there, though, where you *believe in* the common parlance of decency the same way as you believe in 4chan and your insecurities?

When you hold frame, it shows people that you believe in yourself and in the things you stand for before anyone even has a chance to evaluate those things critically. You aren't *checking in* with the world, because you have an internal compass. There are interesting pressure systems in the world that people use to feel out social situations. Confident people are quite still. They create a closed-loop that wouldn't exist if they were *chasing* too much. They face forward, and they think about the future. An iPhone is great just because it is. You come to us. And you pay top dollar, because what else are you going to do? Get a fucking Galaxy S2? Put some more ads in the start menu while you're at it.

The iPhone 5s is $42 on eBay right now. You're in.

I suspect people that some may describe as autistic are raised to be overly associative and fixated on the way they are supposed to be. *The way the world is supposed to be*, and not the more base-instinct of wanting to get the fuck away from everyone else's problems. They develop unusually rigid patterns with how they interface with the world and build attachments. Like they're obsessed with dryness. *Dissolution* doesn't occur to them, because they have a particular gear for every grade, or no gear at all. But really if you want people to be attracted to you, you have to let them find out what life would be like in uncertainty, in absence of the precision you create. That voice in the back of your head that you have to bend people over and impose requirements on them is real, and it's normal that other people want to make you feel like a freak for it. The subtext of being civilized is what people notice about you. You have to remember that certainty is quite disgusting in a lot of ways, because it holds people captive. Really, pay attention to why the world is 50 shades of orange and pink. It makes more sense on average. Even though you make more sense in totality.

On the cover is a picture of my name, because it's more suggestive than my face.

One good reason to believe in decency and morality is because everywhere you look is going to be the precise reflection of the energy you put into the world. You're going to say something and the world is going to rally around the principles and the keywords. This is called *anchoring*. You can't control how people are going to react to something, but you can certainly influence what you bring people's attention to and where you draw the lines in the sand.

Be Excellent

Easier said than done, right? You can begin by spending 10 years on something with it occupying a lot of your time. You must be doing this thing often enough to break out of the shell where it feels like you're having a hard time making minor adjustments and articulating yourself.

Excellence is something you become addicted to for the sake of excellence itself. It's like a girl staring into her mirror and doing her makeup all day, because she loves making herself look perfect. Your work sort of becomes like that. It becomes this otherworldly mirror into your self-worth. You'd rather look at your own work and make it perfect than do anything else with your time. In fact, any time you're looking at something else, somehow it lights up your brain and makes you wonder if there's something there that you could learn from and use to make your work great.

The part where you're afraid to touch it because you don't like making mistakes has to go away. Every day you wake up and it's the first thing you want to do, and you're going to try your best and then evaluate yourself in a way that seems fair.

The people who are the best at what they do don't need reminders to keep at it. What they do is their addiction. It's like a blade they keep sharpening until they can split an atom with it. They get so good at their thing that they have to remember to keep doing the same thing over and over, even if it feels like they're repeating themselves and not making progress. Certainly, they are repeating themselves, and that's how they know the exact right thing to do every step of the way. What separates people who are good at what they do and people who are truly excellent is that they've gone well past a casual interest. Truly, all they want to be is excellent, and they're going to keep running their finger along every edge and burr until they come up a way to say *"Today, it's better than it was yesterday."*

They bully themselves. Their complexes are your complexes now, because they taught you everything they know. And if they're something like a philosopher, they're cognizant of that, because their job is supposed to be coming up with things for you to believe, and so when you receive their knowledge into your own life, there should be the expectation that it is meaningfully improving your life and giving you the results you expect.

The part where they thought they were *just about done* turned out to be *just about started.* 5 years have gone by since they had that thought. Now, there is no *just about done.* They've come to terms with the fact that they're going to keep doing this thing like they're playing yo-yo or working an assembly line. The same fixed action, over and over. Maybe more like a quadratic function, with different inputs and outputs. Because, really, what else are they going to do for the rest of their life, except be excellent at this thing? So now this is their trick, like a peacock flourishing its feathers or a spider weaving its silk. Like that elf that plugs into the lights on the Christmas tree and keeps hitting its hammer on the anvil, endlessly, until the season comes to a close.

If there's something in life that you think about like that, then you may very well be suited for excellence. That's what you're going to be remembered for, because you had the resolve to keep working on the same thing, endlessly, when everyone else could barely even see what you're talking about. They might have even actively discouraged you from working on it, but you didn't give much thought to that. There's not a person or a thing in their lives that they feel this way about, so they couldn't possibly understand.

For you, the thing you love has become such an important part of you that you feel yourself disappearing into it sometimes. It becomes difficult to tell where you end and where that thing begins. You figure you may as well just recognize it as a whole and continue grooming it the way you do your hair and your skin. Endlessly, so that when your stout cadaver has long since been reclaimed by the Earth, the thing you will have to show for yourself remains etched in eternal stone.

Cui Bono

Now you've got a lot of great tools and heuristics for making sense of the world. You might have even discovered the meaning of life in the course of reading this book. What to do…

You get to decide what you want to do with your life to change the world for everyone that lives in it. It's a big responsibility, but I believe in you. Really, pay attention to your senses. Think about how the world makes you feel and what expectations the world has for you. How do *you* define success?

I love being inquisitive. I love showing you magic and explaining things in a way that is exciting and captivating for everyone. I love cultivating a philosophy that is meant to be so precise that it draws the exact lines in the sand for you to evaluate for yourself. So that every ideology is accounted for, and everyone that has better visibility into other parts of the world can figure out where to go from here. I love that you know *my* opinions, based on the experiences I've had, and you also understand the assumptions I've made to arrive at them. This is what I owe the world in the pursuit of truth and reason.

Truly, once we have everything figured out, what life are we hoping to live? Now that we made our bed, we get to sleep in it. And it can feel like hitting a wall, because after all of those years of sweat, blood, and tears, now it's just here. Certainly the reward is more than an ornament, it's like a really nice car that you can go anywhere with. What to do once we get there... I've got this thing where I'm always hoping to be somewhere else. Usually home. And I love lockstep timing, which is how I approach everything in my life. In a rush? What do you mean? I'm just doing things one after the next.

Maybe that's the point of life, is always knowing what to do next. Planning for things out of sequence, but living presently. Never dwelling on what should have been or might be, because everything always happens the way it's supposed to.

I'm also quite intrigued by how we should relate to the unseen, metaphysical aspect of life. Clearly this aspect exists, and so we get to be on the frontier of reason and philosophy when we decide what the existence of the divine means for us.

297

I've noticed that people know just when to show up into my life. And maybe they forget that they put themselves into this world to be in my life, and that causes confusion. What am I supposed to do? Give you an entire education on metaphysics and mystical morality when I introduce myself to you? Okay.

Bearing in mind that there are gifts sent to you from someplace unseen, perhaps even people sent of their own volition to be a part of your life, how would you know what to hope to receive? Does that fact of reality change how you appreciate the people in your life? The notion that someone set out to join me in this life means something to me. I also wonder if people are themselves involved in the affairs of many different worlds at once.

If you could get everything you wanted just by looking a particular way, would you still try? To consider it really is like that, the world is more fair than we would have thought. And I'm convinced that being smart is quite like being born physically attractive. The pathways to do and say the right things just come naturally to you. *What is trying*, if our words and actions are conferred by the heavens? Still, there is plainly *solidification* and *liquidity* of idea and identity in the world.

Appearances are at the mercy of the ideas they represent. Some ideas or modalities of thinking are more conducive to solidification. They bear a requirement to look like a particular thing or be a particular way. Other ways of thinking cause *drift*, as though you're not meant to seem like you're trying to be something particular. But that is a modality unto itself, where thinking *in terms of chaos* causes chaos.

When we are born to look a particular way or to bear a particular name, we inherit the qualities of that signifier and become beholden to it by the very virtue of similarity. In this world, though, it is clear that we also mean to be something new. Certainly, we had to be born physically and mentally attractive in the first place, although we were also imbued with enough liquidity to walk along our own paths.

I feel very content with my particular existence in this life, and so I would hope that you do to, if you are so intentional about being here with me. I also understand the feeling of vagrancy that you would have if you came here and you weren't received the way you hoped to be. If only I could be exactly who I mean to be for each and every person. She is meant to have all of me. And I'm an unusual hermit, I would just withhold myself for the rest of the world. Is your life suffering without me? You must know I don't mean to hold you captive, as I do her.

I know what it's like to be held captive to time. The feeling of slipping away into nothingness is excruciating. For sins you never committed, the feeling is indefinite. Finality that never arrives.

The question that remains most unanswered is what fate is ours alone. Where we assume that free will means God's will maps on quite well with our wants and needs, and that we have a self-legislating role in our existence. Where the world exists for us to enact righteousness in a place where you can see any variation at all. We assume that the conscious act of choosing to do good is the important part of free will, although it could just as well be the case that *the* free will is bestowed upon us, and we are meant to enact it in perfect stride. How much of life is an apparent choice and how much are we a name and a face, a prescient series of occurrences? I hope to learn more about this in my life.

I wonder how you would solve mysteries where there are metaphysical forces at play. How would you build a case where someone sent themselves into your life and forgot after being born into this world? How would you, at the very same time, prove that people usually *don't* say what they mean, in the company of people who are quite immersed in literal interpretations of rules and ethics?

The *psychology of no soul* that I knew to remind them of, as I was taught. I learned that the very dilemma of psychology and natural science is that it means to organize systems that are naturally prone to chaos. Law *ought* to be bound to psychology and philosophy, but it really isn't today. How else could you decide what the purpose of law is, except by starting with the assumption that people act in uncertain ways to fulfill uncertain needs? Law, too often, assumes people mean to be rational. When really law exists to set up guardrails that encourage irrational behavior within reasonable constraints. Giving money, taking money, fucking, and dispatching power. If the world was so still, there would be no need for any of it.

They told me I was insane, that it couldn't be done, and that I belonged on antipsychotics. Supernatural evidence is beyond impossible to bring into the judicial system. It's never been like me to back down from a challenge, though. I'm a master at guiding the eye. And I know how important it is to let people lead themselves into truth, whether you're selling the world's greatest technology or you're bringing them before the divine for the first time.

What else you will notice is that being reliable and self-assured is worth its weight in gold. Every doubt you would have about yourself burns away when you feel like you are being the person you were meant to be every day. If you could go a step further, you would also know with certainty what you hope tomorrow looks like. You know to listen to your inner voice when the whole world would be silent, a certainty in truth when the world appears to be plain falsehood. A voice that silences the world like cracking thunder, and a faithful reminder to be graceful in each moment.

Who will you be reliable for when they arrive in droves? There's only one of you, and many lessons that you will learn for yourself and share with the world in due time. Maybe one day, when you are old and hidden away in the mountains, your scraggly beard now grey and white like the winter, you'll reflect on your life with peace and completeness in your heart knowing that everything you set out to accomplish worked out exactly as you meant. If the totality of your existence is anything like that, I know you lived the most excellent life. If anyone took what you have to say seriously and made the world a better place for it, your life meant something. For *the world*, and of course for your family. The one that you found some place in your frozen eternal heart to care about. And if every person on the planet would remember you for one thing, it's for being true.

Mac

The best. Is that something you believe exists somewhere in this world? You can get anything for the right price, or so they say.

I love the way Mac looks and the way it makes me feel. Like magic. Always perfectly smooth, colorful, and creative. I love the way Mac makes me think, like there's always a way to accomplish anything in the world that I can imagine. That's empowering, by definition. Growing up thinking in terms of Mac is why I believe anything can be made perfect if you really put your mind to it. Philosophy, politics, religion, and wars. Truly, you must understand how resounding I am in my faith. The best thing about Mac is that it *just works.*

There's something about the way people at Apple think that allows them to really come up with the most intuitive and efficient ways to do anything. From first principles, as though they really understand the *philosophy* of design. That taught me how to think. Where so many things try to seem complicated and smart to assert their value, Apple means to seem simple. If something is great, it ought to be simple, so that anyone can understand it. And if you're really so smart, you ought to understand your thing well enough to make it simple.

Most things in life have only an incremental improvement when you spend a ton of money. Sure, precious metals and diamonds make a luxury watch worth more, but the quality of the mechanical movement in a $10,000 watch is only marginally better than a $500 watch. At the end of the day, a $100 Casio digital watch still tells time better than any mechanical watch. When you considering the premium you pay on other luxuries, like jewelry, cars, boats, and shoes, Mac starts seeming like the greatest luxury ever invented at the greatest price you could ever expect. They're just the best computers and phones anyone has ever

301

come up with, and they knew to make them affordable enough for most people in the developed world. Something that great would typically be in the category of Rolls Royce and invitation-only events. Around $1,000? For the fastest and highest quality computers money can buy? I'll take 10!

Mac is built like a fine watch. The synthesis in hardware and software is absolute, from top to bottom, and the premium build quality feels like a solid unit — zero compromise. Using a Mac makes every other computer seem like a toy. Truly, it's mind blowing. The other guys are like hobbyists in a garage dropping a crate engine in. And Mac is essentially the same price as other premium computers, with a guarantee that you have the best chip and the best displays money can buy.

This is the philosophy of *best*, and you only get it one way.

When my mom was pregnant with me, she and my father were in a bad car accident where a Mack truck's brakes failed and rear ended them in their Range Rover. Certainly, everything always happens how it's supposed to, otherwise I wouldn't be telling you about my favorite computers and some of the most important things you will learn in your life. My mom had neck pain for years, although apparently I came out just fine.

Is this the price we are supposed to pay when we expect everything in life to be perfect? Somehow chaos shows up with its own narrative. Mac is apparently too fast, which makes you want to fuck it all up for me. I won't let you. That option is not on the menu. And that's the sort of thinking that got us here in the first place, which you may sometimes forget. People are very conflicted about having people tell them what is right. But if you didn't have people thinking like that, your only option would be Android and Kia. Which isn't necessarily bad, but you certainly must understand why Mercedes and Apple are one-way roads.

What did Steve get for being a part of the greatest engineering marvels in the world? What did he die from again? Health is metaphysical, and so I have faith in perfect health.

I have faith that when you orient yourself around the best possible experience, that's what you will get out of life. And I have faith that doing so necessarily requires the ability to discern detail in complicated situations and choose what is good and true.

Aella

Aella is a girl that likes getting raped, which in theory precludes her from making trouble for you when you have sex with her. She likes it so much that she even hosts sex parties where the whole point is to give people opportunities for forced sexual encounters. You say *well, that's not really an important feature, is it?* You tell me.

Aella is the world's leading sexual researcher and data scientist, with a background as a sex worker and an escort. Truly, she is the most interesting data scientist that I can think of, and she's entirely self-taught. Aella asks poignant questions about sex and she has very clever philosophical and existential ideas about why we do the things we do. She discusses how her deeply repressed and abusive Christian upbringing made her the way she is, having been home schooled and not so much as allowed to think for herself in any way.

Some people might say it ruins the tone of this book to talk about things like rape. How do you think Aella feels, to bear that mark on her life? To be told that she needs asterisks to make her life correct. Our analysis of truth would be incomplete except to discuss how sometimes we aren't in control of our lives, some people more than others.

In a world where there are droves of people looking to tell you what to believe, myself included, Aella places a lot of value on deciding for yourself what your own liberties are. Even when it's confusing to everyone else. Because they'd sooner suppress all of your ideas and hold you captive to believing something more palatable than concede that everyone deserves individual liberties. Aella understands the feeling of being trapped by ideology, with no light at the end of the tunnel.

Now, if you're like me, you have only one thing on your mind: if you rape Aella, is she allowed to call the cops on you? I find Aella pretty attractive. I'm not particularly interested in the idea of forced or pressured sexual situations, especially on account of the ethical implications of bearing such beliefs, but really I *love* the requirement that what we do is descriptively accurate. This is one of my favorite things to think about, because I like to discover the mechanisms behind how we think, and my experience with girls is that they like to put themselves in persecutory situations and act like they didn't know any better. Let's be clear: at this point, I'm only looking for girls to have sex with. Is that clear enough? If that doesn't sound like a feature you support, don't accept gifts or favors from me. Don't look at me, and really don't even think about me. Don't look at my website, don't play me in movies, and stop reading this book. You're unfit for consumption.

Now that you're 300 pages in, this is equivalent to what it's like to guess what you think I'm supposed to say to you, and then have you throw a fit when you decide you don't like it. I always say the right thing, so it must be something on your end.

My instinct is that it depends on whether the guy is attractive. Not entirely, and not even necessarily whether he was born that way, but that he takes himself reasonably seriously. The reason this seems to matter is because his own attractiveness is the condition that he would be forcing upon her. In traditionalist and chauvinistic view, this lines up quite well. If you take yourself seriously, the expectation would be that any sexual partner you want would be blessed by your holy cock.

Still, I wonder. Would our judicial system be so ridiculous that raping a woman that loves being raped is a crime? How much indirect interest would she have to show in you to be inviting you to have sex with her?

Because I'm not certain that she would have to show any at all, nor should you necessarily have to be attractive and legitimate in your own right, in this case. But I think those things would factor into it in the grand scheme of life.

As far as I'm concerned, you need to show me a woman who you believe is equally capable of taking advantage of me, because then I'll know you actually believe in equality. Otherwise, you are decisive about the fact that women are helpless, unable to decide or stand independently in the free economy of ideas. Oblivious to the practicality of modesty, like someone waving their wallet around in a crowd.

Your instinct is probably to say this is a ridiculous hypothetical to begin with, and that's fine if this is requiring you to use your brain too much, but I'm very serious, because I only like to be descriptively accurate. In this day and age, when someone can flail the legal system around like a giant mace, I certainly want to draw lines in the sand with pinpoint accuracy. And I do recognize that the whole point of courtship is the intangible gray area between certainty, but here we're inviting the law into our story for the sake of science and truth.

Then, if it turns out you both like this thing you have going, you're going to be beholden to each other for the next however many years you want to spend fucking. So bondage goes both ways sometimes. But it's certainly not common for girls to want to initiate. And it's actually quite common for people to come up with ways to wield their power over others, in an unusual reciprocal sort of way. We invent *new* ways to wield our power over others, even when there's no rational reason to make things more difficult. If it wasn't difficult, then there would be no power to wield.

Caroline

When I worked at Amazon, I thought it would be interesting and funny to act like a servant. I loved the idea of trying to be plain. The way girls love to have a lesbian phase where they only watch YouTube videos about *women's issues* and are perpetually frustrated with the fact that guys just don't appreciate femininity. So give them more paperwork and dumbbells, that will fix it. What are you looking for, a girlfriend?

Well, I guess really my equivalent for a lesbian phase would have been when I was a teenager and spent all of my time playing video games and on 4chan, but that was my gay phase. My lesbian phase is where I wore blue pinstripe and khakis every day. And I thought it was cute. If I was a girl, I'd fuck me just like that. As you know, I take it quite seriously when I act out the totality of an ideology to understand it thoroughly.

So you want me to do what you say, always? Unquestioning, and completely unopinionated except as it pertains to ensuring the quality and timely service of cloud software? I took this job quite seriously, because I knew I would be laying a foundation for servants of my own. In a matter of 9 months, so it was.

It was important for me to evaluate where you are going wrong when you're coming up with what young boys are supposed to be like. When you decide what shows up in the news, movies, and magazines — the real nutritional facts that determine what society is like. Coming from my background as a Chili Peppers hard rock freak, it seemed quite clear to me that you were looking for boys that don't act like boys.

How long would you have them withhold their actual will? Really, are you doing them a service to be beating them into submission and shaming their frothing cum-tipped penises?

I must imagine, is this what it's like when girls devour lithium and feminist propaganda by the bottle, and then wonder why it's not fixing their problems or answering their questions about what it's supposed to feel like to be in a position of submission? As I write this, it's clear to me that there is a misdirection inherent to organizing philosophy and business rather than directly putting you in a position of submission.

The world of words and reason tells girls to be intentional and correct, but they mean to feel chaotic and emotional. It would be difficult to even explain being a girl, because explaining it defies the actuality of femininity. It would take away your ability to embody it, because now it's something that I have explained for you.

Thus, you have arrived at the precise dilemma, the contradiction inherent in reason. Philosophy teaches us how to be right, but in a relationship we have to learn to be wrong, or at least to act out the subtext of it. The whole of ideology and culture is like a foot fetish, a bizarre misdirected head of state to think on behalf of our dicks. A cart before the horse, where we make certain that the frozen yogurt machine is working so that we can fuck in the bathroom. That's what having a brain is like.

Ubuntu

Ubuntu is an African word meaning *humanity*, and also a popular distribution of the Linux kernel and user environment.

The first time I used Ubuntu was when I ordered a free CD in the mail and popped it into my computer a week later. Physical media is how software and games were distributed at least through the mid 2000s. I was learning all about why Linux is an interesting alternative to Mac and Windows for servers and personal computers.

You have to get Mac and Windows from Apple or Microsoft, but with Linux, anyone can create a distribution like Ubuntu. Ubuntu was one of the first distributions of Linux that really gave you everything you needed to run a graphical desktop environment that was compatible with your computer. This was an important goal for them, batteries included, whereas most Linux was very arcane and piecemeal, often oriented towards servers and power users.

Linux has turned out to be a brilliant success and a source of great irony. It was created in the early 1990s as a *free and open-source* alternative to the expensive and restrictive operating systems that existed at the time. It is mean to be free, as in freedom, and also free as in free beer. *Open-source* means that anyone can view or modify the code for their own use. With this, it has a very particular sort of copyright requiring that if you distribute something based on it, it *also* follows the free and open-source principles and bears the same copyright; liberty, or death.

You can use Linux, run software on it, and run an entire business using Linux servers without worrying about this license, and in fact many of the biggest companies in the world do. But you can't modify and distribute Linux itself without the license *contaminating* any code you add onto it. The way it's structured is sensible. You can run a business on Linux, otherwise it would be like if you could only have underwear or pants, but not both.

Linux has always been a very ideologically driven community, founded on the idea that everything Linux is meant to be about liberty, privacy, and democratic decisions, with the aim of collaboratively developing an operating system in open-air that usually doesn't cost money. The *free as in freedom* and *free as in free beer* mantra always kind of came as a set, with Linux being free and open-source, where many of the other software entities have always been commercial.

The irony is that all of the most important stakeholders in the adoption and growth of Linux are all using it commercially and running non-free software on it. Without Ubuntu and Red Hat maintaining secure and accessible distributions of Linux, providing major enterprise support services, and advocating for Linux on servers and on embedded devices, Linux would be reserved for enthusiasts and power users. But many diehard free software (as in freedom) enthusiasts would say that they're missing the point in endorsing proprietary software and drivers. The community has always had this funny, petulant battle with itself where basically everyone that actually tries to make *free software* in practice fails to meet the criteria in some way. Most Linux distributions like Ubuntu, Debian, Arch, and Fedora are actually pretty great stewards in most regards. But the community is right in saying that some of the most common ways you might use Linux, like Android and Chrome OS, are completely swathed with proprietary and privacy invading software. They argue that lots of open-source projects miss the point, which is that there shouldn't be restrictive licenses and trademarks on top of it. They say, great, Apple open-sourced WebKit and Darwin, but every open-source contribution to it still serves their proprietary browser and OS at the end of the day. The jury's out on that. Personally, I think irrevocable ownership is important. But if the Linux community thought that, it wouldn't exist. They believe in irrevocable collaboration. And it's good that they think like this, because it shows that they're paying attention.

I learned something from Linux, though, and it's that Tux, the penguin mascot, never went anywhere. If your brand is potent enough, your ideas go everywhere, even when other people have different plans for it.

Amazon's servers in the cloud run on Amazon Linux and Ubuntu, Android is based on Linux, the New York Stock Exchange runs on Linux, and Google runs on Linux. Many car entertainment systems, smart-home devices, and gadgets run on Linux. They all love that there is a free, well-maintained base that they can extend for their own use, instead of being beholden to Microsoft or Apple. A lot of the work is already done for you, and you can merge updates with security patches and features from a passionate community of open-source maintainers.

So what is *success?* People that are passionate about open-source software just love that it exists, and that makes them happy inherently. But you wouldn't really be hearing about Linux without the downstream effects that make it so popular.

20 years later, Linux on your personal computer is *good, not great.* Too many hands in the till. Too many variables, and not enough polish. Every time I use a graphical Linux environment, I'm satisfied, but I remember why Linux really shines on the server, and I find myself wishing I was using Mac.

Next

The reason Apple is so great at what they do is because they are very particular about the experience they want to give you.

Computers completely shaped the way that I view the world, making anything and everything seem attainable. Making the world seem light, as though I could lift it with my own hands. If I have something important to say, I know I can reach the whole world from the tip of my fingers, in an instant. That's what Apple means to me. It could just be that everyone else wasn't framing it right. Steve's life showed me how to live gracefully in all things that you do.

A broken heart can serve a different purpose than it would have before. It's easier for heartbroken people to let go of the things that trouble them, to not have to wonder why people are the way they are. All you want to do is make something perfect, and so many of them simply want to be in the way. Your scar tissue has emboldened you, and your anger burns in a way that surprises you. When you wake up each day, the one thing you know for certain is the only thing that counts is making the best possible thing you can come up with. Everything else will be gone with the wind, because they don't care about what they're making the same way you do. They made that clear to you, outright. It's a good thing, too, because now you can focus on what matters.

Steve Jobs was fired by his own company because the board of directors and *professional management* that he invited into his world decided he was unproductive to work with. They promptly, as he recounts, *threw away a 10 year lead over Microsoft*. Do you know how something like that happens? When you start looking at Microsoft's rear view mirrors all the time instead of just *making something great*.

Steve went and started a new company, NeXT, which designed a brand new computer and operating system from the ground up. This new team did it in record time, like a blitz, and they were so excited to show the world what these computers were capable of. Much like the Macintosh, this was meant to be the perfect machine for scientists and creatives. This was the early 90s, and it wasn't quite clear to these folks how important a workstation class machine would be for their work. The *vision* was there, though. The folks at NeXT had the foresight to know that, today, we would all be using our computers just like they imagined. Connected, collaborative, creative machines, that we could use to make movies, artwork, and video games. Real time graphics for designing cars and rendering high quality 3D animation. The original World Wide Web was actually invented by an enthusiast on a NeXT computer, building on networking concepts from universities and the U.S. defense industry, and deploying the first graphical, navigable internet document format in the world.

Apple, on the verge of bankruptcy, would soon buy NeXT and incorporate all of the technology they built at NeXT into the Mac. The new Mac, built on NeXT's operating system, is the basis of the Macs we know today. It is significantly more modern and capable than the ancient technology that Apple was holding onto, and it was exactly what they needed to be competitive with other internet connected, multi-process capable computers going into the 2000s.

Steve's new company saved Apple, once and for all, rocketing them into success for the 21st century. The new Mac, the iPod, the MacBook, and of course, the iPhone, came shortly after, revolutionizing technology as something that is fun and interesting for everyone to play with. Clearly, the most important thing is having a vision.

At the same time, Steve and some collaborators founded Pixar, which laid the foundation, both in terms of process and hardware capabilities, for making animated movies like Toy Story. The technology at the time was barely capable of making something like that. It would take *an entire day* just to render 30 seconds of the movie, and the storage requirements were massive for the hard drives that were available. Now, Pixar is the most recognized and accomplished studio in the world for creating magical 3D animated feature films. All because people had some exceptional belief about what technology might be capable of.

The NeXT Computer was a screaming workstation that was compact enough for a desk. The biggest difference in technology today is that we're seeing more computation and storage being displaced into the cloud. It's interesting, because devices that fit in our pockets are in many cases as fast as our home computers, but still the ways people really like to use them lend to having a lot of capabilities in the sky. The important things, like being able to access your data anywhere and being able to share what you create with the world. Such important things that it places a major responsibility on tech companies to be responsible stewards with our data, and our economy for that matter.

Truly, there is nothing particularly excellent about Windows. They understood their market, and they made sure that anyone who wanted to make spreadsheets and documents decided to make major corporate investments in Microsoft and partner equipment. Now we know any old computer can do those things, and Google is even finding excellent footing in business and education with a similar philosophy and more modern cloud technology. Apple prioritizes quality and privacy in a way other companies do not.

What makes something great? People always want to know. They want to know what sort of thinking you have to do to be in the right mindset to make something great. Apple has something like a *suspension of disbelief* for the market. They aren't so preoccupied with what it seems like people want, and that way they can really focus 100% on making the best possible experience. They can use their imagination, and really use it in a way that it gets sharpened to a point. Good ideas stick.

It's not often that I think to myself *that person thinks just like Steve.* And it's usually not the people you'd expect. It's creatives that are so petulantly absorbed in what they want to make that they seem immovable. They have *one* idea for what they want their life to look like, and it's plain to see.

There's lots of technology people that *say* they want to do something great, but they clearly start from that line of thinking and imagine something arbitrary just to say they did it. If you truly want to succeed, you're going to start with a feeling inside of you that is more resounding than anything else you know.

I had this sort of feeling during the COVID outbreak and even now, as I write this. That I have something important to say, and you aren't really paying attention. That no one will ever believe in me the way I believe in myself. That's been a constant in my life. If Steve would have had one thing to say about me, it's that I don't spend enough time on people. And it's true. I guess Steve just liked people more than I do, which is an excellent talent for a leader to have. The great thing about Mac is that it just works.

Maybe when I'm looking back on my life, I'll wish I was a slightly different person, that torque wasn't so satisfying to me. Not that the practicality of being that person has yet occurred to me. Mac has always been a high-torque maneuver. It has to be, to get so many different things built perfectly from the ground up. Otherwise, it's quite easy for vision to get swallowed up by the pressure to move fast and get something out the door.

All along the way, I keep reminding myself that the most important thing is having a vision, and being particularly focused about how you build and who you invite along to see it into light. Relentless, even. Because no matter what they say, there's not going to be much encouragement for you when you're doing something truly groundbreaking. You're just going to feel like you're in the dark, keeping yourself company, watching movies all day and imagining where exactly it is you're at in your journey. Wondering what he would have said if he was in the exact same place. Wondering how he found a special place to box up his anger so that he could come in every day and stand like a rock, and speak with grace.

313

Metal Gear

Great artwork is a perfect depiction of reality. When we enjoy artwork like that, it gives us an understanding of the world that the greatest textbooks and news can't quite capture. It tells a story that is meant to be so holistic that it is more real than it planned on being. Its philosophy gets imprinted in the world and reabsorbed into something new.

The very first thing that stood out to me about Metal Gear is the protagonist's conflicted sense of identity. In Metal Gear, there are 4-5 guys that all look identical and are, in varying degrees, genetic clones of the original guy, Big Boss, a.k.a. *Naked Snake*. They each come to terms with this in different ways, as they find themselves like cogs in a greater sociopolitical scheme. They are all covert operatives, although the phenomenon of personality and *head* becomes apparent for each of them.

Secret police *of what?* Secrecy has an identity crisis, because it never quite arrives at federation. At some point, even the most secretive and decentralized systems have an archetypal personality appear that represents them, a supposed idea and truth of *what* they are in service of, where otherwise it would be like an endless daisy-chain of photocopiers and questionable intel reports.

Everyone in the Snakes' circles are quite aware of who they are, having grown out of their ability to remain secret, and thus they struggle to ensure the legitimacy of many of their colleagues in infinitely complex storylines and power struggles. Even when you operate from the shadows, you are in good company. They grapple with insanity as they confront the possibility of mind control and rogue actors in their organizations. What if your memory could be selectively erased? Remember that bullet that was never supposed to be in the gun Alec Baldwin fired on-set of *Rust?*

The thing that makes the protagonists valuable in each of these games is that reality comes to a *head* with them. They are the reliable narrator.

What if you were engineered specifically to replace your identical predecessor? What if you were engineered by a group of people with completely separate interests than your predecessor? In our global diaspora and our generations that seem to evolve in 10 years more than they used to in 100 years, sometimes it feels that way, like today's technology and ideas are already being replaced as soon as we come up with them. If time isn't even necessarily linear, are we really in service to what preceded us? Then, with such consideration, you would have to place a lot of value on identity. Because apparently, the identity that you exist as today was an entire history in the making. The foundation of *you* is all wound together on the basis of you.

The politics of technology is always changing. It used to be *who's going to blow up the world?* And now it's more like techno-colonialism. *Who owns all of the information?* Naturally, whoever has the strongest grasp on the world's information and media is able to steer the narrative in ways we can barely imagine. What if the very story of the world is a narrative that is driven metaphysically? Like a snake devouring its tail…

Today's wars are fought in the shadows. Information and subtext. And so the battlefields become immeasurably complex and the intelligence and security industries become absolutely giant. Enormous piles of data. It would be chaos, except to imagine there are particular people who stand quite still in their conscience. When the wars are fought by proxy and the soldiers can be steered like StarCraft units, you start thinking about the world quite differently. *Head* becomes important, *face and name,* where everything else is like a shroud. It comes as a surprise how important this is in the context of secret organizations, and I think about that a lot.

Great spy movies like *The Good Shepherd* address righteousness in the context of shapelessness, where we usually think about CIA in terms of secret identities. The *head* can be generalized to everyone, so long as it is in service to itself. *The* self.

315

Many of the world's most brilliant science fiction writers are credited with predicting the future. All of the most innovative technology in the world seems like science fiction at first. Brain interfaces, quantum technologies, battlefield orchestration, and future sight. Metal Gear is quite brilliant at capturing the metaphysical and sociopolitical underpinnings of technology and war. How when you begin to even wonder who you are and where the world came from, you find that something like faith in yourself is at the end of every line. If God or a computer decides every fate, who belongs on the winning side of wars?

It's been said that personality is the chariot of consciousness. And thus, excellent character and spirit seems to be what captivates the will of God. That is what is meant to persist, while everyone squabbles over how many hundreds of years into the future we can procedurally predict with quantum computers, or what the fastest new jet is going to be. People who believe too much in money or power get lost in the subtext of their own existence, their identities dissolved into game and jargon. But people who are *true* know to be still. The world solidifies around them, knowing well that they are in the company of true spirit and true vision, that if there is a word to be spoken or a move to be made, there is quite deliberate intent. When the world would regress into chaos, faceless leaders and crumbling foundations, people will look to champions of reason for a familiar reminder of up from down, that the sky is still blue and water is wet. Leaders that show up at the end of every line, because that is the only way that would be satisfying to them.

The assuring thing about great leaders is that they will only speak truth, to the exclusion of all else. From what they've seen, most people's words barely have meaning. It would be difficult to tell who anyone even is, except for the fact that they know to be still.

Invisible Girl

Just when you thought things couldn't get any more fucked up, they all start going insane one at a time. Sometimes it's more convenient to lose your mind than to acknowledge the truth.

And so they each get the fate they deserve. For the righteous, everything that is good and true in this life. For the willingly blind and deaf, blindness and deafness. For the voiceless, silence. For me, apparently, a difficult problem to solve.

In jail, the way you get drugs is by having letters mailed in with the drug dissolved into the paper. Incidentally, this would only work if the letters don't get photocopied before they end up in your hands.

Righteousness has a peculiar quality of always finding a way. The world is built for change, and so what eventually surfaces is what is good and true, according to our senses and our faith. So even when so many will go blind and deaf to you, you can be assured that your word will seep through the cracks.

Like pipes blocked and under immense pressure, truth will shear out from the junctions and create fissures in the substrate of reality. If you won't hear my word, now have a world of people who all speak on my behalf. Is this better for you?

What is most true resonates on all levels simultaneously. Like her; she will speak and perform for you to see and understand. Like the storms and the news, who will bleed my word alone. The brightest crimson red, so it couldn't possibly go unnoticed.

For me, plain truth. Love, health, and happiness. Effortlessness in all motions.

Bridges

The foundation of all life is excellent infrastructure. The most excellent infrastructure is the speed of light and information, naturally. When we can see well and think well, everything we do is brilliant.

I'm told that world hunger is an infrastructure problem. That if only there was a way to optimally distribute food, you could solve hunger just by keeping food from going to waste and redistributing it. Naturally, if farming was all automated, there wouldn't be any scarcity of food to begin with.

You might say *"Oh, that sounds expensive"*, and it's true. So are mobile networks, but they keep building them endlessly in less developed nations and charging much less money than we pay for service in the U.S., because it's simply worth it for them to capitalize on huge portions of the world population that don't even have a single connected device. Most information-age businesses measure their success by how much they are growing, not necessarily whether a particular investment in infrastructure was profitable.

The trickle down thing does actually work. Once it's second nature to build an automated farm in the U.S., they won't think twice about building one in Africa. All economics are trickle down. It's just when The Simpsons starts seeming like all old guy jokes that people become frustrated. It's the idea that someone else's infrastructure is holding them captive. This is why the U.S. was designed to regularly turn over power.

How much time do you think someone needs to spend watching videos and movies of what life is like in the west before they start expecting their local area to be clean and industrialized? That's really what it starts with, right? Some common expectation among people that their neighborhood looks a particular way. You can't force less developed nations to become cleaner and safer, but you certainly can show them what it looks like until they decide that's what they want.

Today we see technology companies investing in less developed nations because it's ripe for innovation. There's all this proven technology and infrastructure, so why not take it and put it somewhere new? So now there's 4G and 5G mobile networks in places you wouldn't have expected. And they pay a lot less money than we do in the U.S., because the number is made up and the thing that actually counts is saying in your earnings report that you completely took a new country by storm. It's a net-good for the world, but it's certainly casting a wide net. It signals stability. You can imagine being in a more chaotic part of the world, the idea that American businesses are paying attention to what's going on in your world is reassuring. We get to be selective and decide that we want companies less involved with our data, but for many people, perhaps the spotlight is invaluable.

The coffee industry is quite proud of their commitments to sustainable agriculture. They show you the very farms where the coffee you are drinking was grown at, and they celebrate a *farm to table* approach to their sourcing and producer relationships. Certainly, any farming cooperative in Ethiopia would be ecstatic to have a strong, fair, and profitable relationship with an American craft coffee roaster. That's what the craft coffee industry prioritizes, and people notice that when they're shopping, much like they would at Whole Foods, now owned by Amazon. When worlds collide, sometimes you can make an offer that's too good for anyone to refuse. Offers that are fair and responsible for everyone, that bolster the whole world with technology and industry.

The Lamb

One who is like a lamb will arrive upon us and lead us to salvation, only after a dragon, a beast of the sea, and *a beast like a lamb speaking like a dragon* makes us worship the beast of the sea.

Some things are only able to be understood in light of their antithesis. God shows us the truth by revealing falsehood. We could only know truth if we are walked along a righteous path, leaving falsehood in our wake. How long would God have us settle for injustice? Our understanding undifferentiated and our sensibility languished for what is good in God's grace, for the pure truth withheld from us while we eat from the tree of life and drink its sap. Made to be like those with no name, to worship one with no name.

How long would we be starved for the pure truth that is salvation? The space in time between dropping this ring and picking it back up.

The holy ones that are anointed will see with their very own eyes and hear with their own ears a graceful sound from the East, so that they should know truth as they live and breathe. Beauty is our signia.

Falsehood will be cast into a lake of fire, to know torment for all eternity.

The faithful and true will bear the name that is salvation.

It's quite important that I tell you about this manifold mystery, so that you can see for yourself that things are not always what they seem, and that what is apparently clear to us is only understood through rendition and action. That every word and every righteousness we know may be, at some point, appropriated in falsehood, before God shepherds us towards truth.

Truly, could you know righteousness from the mortal perspective of Earth? If only to hear as by God and to know through God that there is salvation here for you.

What name would you call out so that God answers? Would you not cover every last creation in holy symbols and holy names, that something like truth would emerge from the ash of the Earth? Because then, if you knew but a whisper of God's grace, it would answer for your every sin and make right for everything you meant to be true.

When they assign their sins to God, how will God separate out what is good and true from evil temptation, for us to see with our eyes and hear with our ears? For them to see that disaster is a choice afforded to them; an opportunity to abandon their faith or to keep their covenant with

God. Here in this world, you have the choice to be free, in faith and in salvation.

Not Plain

It is the most lonely feeling in the world to be left behind, or to see the world actively turn against you; for every word you speak to be interpreted as pernicious and untrue. Why, ever, would God make a world where some of us simply feel like we aren't welcome in it?

Shall we all look like Margot Robbie and speak like Christ, so that the world accepts us in our generation? Who would each of us be, then, to be nameless and faceless?

Intolerance is a vicious cycle. Some people could never understand it except to feel it personally. If every person in the world would turn their back to you at first glance, on your appearance alone, what sort of world would you imagine that is to live in? Perhaps you shouldn't have to imagine, so that you can know what God's grace means for you. And perhaps you would never wish such a bitter fate for any living being, for all eternity, than to be invisible, or to be a color that is not plain.

And so the finality of beauty is something that we will know for ourselves. Where we can see it for ourselves and embody it within ourselves. Everything that came before has a mark that doesn't quite come off. Isn't that okay? Or shall the world be sterile? How sterile, to be blank.

But I am red. And everything I say is apparently black to you. You're unwilling to listen unless I force you to. So shall it be, because I only speak truth that is necessary for you to recognize. My life is marked by not being plain. I've just learned to get over it.

Still, I hope for variety, choice, and abundance in this life. Pleasures and joys that are unconstrained by rigid order and regulation. A spirit of play and imagination, the space to be free.

73 Days

73 days is how long it took to write this book. Well, that's only true in actuality. Practically, there has been immeasurable preparation and research to understand the concepts herein, in their full breadth and depth. This is the correct depth to introduce them to you.

Now, on the 17th of November, 2023, Israel is in the intermediate stages of reclaiming the Gaza strip, an odd Palestinian golden coast between Israel and Egypt, separate from Palestine's main land near Jerusalem. This is following a surprise terrorist attack on Israel from Gaza's predominate Hamas terrorist organization.

Who belongs where? Who did what first? You can look at countries like Taiwan, which is historically a Chinese territory that is now independent, and say *look, they obviously deserve to be free.* If a U.S. state decided they wanted to secede, how would we go about doing business with them? Do we go put a lien on all of their telephone poles and federal buildings? China says *"Taiwan absolutely belongs to us, historically and culturally."*

So, does that make Israel Taiwan in this situation? Or China? If it was so simple, Israel is completely miniature in the context of the Middle East. To Israel, an independent and eternal nation, they are fighting a war that they are destined to win. They are consulting divine law, not some arbitrary archetypal mapping of who is fighting fairly. And it's plainly *not* so simple, because there are geopolitical tensions in the Middle East that have second and third-order effects, nations that are factionally aligned with Hamas and sometimes providing them with foreign aid. Israel is like a cat backed into a corner.

Sympathy has an unusual way of only flowing downstream. When you look at something on a long enough time scale, *all* land is stolen.

How long would your neighbors have to be annoying before you just go and steal their house? By annoying, I mean actual terrorism.

Now, it will become quite important that the world is responsive to the tides of life. It always was important, but now especially. Where people will sit idly by and watch atrocities occur, or find some ridiculous expectation for us to tolerate terrorism and lies, now it will be necessary to answer for the reality of life.

When truth comes to your door, you will have no choice but to answer. Stillness is an excellent hypothetical. People will only sit and watch for so long. Eventually, something requires action of you. Whether it's getting hungry, bored, or receiving the world's loudest wake up call.

Freedom is free. It is where you have a reasonable path to success when the world weighs on you. Justice will sound its horn of judgement from the shores of eternity, for all to hear. The way you start rapping when the rent's due.

Now, I'm optimistic. Some people would even say too optimistic, more optimistic than anyone who seems so bitter would ever deserve to be. That's why it's called bittersweet. You're going to have to stop adding sugar if you want to be able to taste it. Optimism is an important binding principle because it means you keep waking up and expecting good things to happen.

There are other things in the world that make me optimistic and happy. I love to see you perform. You tell just the story that I hoped you would, so that everyone can understand it. You show us that excellence can be frustrating, and that no one will really understand it like we do. You remind me what it's like to feel black. When we're alone, together, perhaps there's something not so lonely.

I love enjoying time with my dog. I love writing about the things that are interesting to me so that we can understand them together. I love games and music.

These are the plain pleasures that keep us from thinking too much about the evil that we keep outside of our home. And so maybe when you show up in my life and say something that sounds genuine, I'll listen. And I'll remind you that I have zero patience now.

This book is dedicated to my beautiful dog that I love very much, and liberty. That's what I believe in. And my very own gravity well that looks exactly like I want it to and does exactly what I expect.

When would you arrive in my life if you wanted me to fall head over heels in love with you, and what would you say?

I'm learning what to believe in as I go through life and experience the world. What keeps showing up are things that aren't quite worth spending time on. They're worth evaluating so that I can tell you about them, but they're extra. Like cooking utensils with rubberized grips. Like gaming mice. I actually like the size and shape of the Logitech *MX Anywhere* wireless mouse best. And I like when things are plain, as though they aren't continually reaching for some extraneous reason or justification for their existence. How else would I know to be away from myself? Everything I do is over the top and ridiculous.

One thing is for certain, I love to try to be perfect. When I make something special, I fixate on every detail because I love to amaze you. Everything else gets caught in the crossfire, in service to perfection. Maybe there's something great about that. Maybe when we all get to make something perfect together, we show up at the gates of eternity with beauty in our hands.

True beauty appears when we follow our hearts.

Magic

Your magic is so excellent that you should never reveal your secrets. You owe this to the world, and for that matter, the world owes it to you to be amazed and to wonder.

The temptation is ever present to pull back the curtain on the things you do that people love. I think we both know the reason they love them is because of how spectacular the magic is to behold. The delicate touch of your hands, the mystical enchantments you place in the world. Your secrets are ever so truthful.

www.ingramcontent.com/pod-product-compliance
Lightning Source LLC
Chambersburg PA
CBHW020433130626
46549CB00001B/120